9 December 1988

To Farook

on your birthday

with love from

Janey
XX

XXXXX

xx

Jane x

Steve

Nick x.

To My Greatest Fan —
from
Stephen (Dickie)

"IT'S ONLY A MOVIE, INGRID"

Encounters on and off screen

Other books by Alexander Walker

Sex in the Movies
Stardom: The Hollywood Phenomenon
Stanley Kubrick Directs
Hollywood, England
Rudolph Valentino
Double Takes
Superstars
The Shattered Silents
Peter Sellers: The Authorized Biography
Garbo
Joan Crawford
Dietrich
No Bells on Sunday (ed.)
National Heroes
Bette Davis
Vivien: The Life of Vivien Leigh

"IT'S ONLY A MOVIE, INGRID"

Encounters on and off screen

Alexander Walker

"It's only a movie, Ingrid"
– Alfred Hitchcock
to Ingrid Bergman

HEADLINE

British Library Cataloguing in Publication Data

Walker, Alexander, *1930–*
"It's only a movie, Ingrid" : encounters
on and off screen.
1. Cinema films. Actors & actresses.
Biographies. Collections
I. Title
791.43′028′0922

ISBN 0–7472–0012–2

Set by Colset Private Limited, Singapore

Printed and bound in Great Britain by
Richard Clay Ltd, Bungay, Suffolk

HEADLINE BOOK PUBLISHING PLC
Headline House
79 Great Titchfield Street
London W1P 7FN

CONTENTS

v

For Anthea and Thomas Gibson

CREDITS

Illustrations in the text are attributed, first, to the production company, then to the distributor of record at the time of the film's British release. It may be that some films illustrated are currently distributed by other companies. If so, the author apologises and undertakes to make a suitable correction on the next possible occasion.

The Madwoman of Chaillot   Ely Landau/Warner-
   Commonwealth United
The Lion in Winter   Haworth-Avco-Embassy/Rank
Goodbye, Mr Chips   APJAC/MGM/Associated British
Murphy's War   Hemdale, Yates-Deeley/Columbia
Sylvia Scarlett   RKO
To Catch a Thief   Paramount Rank
The Formula   MGM/Cinema International Corporation
The Saboteur: Code Name 'Morituri'   20th Century Fox/Rank
The Missouri Breaks   United Artists/Rank
Bonnie and Clyde   Tatira-Hiller/Warner-Seven Arts
Network   MGM/UA/Rank
Stavisky   Cerito Films-Les Films Ariane Euro International
   Prods/Gala
Stanley Kubrick   National Film Archive
Ken Russell   United Artists
Joseph Losey   Universal
Olivier and author   Rogers and Cowan
Olivier 'Mabuhay!'   Rogers and Cowan
Marathon Man   Paramount/Cinema International
   Corporation

Section Two

Terence Stamp   Anglo Allied/Rank
Malcolm McDowell   Memorial/Paramount

Michael York London Independent Producers/Associated
    British
Brief Encounter Cineguild/General Film Distributors
Ryan's Daughter Faraway/MGM
Room at the Top Romulus/Columbia
Expresso Bongo Britannia-Conquest/Associated British
Swann in Love Les Films du Losange/Artificial Eye
Bartleby Pantheon/British Lion
King Lear Filmways-Lanterna/Columbia
The Card British Film Makers/Rank
Tunes of Glory Knightsbridge/United Artists
Hitler: The Last Ten Days Westfilm/MGM
The Blue Lamp Ealing/General Film Distributors
The Servant Elstree-Springbok/Associated British
Dirk Bogarde Painting by David Tindle reproduced by
    permission of the National Portrait Gallery, London

Unless otherwise indicated, all illustrations are supplied by the
Stills Department of the British Film Institute. The author is
particularly grateful for the help he received in making his choice
from Marrku Salmi and Tise Vahimagi.

Extracts from the letters of Sir Terence Rattigan are reproduced
by permission of the Trustees of Sir Terence's estate, to whom
the author wishes to express his gratitude.

The passage from Melvyn Bragg's essay on Lord Olivier, which
appeared in the May, 1987, issue of British *Vogue* is reproduced
by kind permission of Vogue's editor, Elizabeth Tilberis, and the
Conde Nast Publications Ltd.

ACKNOWLEDGMENTS

The author expresses his indebtedness to Joseph O'Reilly, his
copy editor at HEADLINE BOOK PUBLISHING PLC, and to
Hillary Bird, who prepared the book's index.

Most of all are thanks due to Sue Fletcher, Editorial Director,
Headline, for her continuous encouragement and advice; and to
Carol Smith for her customary good counsel and patience.

"DO YOU MEAN TO SAY THEY PAY YOU TO GO TO THE MOVIES?"

The question is asked so often that it is as well to get it over and done with before we start: *How did you get to be a film critic?* The "how" is the easy part; the "when" and "why" of it make better starting points.

I remember exactly when. I was four years old. It was my birthday, March 1934, and I was standing on tip-toe to look through the windows across the serene valley of the River Bann at the spring snow on the Mourne Mountains, when my mother said, "I'm going to take you to the pictures today." – "What's 'pictures'? Are they like the comics?" – "A bit . . . but they move." It was a Western we went to, with Buck Jones, perhaps *Riders of Death Valley*. I watched it absolutely entranced, unable to believe the New World I'd discovered in the darkness. Galileo, discovering the Earth moves, experienced the same pang of excitement as I did discovering pictures that moved. Coming home, Mother said, "Humph, galloping round the same bush all the time." *She* was the critic then.

Portadown, our town, lay in the middle of the rose- and apple-growing countryside of Co. Armagh. Linen, hand-woven in strips as long as a cricket pitch, was spread over the river meadows to be bleached to snowy whiteness. It was the kind of paradisal landscape that figures in literary recollections; but any such that I may write will have to wait, because, for me, the town's "picture houses", to use the plain perfect description, were paradise enough. We had three for a population of only 15,000, changing programmes thrice weekly, a double bill daily – 18 new features every six days, more films than open weekly in London's West End today. Films, or "*the* films" as they were known, were enormously popular north and south of the Irish border. But what was surprising was not to find them frowned on in the Protestant towns of the North, the way they were across the water in equally sabbatarian Scotland. I think the reason was

3

they were viewed as "consolation entertainment" for those of us of the majority religion. Ethnically and artistically, the Roman Catholic population possessed a far deeper, broader heritage of cultures to draw on when they wanted to amuse themselves. It was invariably the Catholic drama groups who scooped the prizes at our town's annual fortnight of music and drama. The Catholics would be putting on Synge, O'Casey, Yeats and Shaw, performing them with the tight-knit ease of ensemble acting inherent in their forms of worship, while we more staid and stiff Protestants would be wondering if, this year, we were up to St John Ervine or A.A. Milne. Years later, at a film *première* in Manila, I heard the narrator bring one of his country's bloodier sagas of repeated foreign invasions to an end with the laconic comment: "The Catholic Church brought Christianity to the Philippines . . . the Americans brought the cinema." I thought of Ireland and, being a Protestant, blessed the Americans.

Deprived of a "performance culture" in the North of Ireland, we Protestants took our entertainment ready-made from the screen – hence the abundance of unstigmatised cinemas in our midst. As I grew older, I discovered that different parts of the Province had their *genre* preferences. Our town was wild about gangster movies – a baleful omen, if one could have read it then, of its place in contemporary bloodshed on the northern rim of the terrorist country of South Armagh. Banbridge, in Co. Down, liked Westerns, as befitted a cradle of the Protestant Ascendancy with its stern concern for keeping law and order. Many of the sea-coast towns made musicals their *specialité de la saison*, though Newcastle, at the very foot of the Mournes, had allowed Hollywood to establish a beach-head for horror.

It was in Newcastle that I saw *Son of Frankenstein* one summer holiday. I had worried away at our maidservant-cum-nanny until – being filled with curiosity herself – she gave way and took me in to see it as we came back early from a damp walk over the sand dunes where I knew my father was safely playing golf on the Royal County Down links. I wasn't quite ten years old – and the then "H" Certificate set the permissible viewing age for horror at 16. That didn't at all worry the cinema manager who sold us our sixpenny tickets, took them back, tore them in two, let one half add itself to the tiny green pyramid growing at his feet, and handed back the other to us to legalise our admission.

4

We even took my beloved Scots terrier in with us. I thought I wasn't a bit frightened by Karloff's monster until I discovered, from the whimpering in the dark, that my hands were clamped so tightly around the dog on my lap that I was choking the life out of her. Afterwards, my nanny and I kept quiet about our experience – until she woke up in hysterics that night and, in her babblings over the soothing cup of tea, disclosed to my parents what kind of picture we had been to.

My parents believed that a burnt child either dreaded the fire or, much more practically, adapted to it; and they put no ban on my future filmgoing. Thus by practical experience I grew to be an implacable opponent of all forms of prior restraint placed on people by condescending and prohibitive film censors. Responsibility for others is something I have always rejected and fortunately avoided suffering from myself when I was growing up. This, too, later helped lay down the basics for being a critic. The only responsibility is to oneself and the cinema.

My child's appetite for films was gluttonous and undiscriminating. I saw *anything* that was on (not, for obvious reasons, *everything*) and it would be gratifying to report that at some point quantity began to turn into quality. It didn't – until around 1941, and then as a result of a sad incident.

My mother was almost as keen as I on going to the pictures and every fortnight or so we would take the train to Belfast to catch some new film we'd particularly looked forward to seeing at its city-centre opening. This treat grew harder to enjoy regularly when the war brought the blackout, threats of German bombing and the hazards of travelling even the brief 26 miles by rail to the metropolis. But we generally made it to the early screening on Saturday afternoon, leaving ourselves plenty of time to get home before dark.

On this particular Saturday, as we came out of the cinema a platoon of soldiers was passing by. Someone running along beside the marchers pushed Mother against the wall. Her glasses were knocked off and broke. She had a spare pair which she put on as soon as we reached home, shaken but otherwise unhurt. But they were reading glasses, unsuitable for looking at films, and getting spectacles repaired in wartime was a lengthy business. So for Mother, filmgoing temporarily ended. It was I who now brought back the reports of what I'd seen and delivered elated or dismissive judgments, recounted the absurd or exciting plots, sketched in the stars' roles, acted out how they were played, repeated the dramatic bits of the dialogue – and found I'd turned into a critic almost without realising it.

Unless there is passion in communication, the skills of a critic won't properly engage the machinery. The skills, of course, are much harder to form – like any conscious art. Sometimes they involve a break with old patterns of expectation.

One such epiphany for me occurred the first time I set eyes on *Citizen Kane*, in 1943 or thereabouts. I sat through the opening moments of Kane dying in Xanadu – Bernard Herrmann's music rather overdoing it, I thought, at the *blasé* age of 13 – when suddenly "stirring brassy music" (as the screenplay described it to me much, much later) erupted and the last eerie image cannonaded into the brash opening logo of "News on the March". I whipped round and hissed at Mother, with the *schadenfreude* of a person enjoying someone else's colossal blunder: "They've put the newsreel on by mistake!" We know now whose the mistake was. But it was a galvanising moment in my moviegoing – the first time I realised all movies needn't be made with the same structural orthodoxy. I sometimes wonder if the dislocating jolt to their expectations that my generation experienced on seeing *Citizen Kane* helps account for that film consistently coming out top in the "Ten Best Films Ever Made" lists compiled by international critics. And as this generation becomes a surviving minority among the ranks of movie critics, I ask myself if *Citizen Kane* will eventually be deposed from its first place – though never, I imagine, entirely from the list itself. For everyone like me who saw its novelty unwrapped in front of our eyes for the first time, it remains one of the evolutionary experiences of the movies. The critic's benchmarks for all later claims to revelation were thus set early and enduringly in my case.

It may surprise many people today, but being able to read about films and filmmaking wasn't easy in the 1930s and 1940s. Fan magazines apart, only a very few serious periodicals existed and none of them reached newsagents in our reasonably sophisticated but by no means specialised part of the world. Books in English about the cinema were still rare. Paul Rotha had published *The Film Till Now* in 1930 – not reprinted until

1949 - and in 1937 Alistair Cooke edited *Garbo and the Night Watchmen*, an anthology of American film criticism. Probably these were the best known books on the subject, though our public library had neither. Roger Manvell's *Film*, which came out in the last full year of the war, in 1944, was my first great discovery and joy, followed by the quarterly Penguin *Film Review* which he edited from 1946–49. In covers as solid and bright as tints on a decorator's paint-chart, these quarterlies coincided with the postwar rebirth and expansion of film societies. Each issue sold on average 25,000 copies - a best-seller even today, a super-seller then. Around 1947, I helped to get a film society going in our town. *Ivan the Terrible* was virtually the first foreign-language film any of us had seen - save for Obratsov's children's film, *Land of Toys*, which had come to Portadown in the middle of the war to signify the trust we placed in our Russian allies in those days. *Ivan the Terrible* was perhaps more in key with the Cold War, but its effect on us did not put much strain on the alliance. Film society attendance fell away dramatically after our first taste of "art" and, within a few months, it was back to Hollywood for everyone. That, too, was a seminal influence on a critic who has always loved Hollywood movies, yet hated Hollywood's dominion over his own culture.

Like a man who doesn't realise how poor he's been until he starts making a little money, I learned to appreciate from the Penguin *Film Review* how hugely ignorant I was of world cinema. I got my education from their pages; I caught up on the films later. And I realised how my viewing had been enhanced by my reading - which is a conceit that a critic needs to have.

My entertainment, however, arrived more frequently than the quarterly reviews; it dropped through the letter-box every Sunday in the shape of "the English papers".

By a concordat between the local newsagents and the main Protestant sects in town, the papers were not delivered until people had returned from morning worship. A sensible precaution, knowing the length of sermons in those days. But for a family like ours, which didn't very often wend its way to church, it meant a long paper-less wait. At about 1.10 p.m., just as the roast reached the table, C.A. Lejeune and Dilys Powell arrived with a "thock" on the hall carpet. I had trained my Scotty to pick

7

up both *The Observer* and *The Sunday Times* (it was possible for a small dog in those days: now it is hardly a feat for a grown man to attempt) and bring them to me at table. The rule of "no reading while eating" was relaxed on this occasion only. Both film critics formed my appreciation of what critical writing should do. Both writers "communicated". They gave their articles a "writer-to-reader" directness that was for me what an altar call was to Catholics. Dilys, I thought, took movies slightly more seriously; Caroline (as I discovered later on was what the "C" stood for; the "A" remained an eternal mystery) was ruder. Dilys, I envied: Caroline, I emulated. For apparently I was a rather direct child whose comments were sometimes charitably attributed to "impatience". I took after my blunt father in that respect. My mother would urge patience and bid me try to understand some disagreeable subject ". . . so that at least you can talk intelligently about it." (That kind of advice also serves a critic.) I had shown an early fondness for taking up quite perverse attitudes on conventional issues. At one time, aged seven or eight, I implored the other children around me to sit on their hands and not clap when our resuscitating applause was petitioned by Peter Pan to save Tinker Bell's life. I will put it no stronger than to say I was not a sentimental child. Reading C.A. Lejeune, I fancied I detected a ruthless streak in her, too.

But neither critic wrote with a diplomatic vocabulary. They were first and last *critics*. They praised, goaded, rebuked and championed and did all of it with authority. Reading them, one *heard* them. More by empathy than anything more rational, I learned to listen to the "voice" in the writing.

Over the years, I grew to value something else in such critics: continuity. That doesn't mean consistency. Critics never can – nor should be – consistent creatures. There is no virtue in that, only constraint. A good film can reverse one's judgments and sympathies – and to take off after a film, bent on vengeance, because it doesn't conform to one's own preordained set of attitudes isn't a virtue in my eyes. At its simplest, continuity means a tenure that's long enough to let readers become familiar with a critic's attitudes and to let critics be able to form the comparisons that are the beginning of criticism. At a certain rarefied level, it's tempting for a critic to impose his or her own values on readers. But I prefer to let these seed themselves in the sub-soil of what one writes and to cultivate the top soil for the entertainment of the reader.

You might suppose that I was soon writing off to the newspapers asking for a job as a film critic. I wasn't. I believed that an occupation that seemed better than work could never provide enough work to make a living. The "Protestant ethic" had bitten deeply. Seeing films was a pleasure; work must therefore be something else. For a time, my education set me on quite a wrong course.

A number of new international institutions, were being established in Western Europe, such as the Council of Europe itself. After taking my degree at Queen's, I went on to the Collège d'Europe, which had just been set up at Bruges, in Belgium, by the Council's member-nations to train its future bureaucrats. By the time I graduated from it, I no longer wanted to govern Europe; I'd seen the hours of tedium and compromise it would involve. I turned towards the Americans.

The Salzburg Seminar in American Studies, baroquely housed in a former Max Reinhardt *schloss* that was later used as the Trapp Family residence in *The Sound of Music*, put me in touch with teachers from Harvard (Arthur Holcombe), Cornell (Clinton Rossiter) and the *New York Post* (Max Lerner, their star columnist, who was a Brandeis professor, too). Lerner's combative style of engagement with his students was greatly to my liking – and, I found out later, to his readers'. (This was the "old" *New York Post*, the one edited by James Wechsler.) Max Lerner helped me get a post-graduate fellowship to the University of Michigan at Ann Arbor.

These were the "Eisenhower Years" of the early 1950s, the complacent era of campus tranquillity and "Populuxe" plenty, as Thomas Hine called it in his recent book on consumerism. Prewar America was still visible all around me: not quite Norman Rockwell, but not far off Frank Capra. A real-life Capra-esque villain was certainly viewable on the daily telecasts of the Congressional hearings in Washington DC at which Senator Joseph McCarthy took on the US Army for daring to call up one of his Congressional aides, G. David Schine, and holding him as a "hostage in uniform", as McCarthy alleged. Everything I'd seen in America reminded me of Hollywood, but particularly these hearings. I wasn't surprised when Joseph Welch, counsel for the Army, later starred in Otto Preminger's *Anatomy of a Murder*; and the impression of life aping art was even more strongly consolidated 20 years later, at the Cannes Film Festival when I met G. David Schine and discovered he had "gone into" movies and was now the executive producer of *The French Connection*.

I suppose that seeing a society in terms of its movies prompted my later, and now dominant, interest in seeing movies in terms of the society that produced them. I doubt that I'd have gained this bias had I remained in Europe. The Hollywood cinema is particularly rich in those elements that link cinema and society. A filmmaker working in the European tradition of humanism usually tells one much more about himself and sometimes, like Fellini, Antonioni or Bergman, succeeds in creating a personal vision of the society of his time that goes a long way to becoming a metaphor for it. But the Hollywood cinema responds more quickly – more rapaciously, perhaps – to the movements it senses or can exploit in the society to which it addresses its films; so that when a public nerve is struck or, increasingly frequently today, can be artificially stimulated by advertising hype, the film's reception provides a crude but powerfully suggestive clue to the present condition of the collective unconscious. A critic is part of the information fed into that consciousness . . .

Another bonus my spell in America held for me was psychoanalysis. I still believe the cultured first-generation Russian-American who became my analyst on campus called me – not I, him – since he got several learned papers out of our work together, mostly on the theme of cultural cross-pressures and multi-national attitudes, in which I was apparently fertile. Freudian analysis, I'm sure, is a great aide to being a critic, particularly a movie critic. Character may indeed be destiny; but talent is personality. My first book, *Sex in the Movies*, in 1964, reflected a lot of what I learned while speculating about a life that I frequently discussed in terms of movies I had seen. (Analysts of signs of social change, by the way, should note that Penguin at first wanted to entitle their edition *Sex in the Cinema*, since "movies" was still considered an American "vulgarism" in the mid-1960s! A half-minute's reflection persuaded them not to.)

The belief that writing – or, to be more precise, journalism as Max Lerner practised it – was what I wanted to do was sharpened when I met Lord Beaverbrook at one of his *soirées* at the Waldorf-Astoria in New York. At Michigan, I had been doing part-time lecturing in Government between my own researches into American attitudes towards Europe. Lord Beaverbrook was not impressed. "It is more valuable to entertain the public than to instruct it, Mr Walker," he announced. "It is also safer." He then asked me what I earned lecturing and a third inducement to switch disciplines was dangled in front of me.

My first job in journalism was not with Beaverbrook, however. His London minions were not all of the same mind as he that Walker must be employed immediately. I began on two rival Birmingham morning papers, first the *Gazette* and then the *Post* (into which the *Gazette* later folded). Within weeks of joining the staff of the first paper, I was its film critic. It was as easy as that.

Left largely to my own devices in the features department, I had gradually raised the readers' consciousness of the new films in town from down-page "fillers" to half-page reviews; and I moved with the column to the *Post* when the *Gazette* was closed down to be welcomed by a staid but reasonably liberal deputy editor, Walter Stevens, with the anxious words, "I hope you will manage to review films within our traditions." I had no idea what this meant, since the *Post* at that date hardly reviewed films at all but "farmed out" the Press show invitations to whichever reporter wanted to go to the pictures. The first thing I did was lop off the funereal black borders from the film stills they printed. This was (just about) tolerated. But a protest came from an unexpected quarter – from the compositors, no less! – when I used a still of a bare-backed (*sic*) Jeanne Moreau in a review of Louis Malle's *Les Amants*. The illustration was removed between editions. Thus I quickly learned a lesson not only about printers' puritanism (never mind, readers'), but also about an editor's right to edit. The next time, I didn't confront the latter force: I subverted it. Waiting until the paper's top executives were on their lengthy summer break, I inserted an end-of-column note announcing that from then on "the new films will be reviewed at their London openings". And on Monday morning, I took the train up to town and sat down in the row behind Dilys Powell at the morning Press show. By the time the *Post's* editors had returned to their desks in September, the "London Films" was an established column. (To be truthful, I don't think they

11

even noticed the change of address. If they did, they didn't say anything; the *Post* was a very gentlemanly paper.)

George Santayana said in one of his books – *Dominations and Powers*, I think – that the best way of getting what you want is to learn to like the way things have of coming about of their own accord when you give them a gentle push. I had given them a hard nudge. But in the end I got what I discovered I'd wanted all along.

I moved on to the London newspaper, the *Evening Standard*, four years later, in 1960. Its then editor Charles Wintour had twice suffered my name to be recommended to him. "Suffered" because, the first time, through a misunderstanding between him and the writer and columnist Godfrey Winn, Charles offered me a job on the financial pages – the Sixties bull market was just beginning to bellow. I first accepted the dizzy salary of £25, but after three hours' conscience-wrestling between love of money and love of movies, I turned it down.

The second time, prompted by Kenneth More with a more accurate summary of what benefit I might be to the *Standard* (and, intermittently, to Kenneth More), Charles took the precaution of getting my signature on the contract before I left his office. I had found my "home" with one of the decade's most brilliant editors (and in that respect, my luck has held ever since with Charles's successors, Louis Kirby and John Leese.)

If deadlines exert few pressures on the leisurely doings of film critics – nothing compared with the "curtain-to-column" sprint that theatre critics have to run nightly – working for Lord Beaverbrook, who owned the *Standard*, held terrors of another kind. Beaverbrook was a "hands-on" proprietor. Charles must have had several frights from the follies I committed in my early years. My precipitate – or intemperate – nature was usually to blame.

I would return from lunch in Soho to find the despatch rider from Cherkley, where Beaverbrook had his country house, had delivered the proprietor's tape-recorded commentary on the paper's contents to his secretariat in the *Daily Express*. They had typed it out, cut it up literally into strips and re-distributed the pieces to fall like shrapnel where Beaverbrook had decided they would cause most alarm. Not (at first) having any idea of the peril I was putting myself in, I would compose an immediate reply to some point he'd raised about a film I'd reviewed. A pert and independent riposte. After all, I had seen the film – he hadn't; I was the film critic – he wasn't. I didn't know I was handling high explosives. But Charles Wintour would turn white-lipped as he read the "black" of the text I'd already sent off – and that really did frighten me. "I hope you'll still be working for us next week," he said, chillingly, "but frankly, I doubt it."

But like the story-teller in the *Arabian Nights*, I was spared execution, apparently because I introduced some fanciful new point into my reply which incited Beaverbrook to answer it with a follow-up query – and so, although the agony was protracted, the death sentence was continually postponed. "On the strength of your exceptionally warm review of *Harold Lloyd's World of Comedy*, Lady Dunn (Beaverbrook's long-time companion whom he married a year before his death) and I went to see it. We were obliged to walk out. Your comments, please." – "Dear Lord Beaverbrook, I am sorry that you and Lady Dunn did not enjoy *Harold Lloyd's World of Comedy*. For me, in future, high buildings will hold an additional hazard." – "Your reply is not as earnest as I would have wished. What is your opinion of that form of humour known as the 'wisecrack'?" – "Dear Lord Beaverbrook, the 'wisecrack' is a form of wit much indulged in by Hollywood. I fear it often infects those who have to see too many Hollywood films." And so on, about a fortnight of this torturous free-association, until the exchange came full circle and one was discharged, rather than convicted. "Lady Dunn and I, though sometimes walkers-out when we do not enjoy a film, are generally Walkerites. Please recommend a film we can see at Cherkley this week-end. It must not be too long or too noisy."

I missed Beaverbrook when he died a few years later, a mischievous autocrat to the end; but I had known what it was like for the *Skibereen Eagle* to have had the Czar of Russia's eye on it.

In fact, though I didn't recognise it at the time, it was all good, if high-risk, tutoring in another commandment of film criticism: never second-guess your readers. If one attempts to transplant what the public thinks of a film, one is finished as a film critic.

A film critic's week in those years, the 1960s, was as long or as short as one cared to make it. For a good part of the decade, only four new films opened in London every week. They were shown to critics much the way they are now, except that now there may

13

be anything up to six or eight a week. We saw them on Mondays and Tuesdays, as we still do, starting at 10.30 a.m., frequently in the cinemas where they were due to open a few days later; and then in the afternoon, when the paying public was (hopefully) filling those cinemas, the venue became the private screening rooms of the companies distributing the films. It was a relaxed life – and often a replete one. Almost every week, a critics' lunch would be held, since the distributors persisted in believing that the way to our charity was through our stomachs. Nowadays, there are far, far more critics – sometimes 50 or 60, generated by the media explosion in TV, radio and the "listings" magazines – and there are far, far fewer luncheons. I do not miss the food at all; I should have hated to miss some of the company I kept, though.

One critic I admired was Paul Dehn of the *News Chronicle* (both of them now deceased): a man with a quick intelligence (he was an ex-Bletchley Park cryptographer in the war, and a contemporary of Alan Turing); a very witty revue and lyrics writer; a screenwriter, too, with *Goldfinger* and *Murder on the Orient Express* in his credits; and a critic whose elegant turn of phrase was only matched by his concise perception of a film.

Then there was Penelope Gilliatt (always called "Mrs Gilliatt", which lent her a Restoration dash) who succeeded C.A. Lejeune on *The Observer*. Caroline had fired blowpipe darts into the egos she reviewed, Mrs Gilliatt brought back scalps.

And there was Kenneth Tynan . . . Tynan was unmatchable in virtually every way. Tynan had authority, brought over from the theatre where his *ad hominem* style of criticism resembled the entry of a razor gang into a gentlemen's club. Tynan had met Garbo – a critic meeting Garbo, *imagine!* – and he caught her uniqueness in words of prismatic brilliance the effect of which I have never seen equalled by anyone seeking to refract that lady's singularity into all its colours. Tynan's film criticism felt slightly flatter than his theatre writing; but then the material he had to work on was usually baser. Tynan fed on flesh, not celluloid.

What Tynan taught me was a concern for the interaction of personality and *persona*, on- and off-screen; and I hope this is reflected in some chapters of the present book. Tynan didn't just describe what was in front of his eyes – though he was a superb recorder of appearances, too. He traced the cryptic origins of talent and sometimes found them in very strange places. Before the profile writers took over the world with their backpacks of hand-out material, Tynan explored the dark continents of personality for its essences, with no map to guide him but his own instinct and judgment. Reading the book *Persona Grata*, which he co-authored with Cecil Beaton, in 1953, I recognised in him exactly the same alloy that he judged made others eligible for his hallmark of inclusion: "craftsmanship, energy, elegance, with a dash of the unpredictable".

It saddens me to think how few original books Tynan wrote: *He That Plays the King* (1950): *Persona Grata, Alec Guinness* (1953); and *Bull Fever* (1955) – all the rest were collections and anthologies of reprinted pieces. Tynan wanted to be the performer as well as the critic – which is fine, except that his energies were exhausted and his talents removed from the sphere where they were best employed. He became literary manager (at the National) and impresario (with *Oh, Calcutta!*); and he let himself be seduced by chimeras as well as charisma. He squandered what pitifully little time he had left in a life that lasted only 53 years on actions and enterprises patently unworthy of him. As Peter Kemp wrote, cruelly perhaps, but justly, in the *Times Literary Supplement* when reviewing Kathleen Tynan's biography of her late husband, "For a decade or so [he was] genuinely distinguished, then settled for being merely conspicuous."

It was my good fortune to know Kenneth Tynan in those "distinguished" decades when he combined intellectual authority with resplendent phrase-making. I see I have quoted Tynan frequently in the following chapters. I hope his matchless perceptions will encourage people to re-read him – and, even more important, publishers to reprint him.

Tynan taught me that one must record for posterity, not just for today. By his example, he handed me a longer lens and a wider viewfinder. He'd written that he realised "theatre was a branch of sociology as well as a means of self-expression". I believe this is even truer of films. If entertainment is the active ingredient of film reviewing, one must never forget the dormant elements in the films: the politics, morals, life-styles, economics that a movie can reflect and sometimes even change. For movies define their times far better than statesmen do.

Pauline Kael, in a famous running commentary stretching

15

through several *New Yorker* film columns and published in finite form as *Trash, Art and the Movies*, wrote: "Part of the fun of movies is in seeing 'what everybody's talking about', and if the people are flocking to a movie, there is a sense in which we want to see it, even if we suspect we won't enjoy it, because we want to know what's going on." Exactly. To my way of thinking, that's what film criticism should provide for; it should tell people "what's going on" in the deepest sense of the phrase, not simply what's on the screen.

A critic must try to guess *why* it's going on, which may lead him or her into matters of social or political change, sexual revolution, personality (or, as we now prefer to say, celebrity) cults, generational shifts in taste and international shifts of mood in countries where films are made (or, for various shameful reasons, *not* made). This sounds portentously self-important; but after a time it's something a serious writer on movies does like breathing: sometimes taking a deep breath (in writing books); sometimes panting lightly (in journalism); sometimes holding his breath (not knowing what's happening); and sometimes having the breath knocked out of him (by the total unexpectedness of something happening).

Film critics are performers in their medium in the sense that actors are in theirs; and acquaintance with the text is essential to both sorts. But it's their interpretation that the respective audiences pay to enjoy, to have their feelings appealed to, their curiosity satisfied, and be sent away, at the end of the last act, or the last paragraph, maybe that little bit more fulfilled or illuminated. A good critic learns to do that with trash as well as art. To quote Ms Kael again: "If a movie is important to other people we're interested in it because of what it means to them, even if it doesn't mean much to us."

"It's only a movie, Ingrid," Alfred Hitchcock once said to Ingrid Bergman, when she was being "difficult". But it's not true. The book in which he is quoted, François Truffaut's *Hitchcock*, makes it plain how much Hitchcock resented – feared, even – the efforts others made to find his mind's construction in his movies. It also underlines how narrow his sensibilities were, how niggardly or non-existent his praise was for fellow filmmakers. Hitchcock made some great movies, but one wonders if he really loved moviemaking in the widest, most generous sense. A critic must love movies with that kind of passion, even though he doesn't make any movies.

A film critic's work-load in the 1980s now reflects the expanded place that movies fill in people's consciousness, though not always (or even primarily) in the cinema. Between eight and ten per cent of the "old movies" shown on the two TV networks in Britain are compressed into the fortnight's holiday that the British take over the Christmas and New Year period – an amazing 143 in the 1987–88 period. Film festivals have mush-roomed, too: 287 of every size, duration, character, prestige and ambition at the last count, in 1986. Berlin, Cannes and Venice, in calendar order, are the three that it's hard not to attend – two at least – and still call yourself a critic. They are a good place to stand and see what films the rest of the world is making. Cannes especially is the best observation post for noting how creative energies flow from one country's film industry to another's or how a generational coming-of-age or political liberation or repression can assist or stem the emergence of a national cinema.

None of us who were at Cannes in 1959 will ever forget the night that the *Nouvelle Vague* broke on our consciousness with Truffaut's *Les Quatre Cent Coups*. Packed into the crowd on the rose-marble steps of the old Palais des Festivals, I applauded till my palms tingled. Jean Cocteau had sniffed change on the wind even earlier and before the film ended he had telephoned Picasso to come down from his studio in nearby Mougins and enable both of them to play godfathers to the new movement. Thus I witnessed little Jean-Pierre Léaud flanked by the poet on one side of him and, on the other, by the painter who in spite of his Communist liaisons had changed into a *smoking* for the occasion and added an incongruous touch of *un gentleman* with an Eng-lish bowler hat. Truffaut followed a few modest paces behind them, looking not at all like a man initiating a new era in cinema. It must be recorded that the Cannes jury that year also lagged somewhat behind: Truffaut took only the Director's prize, the *Palme d'or* going to the traditionalist Marcel Camus for *Orfeu Nègre*.

A few years later, Cannes received Antonioni's phlegmatic *L'Avventura* with yawns and jeers, but soon that film had set the somnambulist style for all those alienated movies of the 1960s

17

about the sick soul of Europe. At least we recognised what was happening to us when Fellini's *La Dolce Vita* signalled the U-turn that Europe was making from postwar austerity to sensate gratification – the *sin* of the times, all right. We felt new blood stirring in Czechoslovakia's political arteries with the fresh-faced and sexually liberated movies of the "Dubcek spring" – which Soviet repression so speedily ended and, with it, virtually a whole film generation.

The first years of the 1970s at Cannes alerted critics to the overkill of the Aquarian Age: every cinema in town seemed to be screening soft and hard porn. The chief of police shrugged help-lessly and declared the place a *ville ouverte* for the duration. Later we saw the creative flame borne by an unlikely runner called *Picnic at Hanging Rock* – from Australia, of all outposts! But that sub-continent soon became a hesitant and then a swag-gering contestant on the *Côte d'azur*. And even more recently we've felt the neo-conservative yearnings for the old established values of story and stars as the Cannes movies of the 1980s react against the deconstructionist abandonment of form and content that followed the "Youth Revolution" of 1968.

A film critic has thus to keep his bags permanently packed and ready to follow his instinct – as far as his expenses allow, any-how – if he's to do his duty by his trade and report back from where the newest "new cinema" is to be found.

But the national cinema that all other countries have to learn to live with is Hollywood's. Hollywood is America's overseas empire – with minds to colonise, not territory. The local resist-ance movements of indigenous cinemas are fighting an unequal (and losing) battle, I'm afraid, but that's no reason why critics should shirk their special duty to their own film industry. In Britain, that's often a bitter experience. I've followed the ebb and flow of British film fortunes in two books already: *Hol-lywood, England* (1974) and *National Heroes* (1986). A third book to come, in the 1990s, will be called *The Betrayal Years* – a title that tells all, or most, of the shame that should stain our cultural pride at the way we have let our patrimony be sold to foreigners. But that's another story . . .

A film critic can choose to get to know hundreds of people in the industry, or none at all; it all depends on his or her inclina-tions. My own tend towards the promiscuous, though friendship is the aim, not courtships, and the best relationships are those that invite criticism, not flattery.

Part of the reason for writing this book is to preserve some of the pleasures such encounters have brought me – though, as it's part of my character, I've admitted a fair bit of sardonic scepticism into the record, when it's appropriate. The emphasis is on meetings with remarkable men and women; for the second question most commonly put to a film critic – after the "How did you become . . ." one – is, "What is so-and-so really like?" There are as many answers as there are so-and-so's, but I've concentrated on the unique performers and performances and tried to explore the conjectural links between their personalities, talents and careers. And I've included some random reflections on other parts of a film critic's trade.

"It's Only a Movie, Ingrid" is a book of self-indulgence that I hope will preserve and maybe stimulate a remembrance of things and people not too long past. By the end of it, I'd like to think you'll share my view of Hitchcock's condescending little remark. His words don't even begin to tell the truth. It's always *more* than a movie, Ingrid.

"NAME THE SIX BEST FILMS YOU'VE EVER SEEN"

"What do you work at?" Not "do", you notice, but "work at". Reticent English people in a Mayfair drawing room would hardly have got round to finding out what I "did" before the time came for us to say goodbye. Americans are different. "Work" was how I had to define myself, early and unashamedly, and the question was put to me head-on. Not in any unfriendly fashion – simply in the manner that people would adopt to a total stranger who was going to be their supper companion in five minutes or so.

I certainly didn't need to ask what William Randolph Hearst Jr worked at. The publisher and his wife were sitting on a sofa, facing me, looking formidably solid and curiously impassive – the way that intimate friends of David Hockney emerge from his paintings of them. For people still experiencing the baleful public notoriety of their "outlaw" niece, Patty Hearst, and her trial and imprisonment, they both looked impressively composed, though I suspected it was the natural wariness of public faces passing transiently among strangers in private places.

"I write," I said in reply to Mr Hearst's question. Silence. I was compelled to give away a little more. "I am a film critic." Exactly like a "Speak Your Weight" machine, Mr Hearst said, "Name the six best films you've ever seen."

Now this is a question that most film critics encounter some time or other. Either that or "What's the best film you've ever seen?" For various reasons I usually try to avoid answering: it's a question that requires a brutal, trivialising, patronising or just plain troublesome answer. Anyhow, I have an antipathy to list-making and harbour a particular scorn for list-makers who are regarded by some people as cinema historians.

But on this occasion there was no escape from an interrogation that required me to return six balls in place of the one that had

23

been lobbed over the dividing net. "Well, Renoir . . ." I began (always safe). *"La Grande illusion?"* queried Mrs Hearst. – "I prefer *La Règle du jeu.*" – "Really?" (Plainly, Renoir was not so safe.) "And Chaplin . . ." – *"The Gold Rush,"* she said. – *"The Kid,"* I countered. "That leaves four," said Mr Hearst, not a shade of expression on his large, powerful, heavy features.

Now it sank in that this was more than simply a way of satisfying a casual curiosity. For was I not speaking to the son of the tycoon of the same name who had featured as the eponymous model for Orson Welles's *Citizen Kane*? That film had always struck me as being about a man who behaved more like a film mogul than a publishing tycoon, and the envy that Welles patently possessed for the flamboyant life Hearst led transcended the calumny to which the latter had been subjected by his film. But in the present circumstances there wasn't going to be time to explain such niceties. I began to feel that "Name the Six Best Films" was an inquisitorial game that the Hearsts may have played on previous occasions. True or not, for me it resembled the "Get the Guest" gamesmanship that so enlivened the evenings with George and Martha in *Who's Afraid of Virginia Woolf*?

"Kubrick," I said, playing for time, hoping supper would be announced before the list was complete. "I don't know his films," said one of the Hearsts – I forget which. *"Dr Strangelove,"* I prompted, hoping it would remind him/her. There was absolutely no response. The countdown had now reached an interesting stage. "How about Buñuel?" I asked. They waited – well, how *about* him?

In my eyes by now, Mr and Mrs Hearst had ceased to be Hockney figures, two-dimensional and immured in the moment of their commitment to paint; they had become George Segal sculptures, ominously life-size simulacra of flesh and blood, though drained of familiar coloration.

"The Discreet Charm of the Bourgeoisie," I said. No, on reflection not Buñuel's greatest; yet in its deft, witty, and eventually savage demonstration of how our nightmares invade and possess our normal daily composure very much a prophetic film – certainly one with which I identified in my present impasse. No word was spoken, but it was clear that we all three

knew what was in each other's thoughts. As if conducting a criminal interrogation, they were only waiting for the suspect to crack.

Suddenly I began to enjoy it all. It was the "Who Blinks First" syndrome in a domestic set-up rather than a business one. If placed in such a dilemma, I've always believed the best solution is to *wink* first.

I nominated Fellini as my fifth choice, adding that *La Dolce Vita* might not be a "great" film, by the strictest standards, but its maker's timeliness in giving life and, more important, a label to the materialist orgy of the Sixties would surely entitle it to a place on the short list.

"And what's your sixth?" asked Mr Hearst. The crunch had come.

"Well," I said, trying to look as if I'd been in mischievous collusion with them from the word go and had deliberately been holding back the card they knew full well was in my hand. "Well, how could one possibly leave out *Citizen Kane*?" Mr Hearst said nothing – nothing at all. Afterwards, this struck me as shrewd of him. Whatever he thought of the movie that traduced his father, he certainly wasn't going "on the record" about it now. I can find no evidence that he has ever done so, though surely there must have been numerous requests from interviewers and researchers, more or less serious, more or less scholarly, trying to elicit some recollections of what the Hearst dynasty had thought of *Citizen Kane* at the time – or, at the very least, thought about it *now*, when, as I remarked in the previous chapter, the movie consistently tops the international polls of the "Best Film Ever Made" that are periodically taken by serious cinema publications.

But it was left to Mrs Hearst to give me what little gratification my integrity, boldness or plain cheek entitled me to. "A somewhat overrated film, I've always thought," she said. And that was the end of that. The butler entered the drawing room at that precise minute and announced that supper was served and we all found ourselves different partners around the table.

I never got to say goodbye to the Hearsts. They took their leave before I did. Xanadu keeps its secrets still.

CHARLIE'S ANGEL AND THE CULTURE MINISTER'S WALKING STICK

He was 82 and, I must say, looked it. Charlie Chaplin at the end did not wear well. I was surprised and dismayed when I saw him off-screen, in the flesh, for the first time, at the Cannes Film Festival in 1971.

I knew people much older than he – my own father for one – who had retained the elasticity of limb and alertness of eye of men half their age. Chaplin moved like a toy in need of new batteries. He stared ahead, unnervingly, like a man who could see but can't quite transmit what he sees to the place in the brain where it makes sense. His festival hosts had taken him round to the back of the Palais des Festivals in a wheel-chair. Then they decanted him into a human "sedan chair" and carried him up the bare cold backstairs and into the wings of the stage on which he was due to be honoured by the Minister of Culture. France was determined to slip the halter of a *commandeur* of the Legion of Honour over his tortoise neck, stick the scarlet *bouton* on the old man's lapel like a fresh rosebud from one of those blind flower-girls whom the younger Charlie encountered and sighed for in his films, and plant on those perished cheeks of his an official "kiss of state". There were those of us in the audience that night who felt it would have been more appropriate if we had been attending an embalming, not an investiture.

Even the huge heatwave of applause that rose from the audience as he shuffled mechanically on stage to the *Limelight* theme, accompanied by Robert Favre LeBret, the festival's president, didn't seem to take the chill off Charlie Chaplin. He really wasn't enjoying anything about the occasion.

Seeing an old friend who has suffered *un coup de vieux* is always an uneasy experience; but when it's the Cinema's greatest practitioner of slapstick, a kinetic mime whom we've seen employing every one of his artful physical faculties to infuse inanimate nature with the gift of mischievous life, then it is

29

unbearably painful. According to David Robinson, in his massive and definitive biography, Chaplin had tripped and fallen during the shooting of *A Countess from Hong Kong* at Pinewood Studios, in 1966, and broken his ankle. It is possible that from this time on he began to suffer a series of very minor, almost imperceptible strokes which eventually led to such a catastrophic set-back in his physical and mental agility.

Whereas a comic like Keaton worked out his tricks by intellect and forethought, Chaplin got some of his best ideas by touch and intuition. He had only to take something in his hands and he worked a lightning metamorphosis in its function and nature. The objects, you felt, discovered what they *should* have been when they passed into Chaplin's grasp. A bowler hat in a cage realised that its destiny was to be a bird; an alarm clock with wonky works was reincarnated as a sick baby being examined in a clinic for the city poor; a stack-a-stick pile of chairs on a waiter's shoulders discovered a fraternal affinity with a porcupine. "Touch" was Chaplin's talisman. Like a blind person reading a message written in Braille, he made palpable the second nature of things. Dexterity might accomplish the dazzling physical trick, but touch transmitted the transforming inspiration.

Now, at Cannes, his touch had vanished. He simply looked, well, stricken – a victim of creative sclerosis. Better death, we thought compassionately, than disablement.

He was positioned (unhappily) centre-stage where he looked even more exposed. Favre LeBret hovered uncertainly around him – waiting to catch him, maybe, if he fell? Then Georges Duhamel, the Minister of Culture at that time, walked on from the wings carrying the Legion of Honour insignia in a velvet box – or, rather, the Minister limped on.

Duhamel was afflicted, too, but in a minor way. He was leaning on a cane – whether the result of a natural disability or a recent accident, I was not sure.

There were the usual ceremonial speeches, utterly devoid of wit or comedy. In these circumstances, it seemed like serving the goose without the stuffing; *la gloire* was not going to be denied *its* curtain-speech. And still there was no reaction from Chaplin. The scene, already morbid, began to assume a mummified aspect as the formalities imposed their own stiff postures on the participants. The Minister finally concluded his *allocution*, then handed the velvet box of the Legion of Honour to Favre LeBret, reaching round behind Chaplin to do so and seeming, the pair of them, like a couple of tailors sizing the "Little Fellow" up for a new suit. And still Chaplin stared straight ahead.

Favre LeBret picked up the *collier* with its dangling order and handed it back to the Minister who prepared to pass it round Chaplin's neck like a thin red bib and secure it at the back . . . And it was then, mercifully, that things began to go wrong.

To pin a *collier*, one needs two free hands. M. Duhamel had only one hand free, for he was holding his walking cane in the other. Favre LeBret reacted quickly and went to his help. Each man took an end of the riband, passed it round Chaplin and started to pin it at the nape of the neck. Impracticable! As they fumbled, the audience started to chuckle. Then a ripple of titters spread. It didn't occur to either functionary that their efforts, when viewed by the audience from the front, resembled executioners garrotting a condemned man; for the material was now stretched into one of Chaplin's chin-folds and it looked as if his supply of air was being cut off. The packed auditorium began reacting audibly and risibly to this piece of *petit guignol*, made all the funnier by the victim's total lack of animation. I found myself thinking of that marvellous piece of mime in *Shoulder Arms* when Charlie, camouflaged as a tree, tries to "act" one, too, and becomes a sort of vegetable with hilarious animal attachments. Suddenly Duhamel broke the deadlock. He shooed Favre LeBret away and gave himself back the use of his own two hands by abandoning his prop. He hung the crook of his walking cane on the nearest thing that would lend it temporary support – Chaplin's arm.

The comedian had reflexively reached out to the microphone-stand in front of him in order to steady himself against the assault of these two bearers of honours, and now he gave a stiff little sideways glance at the cane that had suddenly, miraculously, appeared on his arm. Slowly, across the dry-freeze look on that old face, something like a grin began to form . . . and spread. Another man's walking cane was a borrowed sceptre indeed; but he lifted it off his arm with his own free hand. He swung it lightly. He swung it faster. Applause broke out. He now had it going round like a St Catherine's wheel firework. A deep roar began to swell up out of the auditorium . . . mounted . . .

became a huge thunder-clap of noise that supplemented the clash of human hand-palms. People started to rise to their feet. The whole house was standing and Chaplin was grinning – both he and the audience in mutual and joyful recognition of each other.

But I'll wager that it was touch and not hearing that transmitted the message back to wherever "The Tramp's" identity resided in Chaplin's creative being, animating it the way an induction coil passes energy through matter. With a cane in his hand, Chaplin came to life. Wanly comic, maybe, still pathetic, but given back the gift of cheeky semaphore to cut through the pomp and circumstance of the ceremony with a timeless twirl of this stick. He held onto it, too, when it was time for everyone to leave the stage. Duhamel was obliged to limp off into the wings unaided, but radiating a sort of emotional relief that in the end all had turned out well, so that his own pain seemed nullified – probably the way a believer feels who's been emboldened to abandon his crutches at Lourdes.

But the greater miracle that night belonged to Chaplin. Like Lazarus, he'd come back to life before our eyes, raised from the living dead by a touch of the wand that had once helped him extend his comic misrule to every part of the tangible world within his reach. On that night at Cannes, I knew what it was to cry with laughter.

The next time I saw Charlie Chaplin was in 1977. This time I was closer to him, but he was further away from me then ever – and from everyone else, except those in his immediate family circle.

He'd come to London from Switzerland to promote his illustrated autobiography entitled *My Life in Pictures*, which Francis Wyndham had skilfully compiled from the Chaplin family albums and any scraps of the old man's memory that could be stretched to picture-caption length.

The story was later told to me – though not by Wyndham – that extracting even this bare modicum of nostalgia from the shrunken and sometimes irascible little white-haired man was more exhausting to his tender inquisitors than it was to him. A routine developed in which they would show him a snapshot or, more usually, a film still, then wait for something, *anything*, to swim into sight in the developing tray of that dark-room which now formed his memory. On one occasion they were relieved to see a still from *Modern Times* of the "Little Fellow" in a factory setting with "The Girl" beside him arouse Chaplin's immediate interest. In fact he became quite excited over it. "That girl . . . that girl," he kept repeating, "I know her . . . I know her." Wryly, sweetly, they told him that so he should. She was Paulette Goddard; he had been married to her for almost nine years.

At the Publisher's reception for *My Life in Pictures*, they showed a Chaplin film and, for some reason or other, he himself sat through a movie he must have seen hundreds of times. It was *The Kid*. It reduced all of us to unashamed tears. But Chaplin sat staring "sightlessly" ahead, as I'd seen him do at Cannes, so that there was no way of telling whether or not he even saw a film in front of him, never mind one in which his younger, perkier self "parented" (as we must now say) the infant Jackie Coogan.

Some years later I learned that Coogan had appeared at the champagne gala in New York with which Lincoln Center had marked Chaplin's return to America in 1972 after his troubles in the 1950s with the Communist witch hunters of the Un-American Activities sub-committee. By then, the former "Kid" was a paunchy bald man of 58, better known as the ghoulish "Uncle Fester" of *The Addams Family* television series. As the story is told by Aram Saroyan – William's son – in his curious book *Trio*, Chaplin didn't evince a flicker of recognition when Coogan introduced himself. After Oona Chaplin had tried prompting her husband to take note of his one-time infant co-star, she finally poked him hard and hissed, "Charlie, it's Jackie Coogan . . . it's 'The Kid', darling." Chaplin swivelled his eyes away from the infinity he was intent upon observing. "Stop poking me," he whispered. "He wants residuals."

If I'd heard that anecdote at the time we were all responding so moistly to *The Kid's* temporal misfortunes and providential deliverances, maybe I would have been drier-eyed when the lights went up. But, again, maybe not.

After the film, a few of us were introduced to Chaplin. He must have had many such agonies to bear in his life and only his physical disability, I think, prevented him from quite rightly sending us packing on this occasion. I asked him if we would ever get a chance to see *A Woman of Paris*, the Lubitsch-like social comedy he had written and directed in 1923. This was the only

33

film of his silent period in which he wasn't the star (although he had a walk-on role as a railway porter whose churlish unshouldering of a passenger's travelling trunk encapsulated all the indignant manner of a disdainful Sisyphus). I half hoped that my mention of the title *A Woman of Paris* would be the pebble tossed into the well of Chaplin's memory that might produce some interesting ripples of remembrance about the film. No such luck. "Too long . . . too long," he finally whispered into my ear-drum – an echo from the Moon.

As it happened, the film did reappear, but not till after Chaplin's death. I rushed to see it at the revival by David and Barbara Stone, two of London's most innovative film distributors at the time, who had scooped their rivals. I cried again watching it, this time with exasperated admiration at the new areas of talent which Chaplin had only begun to explore with that "serious" social comedy whose total commercial failure turned him back to his slapstick style.

A Woman of Paris reminded me of Chaplin's seemingly effortless visual shorthand which enables him to suggest a whole life-style and comment on it in a single brilliant stroke of direction. It makes many of today's movies sound like what they are – over-talkative radio plays. The maid handling the pile of fresh laundry lets a gentleman's collar slip out, to the consternation of her mistress's ex-fiancé – so this is the state of sin she's living in! A man-about-Paris swaggering into the same lady's apartment finds himself short of a hanky and making straight for the bureau drawer helps himself to one – so this is the one who pays the rent! A muscular masseuse summoned to iron out the wrinkles of the night before tells us by her disapproving pummelling all we need to know of the morals of the socialites gossiping over her client's unseen body – so this is how the idle rich live! If such strokes still impress us today, how revolutionary they must have seemed in 1923! Chaplin's social realism is mercilessly cynical. His own mistress, Edna Purviance (for whom he intended *A Woman of Paris* to be the launching pad to a star's career), is quite ready to let herself be ruined by luxury, but not so quick to let marriage to a poor man ruin life for her. Was it his experience of Hollywood that engendered this cynicism in Chaplin – or was it always there? His son Michael Chaplin, an early teenage rebel of the 1960s, compared his "life with father" to that of someone

34

brought up in an orphanage, which is sinister indeed coming from the son of a man who himself had been brought up, however briefly, in a workhouse. On the other hand, Chaplin's cynicism has the characteristic "He wants residuals" reflex about it that Hollywood breeds. In most of his "comic" comedies, it is redeemed by sentiment; but not in *A Woman of Paris*. There is no sentimental sell-out here, and the box-office take was correspondingly meagre.

In Adolphe Menjou, too, Chaplin found the *alter ego* he admired most. We tend to think Chaplin loved "The Tramp". In fact, he loved "The Gent" even more – off-screen anyhow. Menjou's character in the film is not so much *alter*, either, if we are to believe the gossip about Chaplin's habit of losing his heart to a woman, and then the emotion being superseded by his heartlessness to her. Sentiment and cynicism were central constituents of his idiosyncratic alloy. Worldly, witty, shrewd in the ways of womankind, Menjou's guilt-free *bon vivant* is nearer to Chaplin's own reality than "The Tramp" was ever permitted to be. Curious how it's forgotten that Chaplin was poor, really poor, for only a very few short years of his life; he soon became a well-paid, and then a highly paid music-hall entertainer. Yet it's "The Tramp" on which he supposedly impressed the watermark of his experiences. The evidence of his own life points, on the contrary, to the Menjou character, himself looking like a trial run for Monsieur Verdoux, as the one that's inhabited by the real Charles Chaplin.

Again and again in this film, Chaplin delights in shredding sentiment by showing up human shortcomings. When Edna in a petulant fit flings the pearls her protector has given her out of the window into the street, she savours her "virtue" only for as long as it takes her to see a beggar picking the necklace up off the road – whereupon she rushes outside to grab it back. If the barking dog that pursued the lady up the street is a Chaplinesque concession to slapstick comedy, Edna's sudden exhibition of the "conscience of the rich" in bestowing a measly tip on the hobo from whom she has snatched back a fortune is Chaplin's totally unexpected bonus of realism.

The amount of psychological realism he could refine out of social melodrama is breathtaking. How relieved Ernst Lubitsch, the leader in that line of cruel and witty cynicism, must have been when the audience's rejection of the film (they had expected to see a comedy starring Charlie) hit Chaplin as killingly as silence in a packed theatre that had once given him unstinted applause. The withdrawal of love, we're told, is what kills stars – for stars are by definition people who are loved. *A Woman of Paris* was put away in Chaplin's vaults for over 50 years – and two years after he made it, he regained his audience's love with *The Gold Rush*. What a social realist we lost, what a sardonic critic of humankind!

A Woman of Paris was the last of his old films that Chaplin pulled out of the vaults at the Swiss manor house at Vevey, where he'd eventually come to rest after his self-exile from America, in order to refurbish it with a music score he had composed himself. Work like this obviously clarified his memory – mere "mental" remembering was not enough.

Chaplin died on the worst of days, if any day is worse than another to die on – Christmas Day, 1977. His death was announced to the world – or, at least, the Christian part of it which took the day off. But the mass media not infrequently now take more than "the day" off. Newspapers have their post-Christmas features pages pre-empted by articles already set up in type or locked into the printer's frame (this was before the age of computerised setting) and so several days elapsed before the specialist writers overcame their Christmas blocks, or returned from their vacations, in order to pass a valedictory judgment on Charlie Chaplin's life and career. Television was taken even more embarrassingly by surprise. Not until the end of the first week of January, for instance, did BBC Television find an unspoken-for slot in its prearranged programming long enough to slip in a Chaplin tribute of any worth or substance. (Die on a Friday afternoon, early if possible, is advice that the famous and talented would do well to heed; it gives the next day's morning papers time to do them justice, yet still leaves the Sunday Press with an obligation to their memory.)

Ironically, what happened to Chaplin almost immediately after the life finally left his body got almost as much space devoted to it and certainly resulted in more instantaneous attention being paid to him.

I remembered it well nearly three years afterwards, when I sat

36

with Chaplin's widow, Oona, in pale September sunshine on the terrace of the Manoir de Ban, the 18-roomed house she and her late husband had made their home at Vevey-sur-Corsaire. They had lived there for 24 of their 34 years together.

The gloaming was already beginning to creep up with the mist from Lake Leman, but it was still possible to see the bright hues in the family snapshot album on Lady Chaplin's lap. It was open at a page of photos she had taken not long after Charlie's death. One snapshot showed a rural scene just 12 miles from where we were sitting. It had the vivid Fauve-like hues that the sun gives an out-door setting immediately after a storm. A violet mountain back-ground, clumps of emerald trees in mid-distance, a lime-green swathe of meadow and there, in the foreground, looking as if it were made out of two sticks of rough-hewn firewood, a little Christian cross about two feet tall planted in the crop-land. A photo of it in close-up allowed one to read the words hand-written on it in inky irregular capitals: "ICI DORMAIT, EN PAIX, CHARLIE CHAPLIN": "Here slept, in peace, Charlie Chaplin."

The unprompted tribute of the farmer who owned the land com-memorated – and, for all I know, still does – the spot where two grave-robbers, Polish and Bulgarian garage hands, with a turn of mind more grotesquely funny, surely, than gruesome, had stashed the coffin containing the "Little Fellow" which they had stolen from the Chaplin family vault in 1978, while they tried to screw 300,000 Swiss francs in ransom money out of his widow and children in order to set themselves up in the motor trade.

I thought at the time that it was exactly the kind of comic business you'd have found in a silent movie; surely if ever a bit of buffoonery needed a tinkling piano accompaniment to pace its *grotesquerie* and cue the audience in on the funny side of mortality, it was this foredoomed little plot. Nevertheless, it caught the attention of the world's media and held it until the miscreants were apprehended and the *corpus* of such comic jinks was allowed to settle back again into a sense of permanent loss. "Victoria", said Oona Chaplin, referring to her daughter, "said at the time, 'It's so beautiful a place the robbers buried Papa in that it's almost a shame to bring him back to the family grave.' " But the Swiss police – nothing if not correct – insisted on Chaplin being returned to legitimate peace: can't have corpses cluttering up the cantons.

The snapshot in the Chaplin family album reminded me of what,

37

in life as in death, the great clown seemed, to me to be seeking most – serenity. Against the odds, it was Oona Chaplin, now sitting opposite me and sending for a camel-hair coat to guard against the gathering chill, who brought him that. She had been his fourth wife and there was a difference of 37 years in their ages when they were married. Looking at her, I wondered about that moment when they had first met. Oona, the daughter of the playwright Eugene O'Neill, was then only 17. I knew that Chaplin, going by the "pessimism" of her father's plays, had expected to meet someone "a little more sepia". But had he noticed how her features, just out of the bud of adolescence, must have hinted at a face that would be so extraordinarily like his own when fully formed that she could have been mistaken for his daughter? The same large teeth, the extra-wide mouth, the slightly slitty eyes that are constantly quizzing you . . .

Chaplin at that time, in 1942, was planning to shoot Paul Vincent Carroll's play *Shadow and Substance*. It would have been his first adaptation of someone else's work and his first non-comedy – an extraordinary break with tradition for such a totally self-created comic artist. Regarding the possible reason for this, every single book about Chaplin's life and work is silent including, of course, his autobiography. I should love to know. Oona had already made a screen test for another filmmaker; Chaplin had it screened and saw in her, perhaps, something besides beauty – a shyness, maybe, a becoming obedience. As she herself was the child of a large family with its own turbulent centre, she was prepared for the battlefield that Chaplin's life had become and, later on, for the abrasive father that he sometimes was to their own large brood. Being the fulcrum, the point of rest, was surely the gift that Oona O'Neill brought the man she married.

Her attractive reticence unintentionally provoked a piece of mild slapstick on the occasion I met her – or, rather, didn't meet her, for it was one of those "meetings cute" that Hollywood writers used to strive for as they typed the screenplays of screwball comedies in their plywood cells on the back lots of the film studios.

I had come to see Lady Chaplin at Vevey, one of the first "outsiders" that the manor house had received since its master's death, and I had stayed overnight at Les Trois Couronnes, one of those grand hotels whose comforts are almost killed by their formality. I certainly like a well-ordered ambience, but this hotel seemed like a stage-set without any of the transient players, only the fixed props who resided there in lake-view suites all the year round. These were distanced from other guests by invisible frontiers maintained by unspoken understanding between the hotel staff and themselves. I found only one "comfort" in a long day there: a small bookshop entirely devoted to theatre and cinema tucked away at lake-level almost next door, where for 15 Swiss francs I bought a rare copy of Georges Annenkov's *En Habillant les vedettes* (Dressing the Stars). Could Chaplin's "residence" nearby have attracted such an unlikely little shop to that affluent vicinity?

I was glad when the telephone call came telling me that Lady Chaplin would motor down from her home to collect me and bring me up to the house; and even more glad when another call informed me that she had arrived and was waiting at the entrance to the hotel. I hastened out, walked briskly up to a blue Rolls-Royce drawn up with the back door open, and looked inside. It was empty! Had I passed her in the foyer? But then the chauffeur prompted, "Madame . . ." nodding to the side. Oona Chaplin had already descended from the car and was standing beside it, her tiny frame virtually hidden by its size. Now, eyes downcast to avoid a stranger's scrutiny, she sidled in from the wings, a hand shyly extended. The "sequestered charm" that Charlie had noted in her the instant they met was still there nearly 35 years later.

Oona Chaplin had just entered her 50s, but her schoolgirl figure made her look much younger. The clinging silk dress in a pleated blue-patterned print hinted at the taste of a woman who had grace and elegance in her form and not simply in her wardrobe. There was one surprising note of frivolity: the pair of gypsy-looking sandals she was wearing, chiefly comprised of silver cord.

Chaplin loved his Oona obsessively enough to characterise her in the index of his 1964 autobiography as "O'Neill, Oona ('a luminous beauty')".

The beauty of the girl he had married had had its once unretouched crispness inevitably blurred slightly by middle-age and motherhood. But she was still capable of turning on a grin as "luminously" unexpected as it must have been that day in 1943, in the Santa Barbara registry office, when she heard the clerk, after taking down her own name and age, enquire about her intended spouse who was even then prudently waiting outside: "Now where is the young man?"

In the shyness of her manner I sensed the difficulty that the widowed Oona Chaplin must have had in regaining a sense of independent existence which her marriage to a "difficult" genius like Chaplin had inevitably submerged. Living in Switzerland can't have helped. It is a country that enshrines privacy in its laws (though at its own level the Swiss law can be a very pokey-nosed thing). There isn't the social flux that laps around celebrities who make their homes in, say, Monaco or Paris or Rome. Distinction like Chaplin's also lends dissuasion to anyone trying to take too close a view of famous Swiss residents and the local *gendarmerie* were within easy and willing reach if the Chaplins had ever to call on them to repel the curious. Though their neighbours were "known" to them, they were seldom visited. An exception was sometimes made for other famous people who, like themselves, shared the same distaste for unwanted publicity. James Mason had been one such persona grata; another, rather more surprising one, was David Bowie. After Chaplin's death, Bowie had "dared" Oona to take her first role in a movie – one made in Paris and Senegal by Keith Rothman, the son of the film distributor Mo Rothman, whose canny handling of Chaplin's films in his lifetime and since his death has kept on increasing the comedian's market worth while protecting the "uniqueness" of his image. In return for Oona accepting his dare, Bowie agreed to appear on Broadway in the American production of *The Elephant Man* although stage acting held the same terrors for him as exposing herself to public curiosity did for Oona. It is strange to think of those two world-famous but nervous and isolated souls having to key each other up to public-performance pitch by a mutual dare.

The Manoir de Ban, with its rows of dormer windows and a long elegantly pillared verandah, had the appearance of a country home in one of Chekhov's plays. It stood on 37 acres, though only five of them were of cultivated garden. Green canopies were fitted over the ground-floor widows of the principal reception rooms and added to the "magnificent serenity", as Chaplin called it in the very last two words of his memoirs.

"Even as [Oona] walks ahead of me along the narrow sidewalk of Vevey with simple dignity," he wrote, "her neat little figure straight, her dark hair smoothed back showing a few silver threads, a sudden wave of love and admiration comes over me for all that she is – and a lump comes into my throat.''

I could readily understand that sentiment as I now walked by Oona Chaplin's side. She was like the shy girl in a convent-school crocodile.

We made a tour of the green lawns into which a swimming pool had been tucked discreetly like a blue pocket hanky – ''Out of sight of the house,'' she said. ''Charlie didn't like to see other people relaxing when he was working.'' Or hear them, either. On the top storey of the 1840s mansion were the children's rooms, now almost always unoccupied, which Charlie had had sound-proofed when his sons and daughters were younger and more boisterous. Yet he wasn't averse to having one or more of them with him while he worked on his scripts or composed music for the soundtracks of his silent movies; and he would bounce lines off his children to see if they would ''play'', like a parent bouncing a ball back and forth with his child.

Inevitably our talk turned to *A Woman of Paris*. ''Charlie admired what he'd done immensely,'' said Oona, ''but never, *never* got over the shock of its rejection by audiences.''

''Did he make a habit of watching other filmmakers' movies here at Vevey?''

''Fellini . . . as you'd expect. He liked some of his films very much. Not just for the obvious affinity they both had with clowns and circuses. He liked films like *I Vitelloni*. I think he saw something of his own lonely frustrations in those vital but rather sad young men in the film, looking down the railroad tracks and wishing they were among the city lights.

''But here in Switzerland most films are dubbed into French or German and Charlie never got round to speaking foreign languages.''

''It's odd he never learned them,'' I began, and then her reply occurred to me even before she uttered it.

''But he got on so well at making himself understood without using *any* language that he always thought it superfluous to learn to speak a foreign one.''

How about television? Was the great filmmaker an addict of the small screen that had kept him so popular from one generation to the next?

41

"No, not at all. What he liked best were the news events on television, and the World Cup and the Olympics. Things with action or physical grace and prowess in them."

As darkness fell, candles were lit and dinner announced. Coq au vin with salad, a good Reblochon cheese, red wine, and then we took our coffee into the library where Oona Chaplin put a long taper to the huge pile of chopped wood stacked and ready for lighting in the fireplace. "A good fire gave Charlie such comfort at the end – he felt the cold, even on evenings when it was quite warm. I suppose he knew what a cold place the world had been at times for the likes of him."

In the library was a small oil painting of Chaplin that showed him looking as if he were plucking a note of music out of the air with a finicky gesture. He was wearing what looked like the jacket of a city suit, but a crew-neck sweater coming up right under his tie-less shirt collar added an unexpectedly cosy accent of emerald green to the fastidious pose. It was painted, posthumously, by a neighbour of the Chaplins from a snapshot that Oona had taken, for the family's Christmas card in 1977 – and thus became an unwitting and touching memento of his death on that very day.

I looked around the rest of the room. It was comfortably furnished, but disappointingly like many another domestic library I had sat in. I remarked on how very few other mementoes of Chaplin it held. Oona Chaplin laughed and said, "Don't you recognise something?"

"What?"

"That sofa you're sitting on."

I looked down at it: a sofa large enough to seat the whole Chaplin family clan without discomfort, covered in rough cloth of a dull orange colour. "Yes, what about it?"

"Don't you remember it? That's the original sofa Charlie used for the party scene in *City Lights* nearly 50 years ago: the sofa that The Tramp falls asleep on when the millionaire brings him home drunk, only to get slung out into the street in the morning when his benefactor has sobered up. Charlie always hung on to it. If anything symbolised for him the ups and downs of life, it's what you're sitting on at the moment."

And Oona Chaplin turned on me a sudden grin as heart-warming as the crackling fire.

A DAY IN THE HARD-PLAYING HARD-WORKING LIFE OF A FAR FROM MAD OLD WOMAN

The plan had been for Bryan Forbes to insinuate me sideways, so to speak, so that I'd be there, right *there*, in front of Katharine Hepburn, before her radar instinct for these things told her that a potential enemy had breached the *cordon privé* she erects around herself wherever she travels.

The time was summer, 1968; the place, the lovely old Victorine Studios at Nice which Rex Ingram had intended making his European craft-workshop when he and his wife, the film actress Alice Terry, had moved from Hollywood in 1924 after one of Ingram's many quarrels with Louis B. Mayer, the head of MGM. The tiny, homely studio had declared its independence of Hollywood the day it opened its gates in 1917, so it was a fit place for Hepburn to be filming. But whether the role of the pixillated *grande dame* in Giraudoux's *The Madwoman of Chaillot*, a sort of upbeat and ambulant Miss Havisham, was a fit role for her had yet to be determined. At least John Huston had had no doubts. He had just walked off the all-star production. Bryan Forbes had answered the producers' succinct cry of "Help!" that they had entered in the visitors' book after their "mercy" dash from Nice to Forbes's Surrey mansion in search of a replacement director. I could understand why Forbes hadn't thought much of the screenplay. *La Folle de Chaillot* is a "dead" play, once alive in its time, nowadays saying nothing to us and using a whimsically dated sentimental manner to do so; and it resists resuscitation. Forbes probably knew the best he could do was massage some colour into its cheeks and rely on the stars to animate it with their own personalities and idiosyncrasies. Ultimately, neither rouge nor ruse would deceive anybody.

But as for working with Katharine Hepburn – Ah! *she* was another matter!

At 60, Hepburn could still say (and frequently did) "I am my own master." Though that's a line of Garbo's from *Mata*

45

Hari, it can be borrowed and applied to Garbo's seasoned contemporary.

Hepburn seduced Forbes while managing, as he later confessed, "to look utterly vulnerable herself". From being the arbiter of his fate – for she had "director approval" – she turned herself into bait for him.

The film's cast, already contracted, costumed, made up and waiting impatiently for Huston's replacement to arrive on set and pull their strings, proved a powerful lure to a man of Forbes's appetite. A sometime actor himself, he couldn't resist the line-up. It was more like a menu than a cast. Even then it was rare – and nowadays it would be incredible – to see so many stars on one platter: Charles Boyer, Edith Evans, Giulietta Masina, Danny Kaye, Margaret Leighton, Yul Brynner, Paul Henreid, Michael Wilding, Oscar Homolka . . .

Many of them had been part and parcel of Forbes's weekly filmgoing as a child in the 1930s. They gave him a feeling that wasn't exactly vanity, more to do with fraternity; almost as if they had waited for him to grow up and meet them. Not destiny; nothing as solemn as that. But the sensation of a time-slip that people who have had very long, very distinguished careers in films engender in the newcomers entrusted with their talent.

Much later on Lindsay Anderson was to tell me he had felt the same frisson when he undertook to direct *The Whales of August* in 1986, thus falling heir to 330 years of collective stardom parcelled out among his four principals: Lillian Gish (90), Bette Davis (88), Ann Sothern (77) and Vincent Price (75).

Forbes may simply have totted up the names in his film, not their years, but the total was impressive enough for him to say yes.

I was smuggled onto the closed set, past the suspicious eyes of publicists who had only been told "un ami de M. Forbes" was coming down, feeling a bit like contraband. And for two whole days, nothing at all came my way.

Of the elusive Hepburn there was no sight. She hadn't yet been called for her scenes and obviously wasn't going to put herself on show without a purpose. Eventually, Danny Kaye took pity on me.

Kaye was playing "The Ragpicker". Beware of almost any dramatic part that describes itself generically by trade, profession or vocation. You will be subsumed into the text. You will end up stiff and stylised. Kaye didn't look too happy, and the film had hardly got under way. He had obviously taken great pains with his preparation; all he needed now was an opportunity to exercise it. He wore a *clochard* outfit which was so realistic that his clothes looked as if they had been retrieved from a rubbish bin; he pushed a hand-cart and sported a nose that could have been used to skewer litter like a park-keeper's stick. Stretching out on the couch in his dressing-room, he did an instant analysis of why a straight acting role had appealed to him: "Because the other acts I did had got too easy."

At first it didn't strike me that by "the other acts" he meant the gifted storehouse of physical mime, tongue-twisting versatility and apparently impromptu mimicry that had made him the greatest screen clown of the postwar years. Listening to him now disparage his prowess was like hearing Ben Hur declare he'd prefer to get out of his chariot and walk.

I must have betrayed my scepticism at whether so unfair an exchange didn't amount to professional suicide, for he suddenly jumped off the confessional couch, stuffed a French phone directory under his shirt to help the impression of a pampered, pasta-fed opera tenor and began parodying the late Mario Lanza.

He was in the middle of a soaring aria when suddenly the door flew open – and in, like a greyhound sprung from the traps, bounded Katharine Hepburn. In mid-sentence, without missing a beat, Kaye switched from his defamatory cameo into a premonitory apostrophe.

"Dear Kate," he sang, "please watch whom you address/This is Mr Walk-er/A gentleman of the P–R–E–S–S." The last word he spelled out in rising scales of mock alarm.

But the "alert" was scarcely necessary. Hepburn remained frozen, cogitating, crouching. Would she spring? I wondered. Inhibitingly, I found the line she had in *The Philadelphia Story* flashing into my mind: "Who the hell do they think they are, barging in on peaceful people, watching every little mannerism, jotting down notes on how we sit and stand and talk and eat and move?"

Then the next second, a freckled arm, less like a human limb than a root that's clamped its tree to the earth for ages, was thrust out and I received the first electric how-do-you-do shock of Katharine Hepburn's personality: impulsive, demonstrative, imperious.

But was it just an opening move for something closer, more approachable – or had she already passed sentence on one more of "them"? A kind of "Hello, you must be going" introduction? No telling yet. Less than 30 seconds later, she was gone . . . and I suddenly realised I hadn't really seen Katharine Hepburn so much as *felt* her.

Hepburn's sheer energy is such that it reverses the normal order of perception which comes into play on meeting someone. In such a presence, you tend to avert your eyes in case, just by looking, you incur her hostility. But quite definitely, Hepburn had *been* there, wearing, moreover, the flamboyantly unisex uniform she's worn off-screen (and once or twice on it as well) for nearly 50 years – the wide, loose-cut slacks, a blouse the cut and colour of a bush-shirt, thick off-white sweat socks, chunky basketball boots the canvas of which was already going into holes as their wearer's jumpy temperament had kept them ceaselessly on the go for years. Like the few old and trusted people in her intimate circle, the items she wore looked as if they'd have to drop off her before she'd abandon them. It all lent Hepburn a spartan attractiveness, the sort that male war correspondents discover is possessed by a female colleague who comes dressed like them for the fray.

Hepburn's extraordinary voice is what registers first and lingers longest in the memory. "Deaf people love me to talk to them," she was later to remark to me. "No one who's hard of hearing ever has any trouble making me out." It's not that she shouts, exactly. But words fly from her lips like full-jacketed armour-piercing automatic small-fire, each bullet-syllable having a dead-accurate spin imparted to it by the rifling one suspects exists on the inside of that straight barrel of a throat.

Her appearance before the cameras was set for later that day. In expectation, I settled myself on the edge of the large outdoor set, a period French bistro, which was to be left standing after the film finished shooting – the way streets are in Hollywood Westerns – and become a permanent bit of the Victorine's world of make-believe. It was pressed into service again by Truffaut when he filmed *La Nuit Americaine* (*Day for Night*) five years later. I felt rather like the tethered goat that's used to lure the big game within rifle-range. At least it was a good observation point for the goat.

I soon discovered one of the sources of Hepburn's incredible supply of energy. She devours rich dark handmade chocolates by the bagful; no amount of sugar ever seems to give her constipation or swaddle those rakish bones of hers in fat. She handed the sweets out despotically around the crew and sent a grey-haired woman, who looked like maybe a distant cousin, across to offer one to me. This was Phyllis Wimbourne, her long-time companion, who had once been Constance Cummings' secretary. For a second, Hepburn's official detachment relaxed, as she watched like a bed-side mother to see that I ate what I'd call confectionery and she'd call medicine. Florence Nightingale crossed with Mary Poppins.

I was surprised never to catch her lighting a cigarette between takes. She and Bette Davis were reputed to be two of Hollywood's heaviest smokers. I'd already had one run-in with Davis, by suggesting that the interview we were in the middle of would go better if she could bear to put her cigarette out – it was like asking Boadicea to disarm herself. "You wouldn't dare say that to Kate Hepburn," Bette Davis had said. It wasn't until work wrapped up for the day that I saw Hepburn fly to her cigarettes, then puff her way through a pack of them before dinner like a Foreign Legion trooper on a 48-hour furlough. The habit was totally out of keeping with her brazen air of good health. Kenneth Tynan once called her "the Garbo of the Great Outdoors" – a phrase that celebrates her athleticism as much as her reclusiveness. During my stay at the Voile d'Or, that superb hotel which sits on the promontory at St Jean-Cap Ferrat like a rich dessert on a trolley, I was never up early enough to catch Hepburn at her morning swim. That took place before breakfast was carried up to me; sometimes, I suspected, even before the sun came up on all of us, and the Mediterranean still held the gelid sting of a thawing ice-cube. Though Hepburn was born and raised in Connecticut, she possesses the kind of stamina that once made the Roman Empire tick.

Typically, this imperious woman started at the top. Not that her ascent on Broadway in the early 1930s was exactly an express lift. She played either large parts in short-lived plays or else small ones in plays that lasted (a bit) longer. But she was good casting, even when the play didn't require her to be a good actress.

An independent income supported a temperamental reluctance to compromise. She had no need to do so; hence, perhaps, her lifelong assumption that getting her own way is perfectly natural. She made her own deal with RKO, at $1,500 a week, a lot then, and got the promising George Cukor as her first director and the still distinguished if slightly dog-eared John Barrymore as her first leading man in *Bill of Divorcement* in 1932.

What's important to realise is that this woman came to Hollywood already "shaped" – a stage person. Bette Davis, who was still stage-struck and had no well defined shape at all when Hollywood beckoned, spent many of her early years on a small salary supplemented by a large bundle of try-out roles in order to see what, if anything, she could do best. It took Davis a couple of decades before she gained the respect and earned the fees that Hepburn had enjoyed from the start. At times she must have been wretchedly envious, if not downright jealous of the other woman. If so, she was not alone. Not everyone liked Hepburn then; not everyone does now.

Her apparent snootiness got up some people's noses, and it still does. To others, again, she sounded spoilt and privileged – someone who hadn't paid her community dues. Her full-frontal bluntness didn't go down well in a town where people talked, by preference, behind each other's backs. She even sounded seditious. A few American critics of the time condemned her for having "class sympathies". Robert Forsythe, a man whom the normally tolerant Alistair Cooke once called "a raging Russophile", certainly viewed her from that side of the great divide. "It is palpable nonsense to be concerned about such children as Katharine Hepburn, who will be as forgotten as Mary Miles Minter in a few years time . . . and who so obviously represents bourgeois culture at its apex that she will enter history as a complete treatise on decay." An opinion that recalls Lincoln Stefans' judgment, "I have been to see the future, and it works", enunciated on returning to America from post-revolutionary Russia, as one of the greatest examples in history of wishful thinking being later contradicted by proven experience.

Hepburn sidled round the *Madwoman* set like a shy girl, not wanting to draw attention to herself or distract the other players who were still in the shot.

Then, when she'd positioned herself right behind me, she made a sharp little rush forward and propelled me to my feet. "Get a load of this," she hissed, and pushed me up to the perimeter of the set. Giulietta Masina, another of the film's quartet of genteely dotty *grandes dames*, was beginning a piece of dainty mime. I could see her husband, Federico Fellini, also lurking in the shadows, for once a supernumerary, his big wary face turned towards his tiny wife. I wondered what they talked about afterwards. This ersatz make-believe wasn't Fellini's scene.

Hepburn, however, was radiating a laser beam of admiration that ought to have shrivelled up the waifish little Italian star. Ought to, but didn't, Masina was as professionally detached as Hepburn. But how many professionals like Hepburn would summon a witness to share her praise for another star's display of talent?

A minute later came the words I'd been waiting for: "You want to talk to me?" At last Hepburn and I had "met" – on her terms.

"I was brought up in an age of heroes," was her staccato opening. "Outdoor heroes. Like William S. Hart, Doug Fairbanks Sr – decisive men who never knew a minute's self-doubt. I *worshipped* their kind. I used to dream of being Grace Darling. The lighthouse keeper's daughter. Who rowed out into the teeth of the storm along with her father to rescue shipwrecked mariners. I *owe* my father *everything*. Especially my craze for physical activity. He was a physician. Believed in fresh air, not bottled medicine. We were an athletic family. In those days, the games people played *were* games. Not the crazy psychological torture syndromes they inflict on you now. Father had a great affinity with the strenuous life. '*Accept challenges!*' '*Never give up!*' '*Don't brag about what you've done!*' For Bobby Kennedy to climb what mountain they named after his brother in Canada was a fine thing. He *ruined* it. Told us all about doing it.

"We were encouraged to be individuals when I was a girl. I once played Mary Stuart in a John Ford film. 'Jack,' I said to him, 'I'd prefer to be Elizabeth Tudor. A woman with a head on her shoulders suits me better than one who loses it.' "

"Why do you dress so much against fashion?" I asked. We were now sitting at one of the tables in the Café Français set. At least I was sitting. Hepburn was hunkered down like a Girl

Scout round a campfire. The sun was shining directly into her eyes and she was staring back as if trying to subdue it. The only make-up she wore was a pancake wash – "to hide my freckles".

"I wear the clothes I do to save me the trouble of deciding what clothes to wear. *'Don't clutter your life'*, Dad said. Who needs more than two suits? One to wear. One at the cleaner's."

Her eye, monitoring me, caught me sneaking a look at my watch.

"Don't worry about time on my account. I know when to take my mid-day rest. Always try to be in bed by 8.30 p.m. Edith" – Dame Edith Evans, she meant – "always says I'm sleeping my life away. Don't have much night life, that's true. Don't go out much. Whenever I do, I decide I don't miss much by turning in early."

Hepburn arrived in Hollywood with considerable natural advantages. Her un-retouched looks separated her immediately from the screen's over-groomed pack of leading ladies. Look carefully at her early films. See how the skin on her high cheek bones is stretched as taut as canvas on a pioneer woman's prairie wagon. Her voice, as I've mentioned, echoed the arrogance of her New England class but that had its advantages. The sound recordist who had to grapple with those high-pointed vowels in *A Bill of Divorcement* appealed to Cukor for help: "She's yelling." – "Take her as she sounds," Cukor commanded – and that aristocratic bark of Hepburn's suddenly made all the other ladies seem to yap. The Hollywood *nouveaux riches* possessed power all right but it was power without the confident status that resonates through the shortest syllable Hepburn utters. She has never needed to use strong language to push her side of the argument; she's curiously ladylike in that respect and has never been heard to utter a more indelicate epithet than "Shute!" But then I've noticed many "loners" like her who don't often swear; they don't keep much company except themselves, and consequently don't need to impress anyone.

Hepburn deployed her high-pedigree self-assurance to define the girl she played in those 1930s social comedies in which Hollywood made the privileged world of the "haves" acceptable to the Depression era's "have nots" by showing what a wacky but essentially good-hearted crowd the rich were. Hepburn usually unnerved her man by unsettling his self-esteem. Even when the story has to render her vulnerable, she lets one sense her vulnerability in the way she refuses to show it. Stoicism again. In *A Bill of Divorcement* she played a daughter who fears she's inherited a touch of her father's insanity. It's a more than somewhat stagey picture that hasn't worn well. But Hepburn's performance has – though pop-eyed John Barrymore must have been a trial to play with (and a risk to be alone with). The critics hailed her at the time; it was a dream debut. "A very young actress with the power of a tragedienne," wrote one reviewer.

"Did it embarrass you to become a star?" I now asked. "Some people said the 'retreats' you made from time to time – into the old family home at Fenwick – were spent regretting the talent you lavished on 'flashy' things like movies."

"Listen," Hepburn snapped. "For my Hollywood screen test, I did a scene from *Holiday* – you know, the Broadway hit. A friend read me my cue lines. I seated *him* in a wing chair. Couldn't see anything of *him*. Didn't want *him* signed up instead of me. I played the scene the way I fancied I looked. Tough, independent, spirited, not giving a damn about the world . . . Okay . . . Six years later we make the film version of *Holiday*. I had my old test screened. Just for the hell of it. My God! I never saw a girl who looked more *desperate* to win fame in the movies."

She sprang off her haunches, stretched, strode over to a stack of film flats leaning against the wall and yanked out a ladder she apparently knew was concealed behind them. She slung the ladder over her shoulder and marched across to a small stand of fruit-bearing apple trees. In a few seconds, she had nipped up the ladder and plucked a couple of the ripest fruits. (Does her insurance cover apple-picking? I wondered.)

"Hide the ladder," she said, in a parody of slyness, putting it back behind the flats, "so no one'll get my apples."

There's a branch-line of psychiatry that believes the child we were stays put inside the body and mind of the adult we become. Easy to see the little girl Hepburn used to be; and slightly eerie, too, to glimpse her make a fleeting appearance like this, re-entering the body of the 60-year-old woman. I suspect Hepburn rather enjoys providing evidence of her eccentricity – using it as protective coloration. It provokes surprise and surprise keeps people off balance.

53

Was it true, I asked her, that she used to send her film-star salary back home to her father who, by return, doled out a weekly allowance? And did so even after her short-lived marriage in the 1930s to one Ludlow Ogden Smith, a blue-blooded stock-broker from Philadelphia, who sounds ideal Philip Barry material for Hepburn's fiancé in *The Philadelphia Story*.

She was not displeased by my query, but not disposed to answer it; she just went on munching her stolen fruit. When "Miss Phyllis" called her in to lunch in her dressing room, the apple was only a core – she'd already had half her meal.

In French studios, filming usually begins at noon and goes through the day until 8.00 p.m. But this would have taken Katharine Hepburn well past her bedtime. So she exercised her star prerogative. Now they were keeping "English hours" at the Victorine – i.e. the whistle blew at 5.30 p.m.

That afternoon, I watched her shoot one of the last scenes in the film. In her hobble skirt, lace shawl, feather boa and a flower-bed hat, she moved through the Parisian set as if the Old World was paying a visit to the new on a day-return ticket. Round her was a trio of cronies, somewhat battier than the character Hepburn was playing, but no less decorative. There was Margaret Leighton as a repressed spinster who believes herself escorted wherever she goes by a gentleman companion, invisible to the rest of the world. There was Masina, a powdered and painted parody of maidenly modesty who only goes as far as allowing an invisible dog to escort *her*. And for the first time on the set I saw Edith Evans, a marvellously reverberating aristocrat who haunts the law courts and suggests what Lady Bracknell might have been like if she had sat on the bench as a magistrate.

Hepburn was the flagship in the eccentric fleet. It was now left to Danny Kaye's "Ragpicker" to deflate her gently, to take the wind out of her galleon sails, by alerting her to the dangerous reefs of human greed and duplicity she has been innocently skirting. "Countess," said Kaye, "the world has changed. The world is not beautiful any more. The world is not happy."

Hepburn counted a silent beat. Then: "But why wasn't I told?"

The line is phoney, like most of Giraudoux's, perished along with the theatrical conventions that once made this dramatist tolerable. But Hepburn managed to speak it with a real glistening tear. The lights caught her moist eye; for a split second it flashed like the facets on a diamond. Later, I learned, the tear, though timely, was involuntary – an irksome aftermath of an infection contracted some years earlier when she had had to fall into a canal in Venice for a scene in David Lean's *Summer Madness*. Some bug or other in the stagnant canal had caused her eyes to water ever since. A lighting cameraman has to be careful, for a lachrymose Hepburn is a contradiction in terms. The salt should be on her tongue, not her cheeks.

As soon as she had exchanged her faded *fin-de-siècle* finery for her own deeply pleated slacks and a Pioneer Corps forage cap, she stowed a mini-bicycle into the trunk of her studio limousine, me into the back seat, and, with herself beside the chauffeur, headed into the hinterland of the Côte d'azur. This is her leisure hour. This is when she "raids the territory", to profit from the nursery fields where carnations can be picked up for a third of the price they cost in the Nice flower market. Hepburn says she is no businesswoman. But like a housewife who knows the best cuts of meat, she has earned the wary respect of the Hollywood butchers.

"I don't use an agent," she said. "Nowadays I do only one-picture deals. To keep control of my career that's why. I also own a bit of quite a few of the films I made. Remember *Bringing up Baby*? – the comedy about a leopard on the loose that Cary and I made? Came at the end of the screwball cycle in 1938. Didn't take much money. Well, it's made me quite a bit since – *quite a bit!*" Her voice stretches out the last words, half-evoking the windfall that's come her way, half-mocking herself for even mentioning an *arriviste* commodity like money.

As we drove around the countryside near Vence, Hepburn exulted in the saturated colours of the Renoiresque landscape. It brought back to her, she said, her father's pleasure in the arbutus-scented springs of Connecticut. Her face glowed, its freckled skin almost transparent now that her pancake make-up had been washed off. It was as if she was recharging her own energies after the day's labours by making contact with the fertile earth.

"Isn't it *wonderful* to see people working!" She meant the labourers in the flower fields, culling the bunches of lavender, carnations and *roses de mai*. Her suffragette mother's Fabian socialism blended imperceptibly into her father's love of physical hardihood.

She struck me as a person who likes people who live a frugal life, figuratively as well as physically close to the earth.

I'd injured my shoulder earlier that year, skiing on the late spring snows of Switzerland. Hepburn noticed I was having trouble keeping the not-yet-mended muscles warm in the slipstream of the wind which whipped through the wide-open front windows and into the rear seat of the car. "Here, wrap this round you," she commanded. And out of her bag she yanked the rust-red remnants of what had once been a man's jumper. She seems to keep this sort of rough-and-ready comforter about her the way that house-trained people keep "Band-Aids". Another no-nonsense touch that suggested a childhood spent in a large family. No wonder children take to her intuitively – or that she impulsively welcomes children, from whom there is nothing to fear, as they approach her in simple faith, not with intrusive curiosity.

I later learned that she used to wear the jumper year in, year out, and that it had originally belonged to Spencer Tracy. I wondered wryly at its temporary fate that day – cosseting a film critic.

Tracy and Hepburn were one of the most durable and best-liked partnerships on the screen. Off-screen they were lovers too.

"*Everybody* loved Spencer," is the short, sharp put-down Hepburn customarily gives, if asked about this. The story's often been told – and incorrectly – that on meeting Tracy for the first time, when they were both cast in *Woman of the Year*, Hepburn said, "I'm afraid I'm a bit tall for you, Mr Tracy," and he answered, "Don't worry, I'll soon cut you down to size, Miss Hepburn." Garson Kanin remembers that incident differently – and he was writing the picture. According to him, it was an embarrassed Joe Mankiewicz, the producer, who jumped in quickly after Hepburn's opening sally. Before his two stars could fall out publicly, he interjected, "Don't worry, honey, he'll cut you down to size." The feisty relationship Tracy and Hepburn had from the start already anticipated a scene in any of their eight films together. It was a happy collision of apparent opposites. Tracy was the rock against which her feminist fretfulness broke; Hepburn was the restless fountain of energy that his masculine firmness never succeeded in capping.

56

Tracy died a week after they finished shooting *Guess Who's Coming to Dinner*. "I had 20 years of perfect companionship with that man among men," Hepburn said at the time. Now she let a few more beats of silence pass between us and then said, "There are very few great actors at any time. Spencer was one of them. I'm not in his class. Not remotely. There was a light inside that man. It did a positive disservice to some of the movies he was put into. He made them look even shoddier than they were."

It was Hepburn herself who found the story of *Woman of the Year* and took it to MGM. Propitious timing, though she didn't know it. The studio had just decided to abandon the film Tracy was shooting in Florida – *The Yearling*, which was later made with Gregory Peck – because the unanticipated clouds of flies swarming round the horses couldn't be kept off the camera lens. The studio was desperate to rush a substitute film into production. "I could have asked a fortune," Hepburn said, "but all I wanted to do was act with Spencer. I was already in love with him. I even made sure they played the story from his viewpoint, not the woman's. She was a highbrow, bossy Dorothy Parker-type. The kind who'd get audiences' backs up. I should know. Parts of me are like that."

By the end of the 1930s, Hepburn's style had become a bit too patronising for the audience's changing taste in heroines. She skilfully recycled herself. Having Tracy to administer the gruff put-down was a brilliantly engineered defence stratagem.

The gift each brought the other on the screen was the same element that holds "good friends" together, even more firmly than "lovers". It was mutual affection based on healthy disrespect. Tracy summed it up in his relaxed but wily laid-back look: Hepburn, in her prickly but appealing impetuosity.

"I studied Spencer the way the FBI would study a wanted man. Even screened all his MGM films. Just to see how the woman playing opposite him would be expected to dress!"

"What was his unique quality?" I asked.

"Total concentration," she replied, unhesitatingly.

"In one scene, I accidentally spilled a glass of water. Spencer never blew his lines. Just kept on playing the scene . . . got out his hanky . . . went on talking . . . mopped up the water . . . kept on talking . . . fed me my cue . . . tucked his hanky back into his pocket . . . grinned at me . . . came in on cue himself. George

Stevens, our director, had the wit not to call 'Cut!' – kept the camera going all through – and that's how it is on the screen.

"We never rehearsed together. Didn't need to. If the relationship between us was valid, the spontaneity would be there. It always was. Besides, Spencer was a very quick study. So I had to become quick, too. Where we worked long and hard together was on the script. I was the one for the finicky details of how a scene should play. Spencer trusted the effect to come out okay overall. People often asked why our partnership was so *successful*. The answer is – it was a natural *and truthful* completion of needs."

Tracy was an alcoholic. His consistent earning power gained him continual forgiveness for the one sin that film studios seldom forgave. He never showed up for work drunk, though he sometimes went on a bender in the middle of shooting. Then Hepburn would have to lay down whatever she was doing and nurse him back to work. Inwardly he was as morose as outwardly he appeared successful. His personal life was a mass of shifting sand: he was a husband who'd ceased to get satisfaction from marriage; a Roman Catholic who couldn't (or wouldn't) get a divorce from his wife; and a father whose son had been afflicted with muscular dystrophy from birth. He was impatient, bad tempered, obstinate, sometimes downright malevolent. None of it showed. On screen, all such deficiencies reversed themselves in his performance and showed a silver lining – so that he became a man of apparent forebearance, integrity, compassion and, if ever roused to anger, it was righteous anger.

I imagine Hepburn was often sorely tried. But then saving souls as well as careers is probably part and parcel of her missionary zeal. I often think of Tracy as I watch her and the sloppy, grizzled, stubble-chinned and mean-minded Bogart in *The African Queen* and see Bogart yielding sway to Hepburn's implacable do-gooding which takes practical form in first pouring his liquor over the side of the boat. Life with Tracy, when he was on the bottle, must have provided her with a dress rehearsal for that scene.

Tracy's alcoholism never got written about at the time which shows the Hollywood columnists' respect (or, more likely, knowing that breed, their fear) for the studios' vested interests in the public impeccability of their contract artists. The gossip writers didn't dish the dirt until the pay had been extracted from it in the crushing-mills of Columbia, Paramount and MGM.

Hepburn ordered our limousine to pull up at a roadside stall selling great bundles of scarlet, pink and white speckled carnations. She swept half a dozen of the bundles up in her arms and squeezed them to her face the way that more self-consciously *soignée* women press beauty packs to their cheeks to feed the flesh. Soon I was having to conduct conversation with her through a "wall" of carnations between her in front and me in the back seat.

Another mile or so and *"Arrêtez, monsieur!"*

This time it was the car roof that served her as a platform on to which she hopped with mountain-goat impulsiveness to pick cherries off an overhanging branch. Then she gave herself a ten-minute spin on her mini-bike while the driver, used to her free-wheeling ways, cruised down the road behind her and took her back on board two miles further on. Then it was back to her rented villa on the coast, just up the road from the one Edith Piaf owned.

Her neighbours don't interest Hepburn, famous or not, so long as she isn't exposed to them. Her obsession with privacy is always on automatic pilot. She may sleep; *it* never does. When the production company showed her the house it proposed renting for her, she raised her eyes to the hills above it and saw only umbrella pines. "Can't be overlooked – *good!*"

She was no sooner into the kitchen than she reached for a box of truffles from the best *confiserie* in Nice. Chocolates and cigarettes – God, what a diet!

She indicated a huge French cook, smiling and nodding like a fairground buddha. "This woman has reached the same values as I have." "This woman" didn't understand a word she said, but nodded more vigorously, smiled more broadly.

On the terrace, enjoying the sunset, sat Dame Edith Evans and Bryan Forbes – Edith, in her oversized straw hat, yellow silk dress and spotless cream-coloured shoes: *Ascot-sur-la-côte*. I felt she looked slightly bemused by Hepburn's storehouse of energy and ragbag of garments. According to Forbes, Hepburn had met Dame Edith with an apology on her arrival. "Sorry I won't be able to entertain you much, Edith. Have to be in bed by eight. But Phyllis'll read you your lines, if you like." Edith made no comment, pondering Hepburn's sleeping arrangements, no doubt. Then, after a second or two, in her high, loopy voice she asked, "What do people *do* in the South of France who *don't* go to bed at eight?"

The evening yielded a nugget of this kind when talk turned to writers. So-and-so, Forbes mentioned, "has taken a house in Tuscany to finish a book". Edith was listening, eyes half-shut, giving the unnerving impression that she had dozed off. Suddenly, she opened one shutter and asked, "Oh, what is she reading?" We all began to talk very quickly.

I told the story of hearing a voice, unmistakably Gielgud's, at the counter of a London West End store. A pair of white trousers was being purchased and eyed askance. "Aren't they rather tight?" – "Oh, Sir John," said the counter boy, "you can have them as tight as you like these days, so long as you're going south."

Hepburn mixed our drinks in inventive dollops. A gesture that showed she was either not very experienced, or else had an exaggerated respect for her guests' capacities.

The talk circled round to acting. "What counts there is personality," Hepburn said decisively. "I mean, you can diversify your roles, but only within limits. Your personality must stay a familiar event. You have to resist the temptation to change. Me, I'm like the Flatiron skyscraper. A nice old building nobody wants to see torn down. Spencer hardly changed at all, *whatever* the role. Remember when he had to play the Portuguese fisherman in *Captains Courageous*? It worried MGM, how he should speak. For God's sake, who knows *how* a Portuguese fisherman speaks English? But of course MGM found a Portuguese fisherman and made him come to the studio to coach Spencer. 'How would you say "fish"?' Spencer asked him, very carefully. 'Would you say "feesh"?' – 'No,' said the man. – 'Then what would you say?' 'I'd say "fish".' That was the end of Spencer's elocution lessons in Portuguese-English. He was the salt of the earth in homegrown yarns like *Boys' Town* and *San Francisco*. Why shouldn't the same Spencer be the salt of the sea in the Kipling yarn?

"I'm like Spencer. I like a lot of concentration, not a lot of acting. Audiences today are smart. They concentrate, too. One kind of concentration meets another lot. And then, WHAM!

Think of Margot Fonteyn dancing *Romeo and Juliet* at her age. Think of Edith" (we were now a little way off from Edith Evans, who had fallen into her waking sleep again) "playing Rosalind in *As You Like It* – At the age of 49! Remarkable . . . remarkable! Put it down to concentration. Edith could look up – and fall in love like a girl. *Comme ça!*"

No wonder Hepburn became an early mascot of the Women's Movement, though she never turned out for its parades. She always stood four-square against the convention that women who were still unmarried when they had reached a certain age must be screwed up old spinsters. Though she *has* been married, it's as a single woman, or, rather, as a "woman alone" that audiences perceive her off-screen. And she's shown such a woman can possess independence, wit and intelligence and control her own life: in an abrasive way, perhaps, but not end up a neurotic victim. She's avoided the trap that other stars of her generation all too easily succumb to when roles get scarcer and pay packets slimmer, namely the vulgar refuge of the horror film. Katharine Hepburn has never needed to wield an axe on someone, laughing maniacally, to demonstrate she's still a lady to be reckoned with. She's never performed in any of the menopausal melodramas cast from the ranks of ageing stars desperate for love from young studs to prove (to herself) that she's still a doughty woman. *Old* studs, maybe; but that's an entirely different matter. That's matching one champion against another. Going the distance with Hepburn has re-invigorated quite a few of those vaunted "men's men", like John Wayne in *Rooster Cogburn*.

Casting the pair of them in the same film left many gleeful prophets rubbing their hands in anticipation of the collision between the lady liberal and the chauvinist patriarch. It didn't happen. Professionalism is stronger than politics. Wayne and Hepburn stepped very, very slightly aside from the characters they were playing to wink at the political stance they were expected to assert. They managed to cod together, with straight faces, the values they'd come to stand for singly.

I left the terrace to return to my hotel just as the disappearing sun was turning Hepburn's tawny compound of wind, weather and freckles into a red-gold complexion of singular richness. She looked as if she were being eroded, gradually and with imperceptible kindness, like one of those Venetian *palazzos* that pass by degrees into a stage of decay so glorious that they still look princely.

I wasn't to meet Katharine Hepburn again for another 18 years. This time it was spring, 1986; the place was New York. I'd written to her, telling her I was researching material for a life of Vivien Leigh. I knew she hadn't been exactly a close friend of the worldly Vivien's; but she had been present, and, indeed, an active participant in some of the manic-depressive crises that had made the English actress's life so pitiful and unnerving. I'd been told of the immediate generosity Hepburn had shown, reaching out to succour the poor afflicted Vivien by finding medical help of a kind that, at that date, wasn't too readily available to people who needed a physician as discreet as he was trustworthy. My enquiries were blessed by Jack Merivale, the man who had been closest to Vivien for the last seven years of her life. Even so, I knew Hepburn's views on such enquiries, and I wasn't any too hopeful.

The telephone rang at 8.15 p.m. in my room at the Algonquin. The voice still had its metallic scouring-powder rasp, clearing away polite fripperies in one go. "Katharine Hepburn here . . . You want to see me?" – "Yes, please." – "You had breakfast?" – "Yes" (I lied) – "Can you be here in half-an-hour?"

I knew I could hobble over to her 44th-street home in half that time, if necessary. I even found time for a detour to the best chocolate shop on Fifth Avenue, in case she needed some energy to top her up. After all, she was 79, and had been afflicted for some years with Parkinson's disease. Mercifully, this had not been too evident in the film that had won her a third Oscar three years earlier, *On Golden Pond*, a benign comedy about the generations not so much clashing as nudging each other. It contained its own mellowed reality in the presence of Hepburn and Henry Fonda. Oddly – and satisfyingly – it was Fonda's last role, just as Tracy's appearance with Hepburn in *Guess Who's Coming to Dinner* had been his. Fonda was a good stand-in for Tracy; Hepburn's whimsical attitude to life and death cannoned off his grumpiness in just the same way.

But since then, Hepburn had come out of semi-retirement only once, and then it was obvious what palsied inroads the disease was making into her appearance – and judgment, too, perhaps. I saw its ravages in a role she misguidedly took in a silly so-called black comedy, *The Ultimate Solution of Grace Quigley*, intended, I assume to show that voluntary euthanasia was preferable to the living death of the retirement home. In retrospect, I can see the Roman stoicism in the idea that may have attracted Hepburn to the script; but nothing was made of it, the ultimate effect was all the more unpleasant because she now somehow seemed compromised by her innocence, rather than enhanced.

I wondered what I'd find as I lifted the latch of the little wrought-iron gate and stepped into the narrow forecourt of the old 19th-century terrace house in the part of Manhattan known as Turtle Bay. Like most houses in the row – Stephen Sondheim's is next door – it has a narrow frontage, and is modestly proportioned, but the first-floor (second-floor, if one is an American) living-room runs from front to back of the house, giving it depth in place of spaciousness.

The door was opened by the same "Miss Phyllis" of 23 years earlier, as grey as before, and, thus, not a day older looking.

It was a cold day for April, overcast, too, and rainy; and after climbing the stairs and entering the reception room, I didn't at first see Hepburn anywhere. She was down on her knees, her back to me, holding up a double page of the *New York Times*, the better to make the chimney draw a flame out of the wood-and-coal fire she'd just finished lighting. She had on a shapeless smock, grey track-suit bottoms and basketball boots that looked like sons of the ones she had worn in Nice a quarter of a century before.

The room reflected her temperament – early American, comfortable, respectable, and rural in sympathy rather than metropolitan. Oil lamps would have become it. Chairs were either covered in loose white drapes or were of uncushioned polished wood that it would have been blasphemy to cover. Persian rugs on the gleaming wood floor boards; a clock Ethel Barrymore had given her on the marble mantelpiece; decoy ducks, more ornamental than utilitarian, on the side tables; and a big goose carved in wood suspended overhead and craning its neck impertinently down at Hepburn's territory below.

She saw that "Miss Phyllis" made coffee – for me; she herself drank nothing – and alluded briefly, stoically to our last meeting on *The Madwoman of Chaillot*: "Well, we sure didn't make a success of *that*!"

She settled herself in a high-backed chair that she could rest her head against. I was heartened to see that the implacable shaking, as if her neck were spring-loaded, which had compounded the distress of the *Grace Quigley* film, was now almost unnoticeable – brought under control by medication or remission. She sat at an angle to me, turned away, but facing the thin light from the street as before she had once faced the blazing Mediterranean sun: a ladyhawk, somewhat moulted, but proud and perfectly capable of pouncing and seizing the passing scene (or visitor) in her talons.

Vivien Leigh had found the sort of saviour in Hepburn that Tracy had, too. Listening to her story, I once again had the impression of how strongly stricken people touched her practical sympathy; the compassion of a nurse hid behind the countenance of a châtelaine.

It was Hepburn who had traced a Los Angeles physician qualified to give electro-convulsive therapy to Vivien Leigh in 1966, when she had collapsed while filming *Ship of Fools*, and so restore her to temporary normality. It was Hepburn who drove with Vivien and Jack Merivale to the doctor's, lying down prone out of sight in the back of the car, lest her own unmistakable profile caught the eye of someone who might then wonder where Leigh and Hepburn were off to together, and why. It was a brave act of charity.

I don't think Vivien Leigh and Katharine Hepburn had very much in common, except maybe George Cukor, a director they both adored. But each recognised a great spirit in the other.

Listening to Hepburn, I had a stronger impression than ever of a woman who has lived so intensely within her own guarded world, whose boundaries are patrolled by immensely loyal friends, that she has only a small notion of how the other wider world has moved on. Danny Kaye's lines came back to me: "Countess, the world has changed . . ." and Hepburn's reply: "But why wasn't I told?" But now, unless I was mistaken, a slight hint of interest had been awakened in the world's view of her. A new biography of her had just been published. She was careful to say she hadn't read it. As it happened, I had read it; but I decided she ought to gratify her own curiosity about herself. "You should write your own life, if it concerns you how other people do it."

"Most people have lives that are a mess, don't you think?" was her only reply.

I didn't think so. How could I? The evidence was all to the contrary. I was sitting opposite a woman who denied the truth of it in every possible way. She has made the life that she wanted; or, if failing in any area, has learnt, like George Santayana, to live with the way things have of coming about of their own accord, encouraged perhaps by a firm push. Either way, Katharine Hepburn has inhabited her life with the same durable grace with which she wears the serviceable clothes which are a metaphor for it. She hasn't just lived: she's lasted.

CARY GRANT AND THE HARRY LIME CONNECTION

"Are they the same when you meet them?" is a question that every film critic has to learn to bear with unwincing good grace. It is a natural one, of course, for those people who go to the movies, but don't frequently meet those who are *in* the movies. The answer has to be, "Of course not; the stars can't play themselves all the time, off-screen as well as on it." "Themselves" being their *screen* selves - the *persona* "as known", rather than the "also known as" self, which is their off-screen identity and is usually a far dimmer, more crepuscular one.

Yet even as I try to explain this historical dichotomy of stardom, without dashing the illusion that sustains it in the public mind, I find myself recalling the one outstanding exception to it. The man who always played "himself", whenever and wherever he appeared, in public or private, on-screen or off. The man was Cary Grant.

Cary Grant was the same person to meet in the company of his friends as he was to view in the company of his fellow performers in a film. One took his success at playing - at *being* - himself for granted. It was like a conjuring trick that passes before the eyes without penetrating the critical part of the watchful mind, so that the surprise and pleasure that greet it are enhanced because there seems to have been no deception at all practised on us.

Unlike a conjuror, though, Grant never minded revealing how the trick was done. He knew he'd perfected it - and not only perfected it, but patented it. And you'd never be able to spot the join between reality and illusion, however much you strained your eyes.

"At one point in my life, I pretended to be a certain kind of man on screen," he'd say, "and very soon I became that man in life. 'I' became him, or rather, 'he' became me. Anyhow, at some point, so long ago I've forgotten exactly when - but you're a clever film critic, you'll be able to find out - we met up with

each other. And you know something? This will surprise you
. . ." At this point, the grin would broaden, there'd be a fleeting
impression of Grant counting a silent beat, and then he'd deliver
the pay-off. ". . . we're still good friends."

Of course, this was an act, too. (You realised it even the first
time you heard it; the second time, when I overheard it at the
other side of the lunch table, it was still as fresh as the carnation
in his button hole and, I dare say, contributed to the same
immaculate vision of him.) Of course, *why* he did the trick was
better not gone into. Maybe he himself had explored the reasons – perhaps one should say "he" himself, for one wondered
which one of the Cary Grants had examined the other during
those psychotherapy sessions with LSD which he'd undertaken,
under medical supervision, in the late 1950s. But the fact that
Grant had had his own mid-life identity crisis doesn't contradict
what I've just said.

Those who knew him through associates, if not intimately,
over a long period also knew another side of him. He was at times
reclusive, tight with money and wary of women. That might
make you think that the screen persona didn't tell one everything
about Mr Grant. Wrong. Such blemishes (if that's what they
were) could be found in his screen persona, too, there transformed into facets of comedy, as the script rotated him to let
them glitter. "Glitter" is a good word; for Grant had a hardness
about him which kept the charm springy, didn't allow it to
deteriorate into spongy acceptance of the world's welcome. If
you didn't take to Cary Grant – and, incredibly, some didn't –
that wasn't much of a worry to him. He told me once that in
fact he rather enjoyed antagonism on the rare occasions that
he met it – a bit like a best-selling author relishing the letter
from a reader he has failed to please. It was reassuring, perhaps,
to find someone who *didn't* want to be Cary Grant – especially
since he himself used to say occasionally, "Even *I* want to be
Cary Grant."

If asked what particularly endeared him to me, I'd have to
reply – his accent. You could still hear the "burr" of his native
Bristol breaking through the acquired defences of his American
tones. It gave his personality an edge, that West Country sound;
rather unexpectedly so, a bit like the rocks on which his ances-
tors – admittedly on wilder shores than the Bristol Channel –

70

used to wreck the passing cargo ships by the lure of false lights and then loot them at low tide. It gave Grant's voice the sharpness that comedy needs if it's to be slightly dangerous, and that romance exploits if it's to be slightly menacing. If Grant's handsome looks were an invitation, then his voice could occasionally be heard sounding a judgment on those who accepted it. It was a good voice for screen love affairs; it enabled him to keep his amorous distance with the hard repartee of the dialogue until he could choose his moment to close the gap between him and the lady with his lips.

This is one of the reason why the screwball comedies turned out by Hollywood in the 1930s were such a perfect vehicle for Cary Grant. For all their well-plotted efforts to mediate between the lifestyles of the rich and poor, between the "haves", who had survived the Crash, and the "have nots" who hadn't, they retained a privileged selfishness that Cary Grant could occupy without antagonising anyone. Their humour frequently depended on reversing the romantic clichés – the "meeting sour" replacing the "meeting cute" between hero and heroine, a kind of sexual conmanship being entered into between the two of them in which each tricked the other and even the fade-out kiss could be taken as a temporary truce rather than a life-time treaty. Grant was very good at suggesting that kind of ambiguity.

When he made *Sylvia Scarlett* for George Cukor in 1936, he and Katharine Hepburn were like flint hitting flint. They made the vocal sparks fly higher than the romantic ones. Not that *Sylvia Scarlett* was a screwball comedy – anything but! Hard indeed to say exactly what it was – except a dreadful box office flop. It confused and disgruntled audiences accustomed to certain generic patterns in screen comedy. They were inexplicably deprived of such comforts as the film's mood darkened into suicide and with the perversity of Hepburn hiding her gender in male attire for much of the plot – a sex-reversal that now seems mild indeed, but was then unsettling to say the least. (Nowadays, naturally, the picture has become a camp cult.)

Richard Schickel, the American critic, in what is the best-written biography to date on Grant, put his finger on how the Cockney con-man he played in *Sylvia Scarlett* had been shaped by the sort of English low-life Grant had once known and enjoyed in his days as an adolescent tumbler in a circus, when

71

quick tongues and nimble wits, to say nothing of hard muscles, were needed to anticipate the worst that life brought in order to fend it off. Grant's boyhood, says Schickel, promoted the belief in him "that all alliances are shifting and temporary". That undoubtedly applied to most of his marriages. Even they were unusual, though, in that they were dissolved without acrimony and, in the majority of cases, without alimony. You could say that with a (second) wife like Barbara Hutton, who needed alimony? (What Barbara Hutton got from an alliance characterised, rather wittily, as "Cash 'n' Cary", one wonders; though on the occasion I stood outside the gleaming white palace she later bought in the heart of the souk in Tangier, and heard someone asking, "Why would the world's richest woman want to live in a slum like this?" our French-speaking guide's answer was pithier than I'd expected: "Pour la morphine, madame.")

Before Barbara Hutton, there had been Virginia Cherill, who had been Chaplin's blind flower-girl in *City Lights*; and after Hutton came Betsy Drake and Dyann Cannon. The divorce from the latter was probably Grant's most public episode, although he characteristically held his silence as his estranged wife alleged verbal and physical rebukes she had had to put up with and additionally mentioned her husband's way of insulting the annual Hollywood Oscar ceremony when it was on television. Exactly which was the greater snub – to his wife or his peers – was not settled by Grant's evidence; he made no public response at all to the accusations, rather as if he didn't want to bring down more coals of wrath on his head from the sort of spirited woman like Katharine Hepburn, Rosalind Russell or Jean Arthur whom he was always being matched against in his films. There, he was assured of the upper-hand by the screenwriters. In court, it might be different; he preferred not to risk an unfair division of dialogue. His quiet, private and one assumes happy life was restored to him by his fifth and last marriage to Barbara Harris.

I can well believe that his earlier marital experiences reinforced the wary comic style he employed in order to hold his own against the heroines who tried to push him around. He was a lover who preferred to lead with his chin rather than his lips. It was true what Pauline Kael said about him–that he was "the most publicly seduced man in films". Women went for him as if they had heard the starter's gun. (Of course, Grant had heard it, too, and began running even earlier.) It's truer to say that he drew women to him by making them feel that, though he liked them, and by the end of the film would love them, he nevertheless didn't actually *need* them. Even in life, the married man somehow managed to look like a bachelor. He had modelled himself on one such confirmed bachelor, Noël Coward, another urbane Briton who had come from much the same lower-class parentage as Grant and who had also re-invented himself to his own satisfaction. The model Coward provided encouraged Grant to abandon the stigmata of English class; the American milieu made it all the easier for him.

Coward was hardly ever known to lose his temper in public; I can't remember an occasion when Grant did, either. Both men tried to "rise above it", if life made things rough for them. Coward was bland to a mandarin extent; Grant was urbane to a man-of-the-world degree. They once found themselves on the same liner crossing the Atlantic: Coward's eminence then out-distanced Grant's, but confinement aboard ship is a good place to study one's idol and I'd have liked to overhear what passed between them. One occasionally "heard" Coward in Grant's dialogue, in specific words even. For me, the funniest moment in that drawing-room comedy *The Grass Is Greener* comes, appropriately, with the arrival of afternoon tea, which Grant and Deborah Kerr serve to Robert Mitchum as the American tourist who has unwittingly strayed into their private country manor. I always wait for the sardonic emphasis that Grant lays on the invitation, "Have some *Dundee* cake." In the abrasive treatment of that inoffensive place-name, one hears a lingering echo of that other great disrespecter of the provincial hinterland, Noël Coward.

He used to laugh at his own real baptismal name, Alexander Archibald Leach. "Don't I sound a bounder?" I heard him remark, when he was once reminded of it. Alfred Hitchcock liked bounders and must have known a few in his own *petit-bourgeois* youth spent in the same English social stratum as Grant. Both transplanted Britons had a misogynistic side to them. Hitch-cock's bias is well-known and, towards the end of his life, became distressingly pathological. Grant's, on the other hand, never showed up to his disadvantage, for it could always be subsumed into the churning *status quo* of the Hollywood sex-comedies. There he could deliver a punch to a woman's vanity, or even her gender, with such a roguish smile that it seemed like a lover's backhander. In the relatively few films in which he actually played a *serious* romantic lover, he is not as good as you might imagine he would be. He makes you feel that he'd like to cut it up comically, but has to play by the rules that aren't really his. Hitchcock, typically, found a sinister use for his charm by making him a putative murderer in *Suspicion*. But then Hitchcock liked those English murder-cases in which the gentleman turned out to be a wife-beater and worse. Grant never again let himself be cast as a murder suspect after that film. He'd relieve the wealthy of their jewellery for Hitchcock, even steal a taxi-cab from a woman in the lunch-time rush-hour but that was the limit. And he'd gladly pay the penalty for his sins that Hitchcock inflicted on him in a film like *North by Northwest*. A helpless Cary Grant, at the mercy of a lethal "crop-duster" plane, is a humanised Cary Grant, returned, as Richard Schickel says, to the vulnerable state of being the little boy he started life as.

You will gather from all this that there was rather more to Cary Grant than simply the face in every woman's dream or above the cable-stitch cardigan in every mother's knitting pattern. The black hair with the parting ruled into it, the slightly cleft chin, the candid eyes were all real; yet it wasn't an Identikit (or even Identiknit) picture of bland masculinity. One remembers that celebrated cable he once was sent asking, "HOW OLD CARY GRANT?" and his reply, "OLD CARY GRANT FINE. HOW YOU?" But he could, if he'd been less flippant, have answered, "OLD CARY GRANT HARD".

My memory of him keeps returning to *Sylvia Scarlett*, not just for the way he illustrated this observation in his portrait of a personable, but hard-nosed "chancer". The part spawned a curious sequel involving a far more celebrated screen character, one with whom no one would ever connect Cary Grant: namely, Harry Lime in *The Third Man*.

It was Sir Carol Reed who tipped me off to this. *The Third Man* had carried off the *Palme d'or* for Reed at Cannes in 1950. But despite later successes like *Oliver!* his reputation plummeted and when I encountered him, again at Cannes, in the early 1970s, he was sitting forlornly and a little drunk on the Croisette, unrecognised by most and – I regret to say – ignored by some who did recognise him. He hadn't come for the festival. He owned an apartment at Cannes and, grateful for company, he suggested we go on to take tea there. It was a well-sited flat, in a solid building looking over the *vieux port* on one side and the Moorish labyrinth of Le Suquet on the other. Talk turned to Katharine Hepburn whom he'd been vainly trying to sign for a film he eventually never made.

He asked suddenly, "Did you ever see her and Cary Grant in *Sylvia Scarlett*?"

"Yes, of course."

"Did you know I modelled Orson's Harry Lime on Grant in that film?"

Reed said he'd always remembered the way Cary Grant looked when we first see him in *Sylvia Scarlett*, wearing a black hat and a long tight black over-coat, lurking in the shadows of the cross-Channel ferry, laconically describing himself as "a little friend to all the world–nobody's enemy but my own" – a self-judgment that's soon negated by his division of "the world" into "sparrows" and " 'awks". Grant leaves us in no doubt that he's a Cockney " 'awk".

When Reed was directing *The Third Man* and came to do the set-up that introduces Orson Welles as Harry Lime, lurking in the dark doorway in Vienna and being suddenly illuminated by a light snapped on in an adjacent upstairs window, like a cinema projector, his imagination went back to Cary Grant in the other film nearly 15 years earlier. Welles, in *The Third Man*, had a young, chubby face, not unlike Grant's in a few spells of self-indulgence when he'd broken his diet, and the resemblance was sharpened by the same kind of black slouch hat and the long close-fitting black over-coat that Harry Lime wore in and below the streets of Vienna.

Now that Reed had revealed the connection, I was struck by another intriguing parallel between the films – between the cynical division of the world into the predators and the preyed upon, according to Grant's small-time Cockney con-man, and Harry Lime's similarly self-serving view of life vouchsafed from the bird's-eye-view of a big-time drugs peddler on the Ferris wheel in the Prater amusement park.

Such textual coincidences are common enough in movies, God knows. But every time I see *The Third Man*, I find myself wondering what it would have been like had Cary Grant and not Orson Welles been filling those shiny black boots in the doorway. Not that I'd have wished Anton Karas's zither music to make Grant's life a peripatetic misery, the way it followed Welles around the world for years. But Grant could have managed that "cuckoo clock" jibe – surely the most damning and unfair slander ever passed about a nation in any movie – with as much glib relish as Welles, who claimed to have improvised it.

"You have the mind of a pig," Katharine Hepburn's Sylvia Scarlett tells Grant at the end of their film, when he's shown himself unmoved by her father's suicide. To which his Cockney self-survival instinct replies, "It's a pig's world." Harry Lime's sentiments exactly though Grant made *his* career flourish by picking up the pearls that bestrewed the pig's world of Hollywood.

There was another small thing I found attractive about Cary Grant: he could sit alone at a restaurant table and have his lunch by himself or walk unaccompanied in the street in a quite unselfconscious way. Needless to say, there are a limited number of places in which he could do both without fear of interruption. But self-reliance is a rarer virtue of the famous than might be thought. Recognisable celebrities like to be hedged around by company, flanked by bodyguards. And not just for security. Most of them are people with few resources for entertaining themselves, no matter how many millions of other people they entertain. Grant, one sensed, didn't belong to that crowd.

There was another difference: he didn't like things being done for him: he preferred to look after himself. Now this runs totally contrary to the celebrity world, most of whose inhabitants insist on things being done for them. This is partly because it's necessary to be seen to be able to afford large numbers of people to do these things; partly because of the inconvenience of having to do them oneself. Making a relatively simple request for anything from a drink to an airline reservation necessitates a "performance" – an exercise of the persona by which the famous earn their living on the screen. It goes against the grain of most celebrities to give an expensive service for free. (If any money has to change hands directly, then the transaction can be literally costly to them, since the gratuity has to reflect not only the star's gratitude, but the star's status, and some stars are thus naturally inhibited from under-tipping while at the same time resentful of over-tipping.) All this usually results in a huge number of lackeys to whom the star has delegated his or her authority and who are not slow to drop "the Name" when demanding the favour, the deal, the discount. Grant, as far as I know, never worried about such things; all the reports of how he operated in business or private life confirm this.

He could handle himself in public the way he once used to do on the tight rope or on the acrobat's stilts that he manipulated on the stage in his vaudeville apprenticeship. The presence of his public held no fears for him – what he hated far more were hangers-on. He attended to his own needs in daily life. (It didn't always work out in business life; it is ironical that one of the truly revealing books about the wealth and business interests of Cary Grant should have been written by two former financial associates – that rich territory is usually the province of ex-wives.)

I'd been told by American colleagues that they sometimes came back to the desks in their newspaper offices, after lunch or from a Press screening, and found a note that said briskly, "Cary Grant called". If Grant had had a new picture ready for release, that would probably have explained the call; but this was long after he'd made his last screen appearance, in 1966. When the journalists returned his call, it generally turned out to be connected with an item he'd read in a newspaper involving a friend, or something he wanted to know more about – a play or a book usually, rarely a movie. No doubt he derived a sly amusement from such "out of the blue" calls that certainly caused a flutter in the offices where they were received by humble secretaries.

But in his last years whenever he felt a need for an audience – which even he did at times – he used to pick some out-of-the-way town or a campus well off the main academic circuit and make a personal appearance there with not much prior warning. It was while fulfilling just such a self-arranged engagement that he died of a heart attack. In Davenport, Iowa, of all places. Davenport's fame in the necrology of movieland is now secure. I think Grant would have been amused: it has a touch of Noël Coward, don't you think?

About six years before that sad event, I had been researching a book on Marlene Dietrich and I badly wanted to ask Grant to tell me something about Dietrich, with whom he had co-starred only once, in *Blonde Venus*, in 1932.

Blonde Venus is probably the least regarded of the six films that Dietrich made at Paramount for her mentor Josef Von Sternberg. But like many inferior works, it raises more intriguing questions than some of the acknowledged successes, especially about the state of Dietrich's relationship with Von Sternberg. There had been reports of rows; and Von Sternberg's despotism had had to be tempered by the intrusive prohibitions of Hollywood's self-censorship administrators. Dietrich played a fallen woman slumming her way through the flop-houses of the Deep South with a child in arms – not just as an earnest of her maternal feelings, which was meant to feed the censors a redeeming sop, but also as a physical handicap to any immoral temptation to which her implausible plight might expose her. The film is best remembered for its "Hot Voodoo" number on stage, in which Dietrich strips off the pelt of a huge gorilla, piece by piece, emerging into view as her blonde self in a baroque costume of feathers and spangles. Years after I first saw the film, I happened to be in the Secession Museum in the centre of Vienna, which was Von Sternberg's natal city, and in the great Gustav Klimt mural for Beethoven's "Hymn to Man" which is on display there, I saw Marlene Dietrich's "King Kong" monster, surrounded by suitably unclad maidens. There is no proof of Von Sternberg getting his idea from this source; but it is likely. Once one has seen *Blonde Venus*, one can't view Klimt's gorilla without wanting to exclaim, "Come on out, Marlene, we know you're in there."

But back to Grant . . . He played a minor role in *Blonde Venus* and was ineptly cast, as a gangster politico ("He runs this end of town") who makes Dietrich his mistress, thus relieving her of the financial burden of supporting her stricken husband, who was played, with no gratitude at all, by Herbert Marshall. Everyone in the film looked uncomfortable, even Grant. He went through the motions of the role, making not the slightest attempt at the emotions.

Roderick Mann, then a columnist on the *Los Angeles Times*, and, by virtue of his English background, a long-time acquaintance of Grant's whom he used to interview frequently for the London *Sunday Express*, was living in Beverly Hills not very far from the star. He gave me Grant's address and advised me to write to him with my enquiries well in advance of arriving in Los Angeles. I had received no reply by the time I left London. On telephoning Grant's home, I got no encouragement from the butler: Mr Grant was out of town. One has to accept such drawbacks stoically (and hope they won't be too identifiable in the text of the book). After all, I asked myself, could Grant have remembered very much about *Blonde Venus*, even if he'd wanted to? He'd made it 50 years before and perhaps the only lasting impression it had left on him had been the parting in his hair – which Von Sternberg peremptorily, and without any explanation, had switched from the left side of his head to the right before he shot his first scene in the film. Grant had kept the parting on the right to the end of his life; a coiffeur touch in an *auteur* actor.

I'd once asked Herbert Marshall if he knew why Von Sternberg had done this. "To annoy Dietrich," Marshall replied, replacing one riddle with another.

Two years after my unanswered approach to Grant, I was in my workroom in London when the telephone rang. It was mid-morning.

"Is that Mr Walker?"

"Yes?"

"Oh, Cary Grant here."

It was the familiar staccato, direct, polite, not overly intimate, more like a business call, which indeed it turned out to be. He was speaking from London Airport.

"Didn't you write to me about Marlene . . . ? Two years ago, wasn't it? I felt I owed you a reply. I suppose your book about her is already out?"

"Yes."

"Oh, good . . . then I can tell you what you wanted to know about her."

There was a tiny mischievous chuckle; he was enjoying himself.

"You were asking about *Blonde Venus*, weren't you?"

"Yes . . . how was it?"

"Terrible, really, working with Joe [Von Sternberg]. He put

Marlene and me through take after take, just like you've possibly heard. Don't forget it was only my sixth picture" (It was his fifth, actually, but good marks for memory so far) "and I could never get a scene under way before Joe would bawl out 'Cut' – at me, personally, across the set. This went on and on and on. I felt like someone doing drill who kept dropping his rifle, but wasn't going to be allowed to drop out of the ranks.

"When he'd got me thoroughly rattled, Joe would walk over to Marlene, take her aside and talk to her. Very quietly and in German. Then he'd shoot round, fix his eyes on me and yell at me to get ready for another take. He was a demon! What a relief it was to be off that film.

"Now here's the interesting part . . . Many years later, I found myself sailing back to San Francisco aboard an American liner from Yokohama and Joe Von Sternberg was on it, too. Oh, terribly down on his luck now . . . long, long without Marlene.

"I suppose in honour of my being on the ship, they showed one of my films in the ship's cinema . . . *Mr Lucky*, it was. Ever see it? Oh, you should. One of the weirdest I ever made, in 1943 I think. I was a gambler who falls in love with a socialite and enlists in the fight against Fascism. Adrian Scott wrote the script. He was then the tennis pro at my club – later he was one of the 'Hollywood Ten', but that's another story, I'm sure you know all about it.

"Anyhow, when the movie was over, Joe and I took a turn or two round the deck. Joe was very silent. And then he said, 'You know, in that picture we just saw, you were good . . . Why weren't you any good when I directed you in *Blonde Venus*?' The bastard . . .!"

There was a pause. I prompted Grant: "What did you say?"

"I said, 'Because you damn well wouldn't let me, Joe'." Another rasping chuckle. Then: "I must run for my plane now – hope that's helped you."

"Just a minute," I yelled.

"Yes?"

"Do you remember Von Sternberg altering your hair parting from left to right on that film?"

"Of course."

"Did he ever tell you why he did it?"

"Oh, isn't it obvious?"

"Was it to annoy Marlene?"

A snort. "Of course not. It was to annoy me. Joe loved to throw you. Could you do anything worse to an actor than alter his hair parting just a minute before he starts shooting a scene? I kept it that way ever since, as you may have noticed. To annoy *him*."

THE SOFT WORDS OF MR RATTIGAN – THE HARD BLOWS OF MR RUSSELL

Very few filmmakers, in my experience, take the trouble to reply to critics who have rewarded their best efforts with bad notices. This is only right and proper. A slightly larger number, I'm sorry to say, send thank-you notes for the good reviews.

The thank-you's needn't concern us here. Though their writers are probably sincere (or, at least, relieved), their motives are usually suspect; critics, after all, are cynical fellows. Only one filmmaker has ever tried offering me a bribe in advance for a good review. And even he didn't risk a full-frontal approach but sidled up to me. "By the way," this reasonably famous man said, "how much are the advertising rates in your paper?" – "I've really no idea . . . I've never advertised." – "Well, make a guess." I made a guess. "Is that high?" – "It's said to be." – "Okay . . . and if you were reviewing my next movie, how many column inches would you charge for?"

Towards such a proposition, there are only two responses. I didn't get up and leave; we had met for lunch and I was hungry. I picked up the menu and said, "Shall we order?" – and I made sure I picked up the bill.

Strange to say, the man turned out quite a good film and collected favourable reviews – my own included. I'd like to believe he still thinks of me as an honest critic; I fear he just regards me as a poor businessman.

Pressure of a more unusual kind was applied to me in the early 1960s. Unusual because this time it was the kind of appeal that's harder to deal with – not a pecuniary bribe, but a moral one. A plea for understanding. Or so at first I thought; later on, I wasn't so sure. It came from a man whose self-esteem at one time would never have permitted him to do anything of that kind. But times had changed for Terence Rattigan, though not as brutally as playwriting fashions.

He was 52 in 1963, when his film *The VIPs* had its London

première. He was already out of favour with the theatre critics; to his way of thinking, that was almost as bad as being out of health. He was bitter at the way his West End citadel, the "well-made play", had had to yield the stage to the New Playwrights – Osborne, Wesker, Pinter and others. He had been deposed and now he was habitually disparaged. His craftsmanship was still acknowledged, but grudgingly, and put down to the hollow slickness of a social manner. In the critics' nostrils, he smelled of drawing-rooms, not the kitchen. Trying to please – once the dramatist's imperative in his kind of theatre – had become the damning admission of a class toady – Oh, the language was strong in that era! Worse still, he had had the bad judgment to create a witness against himself who had assumed independent life in the columns of enemy critics. "Aunt Edna" was used to indict her creator by citing her clucking approval of Master Terry's comforting confirmation of the dear old thing's prejudices and tut-tutting at any deviation from her straightforward and narrow-minded predilections.

Around this time, Rattigan's physician had told him he was suffering from leukemia and shouldn't count on living very much longer – a prognostication that the playwright repeated often enough for it to become common gossip. Lacking confidence in his power to hold a stage audience and needing to earn large sums of money more quickly than a lame play could bring it home to him, he had taken to writing film scripts. He had a facility for turning them out rapidly and not caring too much what changes were subsequently made in them. Producers appreciated both virtues but somewhat more, I think, the second. He was well paid for his work. For *The VIPs*, it was reported he had received £40,000, or around £450,000 by the values of the late 1980s, when he sold the outline of it to Anatole de Grunwald in 1961. Being fog-bound at Heathrow Airport on his way to Hollywood had planted the idea of the play in his mind. It was an all-star story about the dramas that just such a vexatious delay caused to an assorted group of travellers in the VIP lounge.

Rattigan had never made any secret that he did such scripts for the money. He used to announce to journalists that he was being taxed out of whatever savings he'd invested for his old age, even by the Tories who were then in Government. In my review of the film, I'd made a point of the characters' single common preoccupation, which was not their celebrity, as the titled implied, but a less intangible commodity: "Not only are all the characters straight out of the author's overnight bag, but of all the many intriguing problems that Terence Rattigan could have shown them to have had on their minds, he deals with the only one that he seems to have, to an obsessive degree, on *his* mind. All our VIPs worry about is money. There's the glossy wife (Elizabeth Taylor) of a millionaire industrialist (Richard Burton) who elopes with a gigolo (Louis Jourdan) because her husband can give her only 'cheque-book affection'.

"There's the other millionaire industrialist (Rod Taylor) who must get to New York if the cheque he has imprudently written out is to be covered before the banks open. There is the film tycoon (Orson Welles) who has to be out of the country by midnight or forfeit a fortune in tax allowance. And there is the impoverished duchess (Margaret Rutherford) making her first-ever flight to earn money as a Miami club hostess and keep the thatch on her Tudor cottage. Even the bit players have money on the brain. A passing doctor importunes Mr Burton for a stock market tip. A girlfriend stops in mid-clinch to ask Mr Rod Taylor if her shares are safe. Mr Rattigan's notion of being a VIP, it seems, doesn't get much beyond £.s.d."

Thoroughly warming to my brutal work, I added: "I never imagined the British cinema in the space of two hours could be carried back to where it was on the day war broke out . . . This is a masterpiece of vacuum-packed cosiness and lushly packaged unreality . . . an entire British Museum of prehistoric clichés and burial mound characters. The fact that Mr Rattigan has one character say to another, 'Please don't talk like a woman's magazine' did not save him from jotting down lines like: 'I've loved him . . . but I don't know him'; 'Killing me won't get your wife back'; 'I don't usually drink champagne, but perhaps tonight is an exception'; 'I want to be treated as a wife, not an expensive mistress' . . . Producer Anatole de Grunwald gets any credit that is going for being fly enough to hire actors who can make flat surfaces look round."

Though probably the most hostile notice the film got, my review was representative of the majority of other critics. In retrospect, I think the film didn't deserve quite such an onslaught. But it showed its age and low level of aspiration compared to what previous weeks had brought to the London screen at the time, notably the John Osborne-Tony Richardson *Tom Jones* and Joseph Losey's *Eve*. The British cinema's "New Wave" was about to break. November, 1963, was going to see the *première* of *The Servant*. And Rattigan's style of comedy was going to suffer the same rebuff in the cinema as his plays had already received in the theatre.

To my surprise, shortly after my notice appeared, I received a letter from him at his London address, 29, Eaton Square. It doesn't bear any date, merely "Monday", which was probably September 16, judging by internal evidence and my own dated reply.

"Attacking success", he wrote, "does not make you into a fearless young crusader high-mindedly defending the cause of television or cinema against the Philistine. It merely makes you out of touch with popular taste, probably with Taste – as when you quote lines from *The VIPs* without the context of character or situation. 'Mr Shakespeare's poverty of language is shown by his use, in a single line, of the word *Never* repeated five times' . . . 'Mr Sheridan plainly didn't know the difference between an alligator and an allegory' . . . 'Mr Ibsen puts into the mouths of his characters in *The Wild Duck* such appalling clichés as etc., etc.' . . . This vulgar error of quoting a line about, say, 'not usually drinking champagne' without acknowledging that it was spoken by a secretary living in Hounslow who is firmly established as a persistent drinker of Bitter Lemon always outrages me and always draws me. If the critic should think that certain lines in a film are clichés, he must relate this fact to character before saying so, and then say *not* that they are clichés – which, in dialogue, don't exist, and, sure Shakespeare's Nurse in *Romeo and Juliet* never existed – but that they are out of character, if they are, or that 'she would have found a stronger phrase', if she would . . .

"Critics should be criticised – both adversely and favourably – and so rarely are. Middle age, a long career and an undisputed popular success (in *The VIPs*) give me that privilege with you. Answer, if you dare. But don't ask, 'What has popular success to do with criticism?' because I know the answer. 'Nothing', of course. And 'everything', of course.

Above Hepburn as the Madwoman of Chaillot: like the character living within her own guarded world, she has only a small notion of how the wider world has moved on. **Right** Hepburn at the bat in her lunch hour. "The games people played in my younger days were games, not psychological torture syndromes." For her, they still are.

Opposite O'Toole in *The Lion in Winter:* the fungus masks the too-pleased-with-himself complexion that he can all too easily confuse with charm. **Above** Sprinting for school assembly in *Goodbye, Mr Chips*. **Left** The "mad Irishman" of *Murphy's War*: "all mock gab, low guile, damn-the-consequences devilment . . . he gave a performance with a head of foam on it."

Above Cary Grant as Jimmy, the cynical Cockney swindler in *Sylvia Scarlett* (with Hepburn in boy's disguise and Edmund Gwenn). Carol Reed recalled that black coat and hat when he outfitted Orson Welles for 'Harry Lime''. **Below** Romantic Cary, seductive Grace. The same car ride led to tragedy 25 years later.

Above left A face made for the Godfather of the overworld: Brando enjoys a power-breakfast as the Getty-esque mogul of *The Formula*. **Above right** A lull on the battlefield. Trevor Howard and Marlon Brando put on their best faces for the stills photographer on *The Saboteur: Code Name 'Morituri'*. Between takes, the rivalry was undisguised. **Below** Brando (with peculiar weapon) in *The Missouri Breaks*: the secret, producers find, is not to be afraid of him – sometimes it's difficult.

Above left Olivier making the film for the Philippines (and signing his memoirs, which had just appeared). A critic-turned-director looks on, wondering if he will get the performance he wants. **Above right** *"Mabuhay!"* **Below** A surprise up his sleeve: Olivier as the Nazi war criminal in *Marathon Man*, the first of a long run of "German" roles, not all so resonant with evil.

Hazlitt never despised popular taste, even when it disagreed with his own. And I'd bet (though you may correct me) that Hazlitt never quoted dialogue out of context . . . V. sincerely, Terence Rattigan''.

As Rattigan might have predicted, I received a shoal of letters about my review of *The VIPs* – fairly evenly divided, however. One woman, surely Aunt Edna's blood relative, wrote, "You only like the films of Jellini." A few days later, I replied to Rattigan:

"You are far too good a craftsman, even when you are writing down" – he had admitted in interviews the week of the film's opening that he put his pot-boilers into films and saved his best work for the stage – "to make a film so monstrously bad that it is positively enjoyable . . . I wish *The VIPs* had achieved the same glorious absurdities [as *Grand Hotel*] which it seems too hard to come by in these more cautious and costly days . . . You reproach me for quoting lines out of context . . . [But] the context – the character speaking the lines – is just as banal as the quotation . . . You say that ordinary people formulate ordinary thoughts in an ordinary fashion. I maintain that the aim of art is to shed an extraordinary light on what seems ordinary. Most people *do* get through the day on luncheon vouchers and clichés. But it is not enough to devise things for them to say that are 'in character' – you must also reveal the shades of character we don't expect. In [a certain London store] there's a saleslady who talks to me about films every time I go in . . . Aunt Edna would probably love her. But one day when she was asking me about Hitchcock's new film, *The Birds*, she mused, 'Birds . . . I don't go for them somehow. Don't know why, really. All I know is, when father was dying a big blackbird used to go tapping at the window. I wonder if that would have anything to do with it?' With what Electra complexities buying wares from her at the store counter is now confused! That's what I mean by illuminating the ordinary."

This impudent trespass on land that Rattigan had posted as his own tempted him, as I had hoped, to fire off a second barrel. On September 24, 1963, he wrote:

89

"I know that your leisure is more limited than mine, so you don't need to answer this answer (or our correspondence might stretch out to such lengths that Jerome Kilty might be tempted to make a play out of it). Let me just answer – or try to – a few of the points you raise. The question of writing *down*. Far too easy and glib a critical judgment. No writer I've ever known of is capable of consciously writing *down* – and if they were, would certainly not produce anything successful (I mean popular), but all writers – well, most – we can exclude Tolstoy, I suppose, but then we always can, can't we? – anyway *most* writers from Shakespeare to Anouilh have occasionally allowed themselves the luxury of lowering their sights a little to knock off something designed to entertain not only their audiences and readers but – here's the point – *themselves* . . .

"Quickly to the rest. I am not obsessed with money. As anyone who knows me, including my bank manager, knows, I instantly spend all I make, and much more than I make . . . I wrote *The VIPs* out of friendship for Tolly [de Grunwald], but as it was MGM I also asked an enormous price for my services which, to my surprise (and Tolly's) they gave me! I then, imprisoned by a contract, felt it my duty to try to make money for MGM, which a *Browning Version* wouldn't have done (because it didn't) and because MGM were then (two years ago, remember) nearly bankrupt, and needed a *Browning Version* like they needed a hole in the head (cliché!) Even good notices from Alexander Walker and Penelope Gilliatt would hardly have un-soured their view of 'this goddam English writer' who had bought and furnished a house in Brighton ('Where's Brighton? . . . Well, it's kinda the British Palm Beach') on the proceeds of their ridiculously over-generous payments and then landed them with a turkey ('*VIPs* Slim $3000 in Detroit Despite Boffo Notices' – *Variety*). Tolly would hardly have kept his job. Puffin [director Anthony Asquith's nickname] would never have been offered another Hollywood film (nor would I, and I might just wish to buy another house sometime). It seemed best to try and please my employers, the public and myself, all at the same time . . .

"I'm quite honest enough to admit my 'contemptuous syntheticism' whenever I can find it. The last act of *While the Sun*

Shines, the final scene of *The Winslow Boy*, the speech-room sequences in the film of *The Browning Version* – but I won't admit much more from *The VIPs* than the Margaret Rutherford part. . . . A secretary (played in the film by Maggie Smith) in love with her employer? Yes, a cliché, I suppose so, but I *had* rather carefully described her as 'in the middle forties with thick-lensed spectacles and a nose that becomes unbecomingly red at moments of emotion'. The final kiss from her employer was intended as a humiliation. He went for her lips and slipped up to her forehead, thus telling her and the audience (rather neatly and cinematically for me) what both should already have known – that bed just wasn't on for the poor bitch. MGM made Puffin shoot it both ways (and they were also responsible for Maggie Smith's make-up) and obviously they chose the shot which would go down best in Little Rock, Freetown and Manila. Can you blame them? *I* can, but can you?

"Alex Korda in a pickle with income tax? If he were played by Ustinov, I don't think you would have thought [that a cliché]. Orson [Welles] is a splendid actor, but, as a comedian, is about as subtle as my left buttock, which isn't subtle at all, but, at the moment is rather numb – from sitting so long in the same position and writing so much. I don't think there is any dramatic situation that isn't a cliché (except, possibly, the one about the chap who unwittingly bumped off his Dad and married his Mum) – I mean the one about the chap (coloured) who got so jealous about his wife having dropped his handkerchief in some other chap's apartment . . . I mean we've seen that sort of thing before, haven't we?

"Flippancy apart, I must end . . . by saying that I rest my case by reminding you of the title *The VIPs*. Today's Very Important Persons are considered so by airlines precisely *because* they are obsessed by money – meaning both the airlines and the VIPs. Their author, and creator, truly, is not. A VIP, here, is usually surprised to find himself considered as – and *there* is a fine example of English prose . . . You don't think it's my critics who are obsessed with money, by any chance? . . . Best, T.R.

P.S. I loved your saleslady character – and entirely see your point – but if she'd gone on live like that for two hours, you'd be wanting to shoot her. ('Des Moines Nixes Rattigan's Talkfest' – *Variety*.)''

I answered by return:

"All right, for 'contemptuously synthetic' substitute 'considerately'. I can manage a sympathetic sigh for de Grunwald, a real tear for Asquith and a compassionate embrace for you – all of you seeing your future prospects and employment prejudiced by making a film that would please the critics and mortally bore the public. But where does such considerateness stop? . . . I am probably out of sympathy with any project for re-founding MGM's fortunes by yoking Margaret Rutherford to Ben Hur's chariot – fine though that would be in marquee appeal.''

And *that*, I thought was that; but, as it turned out, not quite.

"This is Mr Rattigan's secretary," said the voice on the telephone. "Mr Rattigan would like you to come round for a drink. He has something very important to tell you – the sort of thing, he says, that can't be put in a letter very easily.''

I was hooked immediately. What couldn't a professional writer put in a letter easily? I telephoned Ken Tynan. "Do you think I should go?'' – "Of course you should. As Oscar Wilde said – who should have – 'never refuse an experience'.''

Rattigan's flat was like a lot of the other stage backcloths that the distinguished actors and actresses who were his neighbours in Eaton Square had, consciously or not, arranged their off-stage lives against. I had a strong impression of a curtain rising when I entered Rattigan's drawing-room. The room was well decorated, though that particular Regency style now looks *its* age – which is certainly not the Prince Regent's. The room was warm and the windows slightly steamed up, blurring the fine Belgravia rain outside even more. A Guardi painting of a Venetian scene kept its patrician distance from an L.S. Lowry picked out in bright supporter club hues.

Rattigan was lying on an olive silk sofa in navy blazer and flannels, one leg up on the upholstery, his head supported by a cushion. Had he not looked so well-groomed and healthy, I'd have thought I was visiting a convalescent. But what were almost his first words belied his appearance and confirmed my impression – "You know of course that I'm dying?"

"Good heavens, no," I lied, for I'd heard the stories of his doctor's diagnosis. "Yes, I'm afraid so – leukemia. My doctor's actually given me a date for the . . . the event. It was to have been three weeks ago. Just as *Man and Boy* was opening." (Rattigan's most recent play) "I'm afraid it's the play that's dying, not me. Do help yourself to a drink. The tray's over there. While you're about it, get me a whisky, would you?"

"I like your understatement," I said.

"What your colleagues would call 'Rattigan's evasiveness', I'm afraid – don't you agree?" He swung his other well-creased flannel-trousered leg up on the sofa and the effect of a sickbed was communicated even more strongly. While he was speaking, he didn't look at me directly, but threw a glance my way every now and then – it was as if he were playing to the audience "out front" yet had to keep up the pretence of addressing me directly. I was to remember this when I met Laurence Olivier a few years later; that was how Olivier operated socially, too, except that *he* would lower his head and shoot a glance up from under his brows, checking on his effects, while Rattigan swivelled his neck as if someone had been overheard speaking sharp words about him in his vicinity.

Rattigan didn't speak with the punchy self-justification of his letters; he was shy, if anything, and social ease came to him from an arrangement of effects, the veneered hair, the cigarette in its long holder, his blazer unconcernedly crushed beneath his supine posture.

He reminded me fairly quickly, however, that a few months earlier I'd given a frosty notice to a television play of his called *Heart to Heart*. It was an early example of "television *sans frontières*" – a Eurovision chamber-drama, commissioned by BBC Television and produced by several other European countries as well, each in its own language, within a few days of the original broadcast. The theme was one Rattigan returned to again and again, the secret life of public figures; in this case, a British Cabinet Minister who's accepted bribes and kept a mistress and now discovers his indiscretions have become known to the TV interviewer who has him scheduled for a "heart-to-heart" encounter.

93

"Did you really hate *Man to Man* so much?" he now enquired of me.

"*Man to Man . . .?*"

He gave a little start – "Oh, sorry, that's what I originally thought of calling *Heart to Heart*, but decided not to – someone would have made a snide joke, wouldn't they? You know, of course, that John Freeman" [then TV's most celebrated interviewer and, before long, destined to become British Ambassador in Washington DC] "was desperate to play himself in it – the interviewer who brings out the 'truths of the heart' (cliché, Mr Walker). He was terribly piqued that Kenneth More got to play him, rather better than life, I think. I'd wanted Richard Burton, actually – I suppose you know that. He'd have been perfect. The man's got to be an utter bastard and Kenny was just too chummy."

"At least you got Burton for *The VIPs*."

"Yes, playing Larry."

"Sorry?"

"Larry Olivier . . . That's who the husband in the film was based on. Didn't you know? The Liz Taylor and Louis Jourdan roles were based on Vivien Leigh and Peter Finch. The whole incident of the woman eloping with her lover came out of Vivien deciding to leave Larry a few years ago and run off to America with Peter. The fog came down and stranded them in the VIP lounge at London Airport. Vivien told me so herself. By the time it lifted and they were called for boarding, she realised how much of Larry, and everything he stood for in her life, was going to have to be left behind and she just couldn't face it. Bye-bye, Peter. She beat it back to London. Burton played the husband the way Larry might have done – you know, the strong-weak man with letters of G–U–I–L–T running through him like Brighton rock (cliché, Mr Walker). I can't think why he and Vivien never did *Candida* together. It would have been perfect for a couple who depended on the idea of each other much more than they loved the reality of being together. I wonder who'd have played Marchbanks, though . . . By the way, you mustn't use any of this in the newspapers."

"We do have libel laws," I said a bit pompously. (At this date, Vivien Leigh and Peter Finch were both alive.)

"And very glad I am for it. A playwright like me depends upon

94

the social dishonesties they uphold. Kick them away, and where would the drama be? That's what makes me hate Osborne. Osborne's incapable – quite incapable – of *implying* things; it all has to come out in a great vomit . . .

"But you know, I often go to 'life', as it's called for my characters – not that a critic like you would recognise that. My characters have their models every bit as much as Master Osborne's. But you see critics like you won't grant me that. Did you see *Variation on a Theme*?"

This was Rattigan's up-dated version of *La Dame aux Camélias*; it had been staged in London five years earlier, in 1958. I hadn't seen it, I said.

"Pity. You know Larry, don't you? I wonder if you'd have recognised the little shit in the boy in the play?"

" 'Larry'? Larry Olivier?"

"Good God, no . . . Larry *Harvey*. I'd always wanted to do a downbeat modern version of *Camille* and Larry's own life egged me on to do it, especially when he got his hooks into Maggie Leighton. You see, Marguerite in the play – my play, not Dumas' – isn't kept by her men: *she* keeps them. But just as she's about to marry a rich man, she meets this boy who's far harder, far more ruthless than she could ever be. Her desire for him is answered by his opportunistic clutch at her – he leaves his male lover for the life of luxury with Marguerite. Just like Larry Harvey. You mustn't use any of this in your newspaper, by the way."

The conversation had now taken a determinedly confessional turn; I realised I was being tantalisingly told things which couldn't be broken to the world so long as the people who figured in them remained alive. There was a sort of mischievous perversity about it all. Rattigan veered off Larry Harvey – "He wouldn't have been a better actor if he'd stayed with his original benefactor, but he'd have been a bigger film star" – and talked of a famous actress whose life off-stage had been fraught with tragedy. It had stirred his compassion, he said, and excited his craftsmanship – "If you'll forgive that dirty word." With his "great play" still to write – "the one that will be performed 100 years from now" – Rattigan said he'd like to choose this woman's life as material. Ibsen would have loved the theme, he added. "He'd have begun the play . . ." Rattigan's finger stabbed the air . . . "just *there*." And he jabbed it into the time sequence of the yet-to-be-written drama.

"People need the discipline of love," he said.

"Do you?"

"Of course. Unfortunately, while I receive all gifts gladly and *most* sincerely, I'm not of a nature to return them in kind. Love-lessness is my great defect."

"And your great virtue?"

"Oh, that's easy – single-mindedness."

"I hear you refused to let Larry Harvey play Lawrence of Arabia in *Ross* when it went to Broadway."

"Yes, I was pretty single-minded there all right. Easy, really. People like Larry always end up hating the people they need – they often begin that way, too, unfortunately. Which is what happened with him and Maggie. Not that he mightn't have been quite good as Lawrence – 'quite', I mean. You need to be a bit of a cold fish to play Lawrence of Arabia. Which is why I didn't take much to Peter O'Toole in the film, except when he said that one word – do you remember it? – 'Pity!' when he found the wireless transmitter didn't work. '*Pity*!' Just like a petulant girl, spitting at someone. He was good then. You know when Puffin and I were going to do *our* film of Lawrence, we had Dirk Bogarde who, I think, would have been *very* good. 'Very', I mean. Dirk has this thing about wanting to show up the flaw in a character, whatever it may be. He's got the courage to be a shit, has our Dirk; now all he needs is the part."

A few weeks later, Rattigan and I discovered Bogarde had at last got the part, too, in the Losey–Pinter film of *The Servant*.

Rattigan had been dead right there, but I later wondered how he had reacted to Bogarde's triumph in Pinter's screenplay for *The Servant*. Pinter thrived on an iron diet of elusiveness that Rattigan never attempted in his stage plays. The latter went for the Rattigan-tat-tat of dialogue. I think his style had been formed by his thwarted ambition to be a great barrister. His characters sounded to me like people taking the strain of cross-examination in the witness-box, their responses being echoed by a sardonic counsel. Pinter's characters had their patterns, too, but they were the inherited patterns of an actor (which he had been) who turns every moment into a "performance" without needing to fit the dimensions of a text. Bogarde caught the cryptic style better than he would have done the cross-examining one.

Listening to Rattigan tell me "things you can't print", I recalled how frequently his plays depended on an act of self-revelation to provide them with the "curtain". I had more and more the feeling that this evening had been arranged as an act of stage-craft. My professional constraint on revealing what I was being told was giving him a sly enjoyment. I was being tantalised by insider information I couldn't use to advantage. At the same time he was demonstrating his artfulness in transfiguring life by making me privy to the reality behind his apparent fictions.

Rattigan had exposed everyone, but kept himself hidden behind an unruffled exterior. It was a "heart to heart" talk without a genuine transfusion. A self-indulgence.

"He didn't bitch much," I reported back to Kenneth Tynan when I telephoned him later in the evening. "In fact, he was rather melancholy, if anything."

Tynan laughed. "Has he rescheduled his death?" he asked.

In fact, Rattigan lived on for another 14 years, until November, 1977; so news of his death was much protracted if not exaggerated. His last years were much happier ones. He was knighted in 1971 and his price on the theatrical stock market rose with Coward's.

But he looked lonely when I left him that evening in 1963. He had obviously no plans for the rest of the evening, except to spend it in his own company or on the telephone to friends. Death was on his mind; not only his own, though. As we passed from the drawing-room into the hall-way, he took me into his study, a room wallpapered in red like a luxurious brazier, and pointed out a very small framed painting, not much bigger than a postcard. It was an abstract work, a few chrome yellow doodles on a white ground recalling the way wisps of a woman's hair might stray negligently over the nape of her neck. An insubstantial thing, quite pretty. I was glad I didn't make the guess he invited me to make about the identity of the artist, for he pointed to three minuscule initials in one corner that looked as if they'd been painted by a brush with a single hair in it: "M.M.M."

"Marilyn Monroe Miller", he said, contemplating this relic of the film actress who had died the year before. She had given it to him when she was starring in the screen version of his play *The Sleeping Prince* (filmed as *The Prince and the Showgirl*).

"She had talent as a painter, too, I think. But of course she never exhibited." And he added with not quite mock irony: "Probably afraid of the critics."

Critics, strangely enough, contribute very little to the unhappiness of filmmakers. I write "strangely enough" because, being at the sharp edge of the process where a picture meets its public, their view of it might be considered crucial, sometimes fatal. But critics have never had the power to make or break a film and what residual influence they retain on its fortunes at the box-office is being eroded by the countervailing power of the commercial hype that precedes a film's release, often by months these days.

Hype overwhelms the small dawn chorus of critics' voices dissenting from the high and mighty and reiterated refrain of the paid-for mass media. Hype, some say, is a contraction of "high-powered". Others say it is derived from "hyperbole", or "undue and absurd exaggeration". Either way, it means promoting a product or person so intensively, expensively and continuously that it's almost impossible for the public not to hear about it and want to taste the experience it represents. Hype is more than mere advertising. It has an in-built neurotic compulsiveness. If one hasn't seen the current colossus of hype, one is considered a non-person. Not all hype is self-identified advertising. The growth of the "profile industry" in newspapers and magazines has progressed at the expense of the critical columns. Nowadays the mass public's view of a film is generally formed well in advance of its *première*, by the "feature articles" about its making and the related "celebrity interviews" with its director or stars. This is generally all part of the hype, too, the product of a mute accord between the subjects and the writers that the latter will insinuate no snide commentary on the forthcoming movie or obtrude no disputatious opinions of their own about the claims made by those interviewed about their own importance or success.

Press, television and radio commit media incest far more frequently today than they used to do. Fear of missing something, of not being first in on the next "media event", as a "big important movie" is now termed, causes them on occasion to diffuse throughout their pages or their programmes – even though those sections that wouldn't normally deal with movies – all the news, views and hearsay that contribute to the hype. *Platoon* was a picture that "crossed over" with phenomenal success in this way: a "must see" event before the film critics had got to it, largely on the strength of well-placed and timed "media screenings" for political, editorial and even "hard news" editors, backed up by phone-ins and talk-shows and interviews by its ubiquitous director, Oliver Stone, whose own obsessiveness was well suited to this kind of media commando exercise. Soon everyone was talking about *Platoon*. Willy-nilly, we are all the agents of hype.

Not that the hype works every time. Long is the list of expensive hypes which have fallen utterly flat: Otto Preminger's casting of the ingenue, Jean Seberg, as Joan of Arc, a piece of hype that only added oil to the flames in which Seberg was roasted, since his calculated gamble was interpreted as personal vanity; or Mohammed Ali's appearance in *The Greatest*, attended by almost total lack of curiosity about a man who needed to appear in the flesh for the hype to work; or Julie Andrews, fresh from *The Sound of Music* and *Mary Poppins*, failing to have her purity-rating successfully reversed by sharing an unwed bed with Paul Newman in *Torn Curtain* and then hastily trying to repair the damage by starring in *Star!* which was one of the most heavily hyped films of the late-1960s and a total write-off; or Rex Harrison turning to talk to the animals, instead of a Cockney flower-girl, in *Dr Doolittle* and meeting with such indifference from the two-footed species that even to get them into the cinema one-by-one, never mind two-by-two, was an achievement; or Elliott Gould, an icon of his own uptight era, mirroring its insanity in the smash-hit *M*A*S*H*, until Ingmar Bergman got him for *The Touch*, whereupon Gould "got art", which so traumatised him that the hype went to his head and his career collapsed in on itself like a black hole where formerly a star had shone; or Liv Ullman, dubbed "Hollywood's New Nordic Star" before she had even reached the place, and for whom it was said the producers of *Lost Horizon, 40 Carats* and *The Abdication* passed over, respectively, Audrey Hepburn, Elizabeth Taylor and Vanessa Redgrave; or Marthe Keller, another candidate for the American popular vote who didn't get it despite hype-by-association with Dustin Hoffman; or Isabelle Adjani who got as far as the cover of *Time*, which is nowadays the epicentre of hype, but little farther; or Marie-France Pisier, hyped by the same magazine in a fatuous cover-article about the "New European Stars", who was glossied up and had the full hype treatment to turn her into an international star in *The Other Side of Midnight* – which is roughly where her would-be American career ended up.

Hype, as that little list of yesteryear indicates, can be a two-edged weapon. But like many aggressive bits of equipment, its manufacture goes on being refined and adapted to the end it is desired to accomplish. We're now, I'm afraid, in a period when hype is virtually inseparable and, even more ominously, indistinguishable from what should be the untainted critical commentary of the media.

Sub-contracting out to firms of "independent" publicists the promotional work on a film that used to be done by the in-house publicity departments of the film companies themselves, has had its banal effect. It has re-distributed power in favour of those who are eager to retain a tighter, narrower, altogether more security-conscious rein on the judgment that others are paid to pass on their product. The publicity departments of the film companies at least dealt in quantity promotion, not quality control; and they really didn't have the time or the budget to promote each picture with the same degree of media penetration given them by the new satellite PR firms to whom they have hived off their office work as much out of concern for economy as a desire for encomiums. The hype hirelings have a vested interest in building up *every* movie they handle, and every moviemaker or movie star who comes with the package, as a unique event that must not have its importance scathed by the slightest degree of advance scepticism about it, much less full-bodied attack.

The Sunday newspapers' colour supplements, both in Britain and America, have also had a great deal to answer for in the downgrading of independent opinion. They play up to the market forces of "success" and "display" rather than upholding the critical canons of judgment. And even they have been infected by the greater sickness disseminated by television when it comes to validating or rejecting the self-aggrandising claims of filmmakers, stars, etc., who are the weekly, sometimes daily food of the electronic gods except that television doesn't devour such celebrities so much as lick them. It nearly always gives the gentlest kind of treatment to its famous guests. If it didn't, then the holy grail of that medium, the fragment of the True Cross, the divine film clip itself, would, upon too frequent repetition of the sin, be withheld from the programme makers and they would be forced to fall back on that ersatz wordy substitute, the mere talking head.

The stars and their manipulative PR courtiers know that one TV chat-show is worth 10,000 printed words and it's safer. It doesn't necessarily matter if the hosts are inarticulate – they generally are – for that probably reinforces the identification between themselves and the viewers for a kind of showcase event whose main object is to let the latter push their noses up against the glass and gaze in without turning a critical ear to the host's spiel or the star's claims. The process holds no great fear for the guests whose lips have to frame replies to their "parfit gentle" host's list of clip-boarded questions; for they have probably heard the self-same questions dozens of times before. The television researchers who prepare them in the first place simply work over the same stock of anodyne material originally contributed by the feature writers in the newspapers or magazines that kow-towed for favours of "access" and "exclusiveness" to the same publicists when the movie was in the making.

Even stars of sound mind, a long career and independent reputation now routinely submit themselves to promotion schedules that sound more like a security operation. It is rare to see an interview by Paul Newman, say, in any magazine that isn't known for the blandness of its opinion, which is generally maintained at the comfortable blood heat demanded by its own unexacting mass readership. Let Newman appear on a TV chat-show and it is almost invariably the tritest of the lot, singled out in advance for its reputation for not disconcerting the celebrities it nets. Even if he submits himself in Presidential style, to a general Press conference – he generally disdains the labour of "one-to-one" interviews – it is with the reasonable confidence that no wounds will be opened by his interrogators. The simple reason for this is that no critic worth his salt is going to savage Paul Newman while his lazier colleagues are standing by to profit from any response the assailant has provoked.

All this subservience to managed opinion has contributed powerfully to downgrading the old judgmental role occupied by the film critics. They now come in at the very end of the manipulative process, like people who have to be squeezed into an exuberant celebration, and who are told to be grateful to be admitted at all and not to spoil the party atmosphere.

On occasions when one or more critics jump in ahead of the game and come out with their opinion on a movie before the publicist has smoothed its way and massaged its public, then the remonstrances are shrill indeed. Twice in recent times, I incurred this kind of hostility, though fortunately without suffering anything more punitive. Once I found myself in Vienna, on business totally unconnected with films, and spied an *avant-première* screening of Bertolucci's *The Last Emperor* at the little Burgkino cinema on the Ringstrasse. I quickly put down my 90 schillings for a preview of a film that had not then opened anywhere else in the world. (The Austrian distributors, using Vienna's English-speaking colony as a test-bed, had decided to put it on in English, and without sub-titles, before the German-dubbed version became generally available.) In due course I wrote about *The Last Emperor* at some length, believing that a judgment on the film was every bit as urgent a news event as the acreage of touristy features which had accompanied its shooting in China. I did the same for the long-awaited film *White Mischief*, when it had its *première* at the Rio International Film Festival in Brazil at the end of 1987. In both cases, publishing a review of these films before the publicists had given the word "go" was deemed akin to the actions of a Fifth Columnist.

Occasionally a publicist's guard slips and a director or a star is exposed to a critic (in the precise sense of the word) whose line of enquiry is so off-beat or off-limits that it puts the whole *entente cordiale* in jeopardy. I am always amused on the rare occasion I read interviews of this nature – the best of them are frequently the work of novelists or even literary critics which may be significant of something. I sometimes follow it myself, if only to vary the monotony of over-exposure that the celebrity has suffered from the line of interviewers processed past him or her in the course of the day.

Sometimes this approach generates its own backlash. The shortest interview I ever did – it was actually so short it never got into print – occurred at one Cannes film festival when I applied to have 20 minutes with an actress who I thought was the most interesting of the new crop in Hollywood, a woman noted (I'd read) for the intelligence and integrity (beloved PR words) she brought to her characterisations.

"You went to Sarah Lawrence, didn't you?" I asked her for openers, to the immediate and obvious puzzlement of the attendant publicist, who would clearly have preferred me to say, "You went to Paramount Pictures, didn't you?" The star, too, was suddenly cagey.

"Sure . . . what about it?"

"What did you read there?"

" 'Read?' What do you mean? Books."

"Sorry, I meant what did you study?"

"Oh, writers . . . poets."

"Oh yes . . .? Which writers, which poets?"

The publicist was now screwing up her face in indignation: what the hell is this, a seminar?

"American, mostly."

"Oh yes . . .? Which ones?"

"Well, Delmore Schwartz, Robert Lowell, Sylvia Plath, John Berryman . . . you know."

"Oh, all the suicides."

At which point, the publicist abruptly terminated the interview. As I left the hotel suite, I heard them saying, "How dare he come in here and talk about suicide!"

Producers are frequently the most rewarding people to talk to, yet they are regarded as the least attractive by the popular media and, unless they have managed to dramatise their personalities in other ways, like Sam Spiegel or David Puttnam, not much loved by the hype merchants either who feel the producers should stand well back and let the more famous members of the family take the bows. Producers are usually resigned to this which is maybe why their talk has the candour that comes from endemic loneliness, not to say unlovedness. They are generally the people who know "the truth" of what went on and often, to my surprise, will freely admit to it. It probably eases the pressure to lay some of it off on the people they had to nurse throughout the film at the expense of their own sanity – or sometimes even their solvency – and can now dispense with at least as far as that bad memory is concerned.

Producers reflect the power structure of the industry, "who's in" and "what's out" being the communiqués they issue once one has a rapport going with them, varying them sometimes to inform one "who's out" and "what's in". There are not many tracks to a film producer's mind, admittedly, but the money one is probably the best signposted that a critic of the industry can follow. Follow the money and you are bound to reach the truth.

The best recent books on Hollywood have not been about stars or even directors, though these remain the most fashionable subjects. They have both been about producers and money: *Indecent Exposure* and *Final Cut*. The first dealt with the tribal loyalties of a major movie corporation's executives trying to cast the dybbuk out of the producer who had admitted forgery and embezzlement and therefore make him whole and healthy again; and the second chronicled the megalomania of a producer-director (but more "producer" than "director" in the area where power is exercised) who used sheer bigness as a promissory attraction until, like the accumulating debt of a Third World nation, his film had to be supported by the very creditors whose collapse it would threaten (and did indeed contribute to destroying). "Real life" dramas like these, unmediated by hype and unleavened by PR alibis, make the weekly fiction dished up to movie critics seem pallid and lacking in vitamins.

I've mentioned that critics seldom hear directly from film-makers to whom they've been less than polite. I'd like to think this is because the latter sometimes recognise the justice of a harsh verdict; but I really think it is because filmmakers appreciate the limited impact even the worst reviews can have on a film and, conversely, the powerlessness of the most glowing reviews to salvage what the public doesn't want to go and see. All the rave reviews that Martin Scorsese's *King of Comedy* received couldn't save it from total box-office disaster; all the polemics launched against Stallone and his Rambo movies couldn't turn them into one.

I recall a *New York Times* review, a few years ago, of one of Pauline Kael's collection of her *New Yorker* reviews. It ended with the reviewer – a filmmaker, I think, though I've shamefully forgotten who it was – saying that Ms Kael no longer seemed as interested in the movies as she once had been. "But then," he added, if I recall his words rightly, "the movies are no longer as much interested in Ms Kael as they used to be." Or in any of us critics.

* * *

The distance that critics and filmmakers keep between themselves, however, is sometimes annihilated at a stroke – or a blow.

Such was my experience on the night of July 22, 1971. Judging by the number of people who claim to have seen the altercation between Ken Russell and myself transmitted live on television that night, BBC viewing figures must have taken an unprecedented leap. The anecdote now seems built into the folklore of Television Centre where it took place, though I believe the recording of it that used to exist has been wiped.

The 22nd was a Thursday, the day on which the *Evening Standard* carried my film review column. Leading the column that day was *The Devils*, the latest Ken Russell film that had just opened that same afternoon. Apparently the *Tonight* team felt that the agenda of world events lined up for their news programme would be lightened by confronting the filmmaker with his most tenacious critic. I don't think it was conceived (or even hoped) that we might be brought into physical conflict, too.

I'd certainly been harsh on *The Devils*. It claimed as its basis the 17th-century demonology trials at Loudun, which Aldous Huxley and John Whiting had already used for a book and a play respectively; but as Russell conceived them, they seemed to owe more to the practices of De Sade and Dachau. The film was a glossary of sado-masochistic rites which appeared to me to use issues of conscience and conviction to flaunt the director's acknowledged flair for graphic portrayals of pain and perversity. In short, it subordinated the analytical function of the drama to the anatomical agonies of the martyrs.

Russell and I were kept apart in separate hospitality suites until the sands of the *Tonight* arena had been raked smooth after the preceding item. This, too, had been a contentious one. It involved Denis Healey, the former Minister of Defence, who is no lightweight when it comes to a verbal scrap. Ludovic Kennedy was the interviewer, and as I was led in to be wired up for sound, I sympathised with Kennedy. Having had to sit through the early afternoon screening of *The Devils*, who would want to end his day by grappling with an ex-Defence Minister? Particularly this man who had written an outstanding book on institutionalised violence, *10 Rillington Place*, about the miscarriage of justice when Timothy Evans was hanged for the multiple murders now thought to have been committed in the mid-1940s by his landlord John Christie.

Kennedy looked relieved as he moved across the studio after the fracas with Healey to begin the interview with us; this was going to be a breeze.

Russell and I weren't seated facing each other, but side by side, so as to favour the cameras, and a mere foot apart; an edgy, slightly unreal disposition, lending itself to "playing to the camera".

The interview began straight off with a thunderclap of indignation from Russell. He opened a copy of that day's *Standard* at the review pages in order to read out my annotated list of the grievous bodily harm done to Oliver Reed's renegade priest – and then alleged that my reports had been greatly exaggerated. His films had always been attacked on such specious sensationalist grounds. They were, in any case, not made for critics. They were made for the ordinary public.

"The public doesn't appear all that grateful," I interjected (No, ours was not a very lofty plane of disputation.) "Especially in America," I added, rather sneakily, since I knew the film had been faring badly at the box-office there. Out of the corner of my eye, I could see the ex-Minister of Defence on the sidelines, smiling broadly at the row. I was reminded of the moment in Kubrick's *Dr Strangelove*, when a similar fracas has broken out between two VIPs and the US President expostulates: "Gentlemen, this is the War Room; you can't fight here."

But this second of inattentiveness was my undoing. In that brief moment, Russell rolled up the *Standard*, lent across and whacked me solidly about the head, three times.

But it wasn't the blows that made the impression on viewers, even though that day's edition of the paper was a thick one. The accompanying language was what did the damage: "Then go" – WHACK! – "to America and write" – WHACK! – "for the fucking Americans" – WHACK!

As I opened my eyes, which I'd involuntarily closed as anyone does when struck, I saw the image of myself on the TV monitor jump as if the cameraman had been goosed. Then Ludovic Kennedy was gulping and saying, "Thank you, Mr Russell . . . Mr Walker. Nowbacktothenewsheadlines." We'd been on air less than two minutes. But the exorcism of Russell's private critical devils had been nothing compared with the effect of his public utterance. The same four-letter word had first been used by

Kenneth Tynan on live TV in the 1960s and events now showed that it had lost none of its primal vigour in the interim. Phones began to ring as viewers called the BBC, jamming the switchboard briefly. None asked after my state of health. The overwhelming number were beside themselves with anger at the attack on their own sensibilities, on those of their wives, their children, their servants probably by That Word. Russell and I were hustled into separate corners, then put into individually summoned taxis and sent home in disgrace. The newspapers made great play of "That Word!" the next morning, while the BBC mandarins deliberated what to do about it all. Eventually I was told that if I were ever invited to appear again with Ken Russell, I must give an undertaking in advance not to provoke him. I don't know what he was told. But Ludovic Kennedy was less than amused when a letter from Russell appeared in *Radio Times* alleging collusion between Kennedy and myself to do him down. This was totally baseless, but the affair rumbled on for weeks in a diminuendo of accusations, libel threats and, eventually, qualified apologies. People still recall it to me; which is why I have taken this opportunity, in writing about the relationship between critics and filmmakers, to put it to rest, though I am ruefully aware that any obituary of mine is likely to make mention of the critic "who was hit by Ken Russell on television". Such events clearly form some arcane part of the nation's collective wishes.

The nice thing is that it produced no greater enmity between the hurt party and his assailant. In fact, I had rather more respect for Ken Russell for forcing his emotions so trenchantly on a critic. The manner of his doing so was, after all, the very embodiment of his filmmaking.

EVEN HOLLYWOOD PRINCESSES DON'T ALWAYS LIVE HAPPY EVER AFTER

I suppose that girls in a hurry today, rushing across town from one modelling appointment to another, carry Filofaxes along with their purses. But Grace Kelly, for me, will always belong to the era when girls going places had hat boxes on their arms.

Not that one would ever have found a hat inside; the box was a cover-up. Inside was all their professional make-up kit: the creams, mascaras, lipsticks and the absolutely essential hair-drier. A hat box was an inspired accessory. Just as an aboriginal woman's graceful stance developed in part from toting bundles on her top-knot; a hat box, carried with the proper aplomb, actually assisted deportment – a word that's now as hard to find in common use as . . . well, a hat box. Moreover, it didn't actually make you look like a working girl. Not that I can imagine a time when Grace Kelly ever did look that way. For one of the characteristics of her life and career was how effortless it all seemed – and still seems.

Think of it: she spent a very short time, a mere six years, in Hollywood – just a stop-over when measured against the itinerary of today's stars. She completed fewer than a dozen movies before she swapped thrones, adjusting instantly and unflurriedly to the life and style of a princess after enjoying that of a film goddess, as if the one were only a slight move down the scale of divinity from the other. Following what was only her third screen role, she received her first nomination for an Oscar; a mere two years later, she won the "Best Actress" award outright. And then there was the rare cluster of leading men with whom she starred: Gary Cooper, Clark Gable, James Stewart, Ray Milland, Cary Grant, Bing Crosby, Frank Sinatra, William Holden . . . good heavens, even Alec Guinness! You could have worked a lifetime in Hollywood and not even have got to *meet* all of these, never mind act with them.

Grace Kelly's short, illustrious career tells us as much about the state of the art of popular moviemaking in the Hollywood of her time, from the late 1940s up to the mid-1950s, as it does about the person herself.

It's true that she'd had to work hard before she gained anything like a leading role. It was in Fred Zinnemann's *High Noon*, playing the young bride, married in the morning to Gary Cooper's veteran sheriff, who looks as if she'll become his widow as soon as the killers step off the train at the noonday hour to settle old scores. But I already have to correct myself. Grace Kelly didn't "work" so much as keep herself busy. She took parts in scores of "live" plays and films on television, but she never had to depend on it to support herself, it was stick-pin money, paid for the "exposure" she earned, not the notices she gained. As a daughter of the union between a wealthy Philadelphia-Irish building contractor and a former beauty queen, there was already money as well as looks in the family when she was born in 1928. A woman who was working as a secretary in a public-relations agency where Grace Kelly used to drop by in those pre-Hollywood days, once told me that she and the other office girls knew, after taking one look at Grace that she was, as they put it, a "social" worker. She didn't need the money; what she did need was the kind of world to which the work introduced her. The office girls envied her looks, which is not quite the same thing as admiring them. They envied the confidence that money can sustain, especially if it doesn't need to have been implanted in the first place, but comes by birth-right. They envied the immaculate clothes sense that money could buy, particularly if it was partnered by innate good taste. They envied the understated look there was about her – this above all else – that betokened money in her background, not merely on her back. All this Grace Kelly apparently had from the start – and used.

Not that it was always *useful*. Sidney Lumet put it perceptively, if a little vulgarly, when he turned her down for a leading role in a television film he was directing. She had "no stove in her belly", he said. No fire, he meant; whether divine or profane didn't matter, but there had to be heat . . . fuel . . . hunger to get the role. But she wasn't going to heap on any coals – for anyone. And so she continued to miss the lead part, the big role, whenever they were casting the teleplay or the film. And you know something? *It didn't matter a damn.*

What Grace Kelly eventually brought to the cinema screen was all the purer for not having been sullied too much by life outside the movies, which can indeed happen sometimes, to young girls set upon acquiring experience.

Had Grace Kelly been born an English girl, it's unmistakable what her fate would have been. She would have corresponded perfectly to all the recognised traits of the "Head Girl Syndrome", along with Audrey Hepburn, Deborah Kerr, Jean Simmons and other girls who combined a patent purity of character while avoiding primness of manner with an attitude of cool and worldly aplomb that could turn men's heads by its well-bred self-possession. Grace Kelly's arrival on the Hollywood screen was as timely as it was fortuitous; she enabled the American cinema to replenish its dwindling supply of what's politely called "breeding" and, more commonly, "class".

Ingrid Bergman had formerly held the patent on that particular quality, which Hollywood has never been able to manufacture in its own workshops, and has always had to buy in. But Bergman had become a "fallen woman" as a result of her scandalous and open affair with Roberto Rossellini and the defiance she'd shown towards American public opinion, which was additionally outraged because it felt itself betrayed by the woman who'd seemed to enshrine all its decencies.

Grace Kelly didn't replace Bergman in the roles in which one might have expected to find the Swedish star. There was ten years' age difference between them, for one thing. But just as in an abdication, the *fait accompli* of Kelly's accession ensured that the same royal line still ruled, even if it was another branch of the dynasty – an American branch and, as such, even more acceptable than an adoptive symbol from abroad.

Kelly was called into being to do for Hollywood what she was required to do for the Grimaldis less than ten years later in the Principality of Monaco. On one, she conferred "class": to the other, she lent dignity. The moviemakers had their treasury replenished; the monarchists had their succession secured. One career was an extraordinary kind of rehearsal for the other; it was as if she had stepped out of the picture into the principality without even needing to change her dress.

The special quality that Grace Kelly imported into Hollywood was well defined by the (unnamed) critic of *Time* magazine when he (we can be sure it was a "he") reviewed her third film *Mogambo* and noted that "her fiery quality is the suggestion that she is well-born without being arrogant, cultivated without being stuffy, and highly charged emotionally without being blatant". When *Time* says that about you – in those simpler days, anyhow – you are on your way.

I test Americans whenever the film *Mogambo* comes up in conversation when we're talking about Grace Kelly. Nine out of ten of them, I find, have forgotten that she played an *English* woman in the movie. She doesn't play her very well, I'm sorry to say. You can actually hear the lady-like airs being put on. She gives orders to a no-nonsense fellow like Clark Gable as if she were directing the head gardener to spray the roses and get rid of the greenfly. Of course their "meeting cool" grows appreciably warmer once he discovers that her charms lie off – well off – the beaten tracks. Equity, the British actors' union, wasn't happy about the casting, either, feeling that there were plenty of home-grown "gels" who could have played the role as well, maybe better. Rough-tongued John Ford, directing the movie, didn't swell her fan club; but having picked her, he endured her and probably thought that Ava Gardner, the other female in Gable's field of vision, would sell the film in those sultry areas that matter most to the audience. But "the roughneck and the lady" was a hallowed coupling in American populist myth. And American audiences could sense the lady of passion in Grace Kelly, even if English audiences (some of them, anyhow) felt that the "lady" wasn't all she could have been.

Fred Zinnemann had picked her out two years earlier to be Cooper's Quaker bride in *High Noon*, on the strength of her turning up for the interview wearing white gloves of the kind a young girl wears for Confirmation. Perfect, Zinnemann thought. It would make her stand-offishness plausible when she initially refuses to stand by her man in his hour of peril. In the event, it was Katy Jurado, as the town madam and universal comforter, who took the audience's sympathies away from Grace Kelly; yet it's Grace Kelly who continued to be the focus of attention, like someone who is seated in the front row, earnest and worshipful, not quite belonging to the rest of a good-neighbourly congregation, yet sure to monopolise the chit-chat on the way home from church. Her inexperience of cinema at this stage of her life probably helped, too; for she'd only done one earlier film, *Fourteen Hours*, in which she played a young society girl who's discussing divorce with her lawyer when a would-be suicide appears on a hotel's window-ledge and shows her by his self-destructive example the superficiality of her emotions. Her slight stiffness in the *High Noon* role adds verisimilitude to the character of a girl who hasn't yet shaken the starch out of her religion and come to terms with life.

I don't think I'm being unfair to her. She later acknowledged her own shortcomings. She told of how she had gone to see *High Noon* in a cinema, on her own, and had looked into Gary Cooper's ageing face and seen *everything* the star was thinking. Then she'd looked into the face of her own screen character – "and I saw nothing".

Scandal-mongering at the time – but especially after her death – has alleged that Grace Kelly was not all *that* innocent – in fact, not innocent at all, but simply well screened from public notoriety by the discreetness and protectiveness that a chaperoned life and the power of money in a family of devout yet worldly Roman Catholics could then purchase. Actually reports about her "promiscuity" went the rounds at the time by word of mouth. Some even found their way into magazines like *Confidential*. But they were not flagrantly disseminated, the way they certainly would be today. In those days – and we are talking of the early 1950s – the conformity of most of the mass-media magazines (a few mavericks like *Confidential* apart) was entrenched in the vested interest that the print media felt they had in colluding with their readers' fantasies, not shattering them, unless the scandal were "contained" in the news framework of an admitted adultery or a public divorce. When *Time* put Grace Kelly on its cover, it labelled the story "The Girl in White Gloves". For her admirers, whatever she did, Grace Kelly would always continue to wear spotless white gloves.

Once Grace Kelly had stepped into the casting void left by Ingrid Bergman's humiliation, it is hardly accidental that the man who moved with an alacrity that belied his bulk to borrow her from Metro-Goldwyn-Mayer, with whom she had signed a seven-year contract, was Bergman's former mentor (and sometime tormentor) Alfred Hitchcock. More than any other single individual, it

115

is Hitchcock who was responsible for the Grace Kelly image; an image that evolved out of his own obsessions as much as out of her appearance, though both worked in powerful combination with each other.

Just as he believed bloodstains were seen to their best advantage on virgin snow, Hitchcock held that putting *blondes* on the torture rack made for a more suspenseful reaction. Purity was all – well, quite a lot, anyhow. Launching an assault on a blonde who was also a *lady* worked best of all. Hitchcock's misogyny is well attested to, and corroborated so often in Donald Spoto's well researched biography that one wonders that anyone should still try to deny it. (Usually, it is the *male* stars Hitchcock worked with who deny it.) Explanations for it are something else, however.

Grace Kelly, I think, reminded Hitchcock of those well-born, sexually distant and socially unattainable English *débutantes* he used to see regularly featured in the "Court and Society" pages of *The Times* or the (now deceased) *Morning Post*, or pictured by society photographers for the "Engagements" section of glossy English magazines like *The Tatler* and *The Sketch*. (*The Times*, incidentally, was the paper he subscribed to until his death; its airmail edition arrived daily in his office, where it was treated as an earnest of his abiding Anglophilia. When I look back, though, it could just as well have been vestigial evidence of his pathology.) To the plump little lower-middle-class Cockney, the posed refinement and impeccable beauty of these English girls contradicted and concealed their sexual appeal; but he suspected (rightly) that they had an earthy side to their well-bred natures turned away from the camera. Humiliating the better-born – well, at least, better-dressed – woman is a recurrent, unpleasant but fascinating feature of Hitchcock's *oeuvre*. For the intimacy that his own nature (and fluctuating corpulence) deterred him from seeking from a woman, he substituted the voyeuristic consolation of seeing her discomforted or even assaulted.

But just as innocence is a legal presumption until the jury returns a verdict of guilty, ladies in Hitchcock's films behave like ladies until proven otherwise.

Hitchcock was possibly the last major film director to feature characters who were "ladies and gentlemen", and recognisably such, in film after film. There is plenty of testimony to the pains he went to in order to rearrange to his private satisfaction the smallest detail of apparel and grooming. Even his male stars had to obey the long-standing dress code. You seldom see a slovenly male hero in a Hitchcock film – almost never a slovenly villain. Even when they go off to preside over the torture of a kidnapped Head of State, his masterminds hook their umbrellas over their custom-tailored arms and pick up their gloves from the hall-table as they leave their mansion. Oh, to have put blood on those white, white gloves of Kelly's – what *fun* that would have been!

Even so, Hitchcock didn't get her quite "right" at first. He had Warner Bros "borrow" her from MGM – whose production chief, Doré Schary, didn't really know what to do with her "type" and was glad to turn a studio profit of $14,000 on the Warners loan-out fee of $20,000 for her services. Hitchcock then cast her as the wife in *Dial "M" for Murder* who is just that little bit unfaithful and has to be punished for it by being made the victim of her husband's murder plot. She is then reprieved after she's done penance in the condemned cell – a characteristic "Catholic" notion of the kind Hitchcock understood so well. But being an intended victim isn't the same as being an intentional *provocatrice*. Grace Kelly's sexual passivity is interrupted only when she has to defend herself. And even the flashing scissors – and how Hitchcock laboured to capture that "flash" on camera! – that she plunges into her would-be assassin remain a weapon and not any deeper Freudian symbol. Hitchcock wanted to create an aura of seductive fascination around her, inviting her own entrapment. *Dial "M" for Murder* simply wasn't that kind of story. The next one was.

In order to work again with Hitchcock, on *Rear Window*, Grace Kelly turned down the role in *On the Waterfront* that Eva Marie Saint eventually played. The latter was going to be shot in New York at the same time as the Hitchcock film. (Four years later, when Grace Kelly was now unavailable, Hitchcock would borrow Eva Marie Saint for *North by Northwest*; his sexual fantasies were cut, like paper dolls, from the same strip of material.)

The Grace Kelly who appeared in *Rear Window* was a fantasised version of herself – a model girl promoted in the screenplay to being a *Vogue*-ish magazine editor, a girl with a Park Avenue manner and all the right labels on those gowns and

117

accessories that Hitchcock supervised with the critical eye of a *couturier* to create a creature he called "the un-haveable girl". Once she gleamed upon his sight, he dangled her like a waking dream in front of James Stewart. Since Stewart was incapacitated in a hip-to-toe plaster casing, any sexual encounters that might have taken place – that surely *would* have taken place – were safely ruled out. In much the same way, and for much the same reason, given his unappealing corpulence, Hitchcock's own fascination with his star had to be indulged in the mind's inner-eye without physical intimacy.

Rear Window established her as – to quote *Time* again – "the tingling essence of sexual elegance". One might quarrel with that word "tingling"; perhaps "teasing" would better fit the image. After all, that was the relationship that many of those who worked on the film observed between its director and his leading lady. Both were "jokey" people, though Hitchcock's penchant for pranks inclined to the sadistic, while Kelly's tended to the flirtatious. This, too, was indicative of their mutual feelings.

The image he created of her travelled well. American women were *au courant* with the society or "town gossip" columns of their daily newspapers, and Grace Kelly's credentials had the suggestion of the *Social Register*, even if her family didn't actually rate a mention in this, the bible of American blue-bloods. Yet she also knew when to let her passionate side show without allowing her dignity to slip. American girls could very easily imitate Grace Kelly in their make-up, hair-style and the way they dressed, even if it was in scaled down versions (and prices). Abroad, too, on alien screens and in foreign-language magazines, she was the epitome of the "American Girl" as everyone imagined that stereotype, with her youth, self-confidence, her faultless yet casually worn wardrobe, and her recognisable but understated sexuality. Had she made *On the Waterfront*, the performance that Elia Kazan would have got her to give might have deepened her character and the way she was perceived as an actress; but it would not have disseminated the Grace Kelly myth. *Rear Window* was the film that effectively internationalised her.

As he was fond – overfond – of telling us, Hitchcock didn't require the people in his films to "act". From them, he wanted obedience above all else. He wanted stars with the aptitude to give him those neutral looks that were the "screens" on which his own fantasies could be projected and "read" by audiences. Up to now, Grace Kelly had provided him with exactly what he needed. But then came *The Country Girl*.

It's often thought among those who knew him only by reputation that interviewing Alfred Hitchcock was a rewarding business. It wasn't. It was interminably tedious in the time it took and, usually, disappointing in the results it yielded. Part of this was due to Hitchcock's refusal to "open up", to crack himself open for inspection and allow one to verify whether the oyster held a pearl and, if so, what the grit was that had produced it. This reluctance is understandable. Many – most – people who create works of art out of private fantasies have a dread of the living autopsy that exposing themselves to an interview may require. The trouble with Hitchcock was that he never used his reputed inventiveness to make an interview very novel; it was the same old stuff slyly aligned with the content of the current film that unspooled again and again and again. He could claim, with some justice, that he was asked the same old questions again and again and again, differing only in the language of the country he happened to be in when they were put to him. But he didn't bestir himself to reveal more than he thought fit – and "fit" in a very proper, Victorian sense of the word. He spoke very slowly, too, so that listening to the answer was sometimes as irritating as hearing a record being played at half-speed. The retarded delivery and the unvarying responses were depressing.

Occasionally, one was driven by boredom to say or do things that entailed the risk of having the interview cut short – or of not being granted one at all the next time round. In such a mood, I once played a small trick on him. He was staying at his favourite London hotel, a place that employed (and still does) many Hispanic room servants whose Latin looks, coupled with the wrought iron grilles around the lighting brackets in the corridors gave the place a slightly sacerdotal air, not uncharacteristic of some of the Hitchcock films where churches figure ambiguously in the plots. I gave £5.00 to two of the Spanish room servants, a man and a woman, and instructed them to kneel down in front of the wall-lights as soon as they heard Hitchcock come out of his suite along with his publicist and myself to proceed to the restaurant for lunch. They did so. Thus when he turned the corner, this most Catholic-themed of filmmakers found himself confronted by what looked like a wayside shrine in a Mediterranean country with two worshipful figures on their knees in front of the lamp-shaded illumination.

He paused a second and then, once safely past the "praying" chambermaid and her male companion, he raised an eyebrow and said, "I wonder what their sins are." I was naturally elated to have drawn one new line of dialogue out of him. But on the way down in the elevator, his suspicious mind penetrated the ruse, and as we turned into the restaurant, he said, unsmilingly, "Mr Walker, he who plays the jokes gets to pay the bill." It eventually cost me much, much more than £5.00.

At that meeting, in the late 1960s, I asked him about his reaction on hearing that Grace Kelly was going to do *The Country Girl*. It had been a bold step for her to take at the time. Playing Bing Crosby's shrewish wife was a role that required "acting". It was also an "unsympathetic" role and, as she was later to tell me, she took it against the advice of most of her industry friends, not because she wanted to have her stardom confirmed – "There were easier ways of doing that," she said – but because she wanted her professionalism validated. She had gone into *The Bridges at Toko-Ri*, playing a Navy pilot's wife, a role naturally overshadowed by the men's action roles in the film, so as to do *The Country Girl* which was owned by the same producers William Perlberg and George Seaton.

When I now put the question about her competence to Hitchcock, he stared past my right ear – a trick or a reflex he'd developed over the years in order to avoid confrontation with anyone who might be "trouble". ("Trouble" was almost always deflected by Hitchcock's intermediaries. For reasons I've already cited, "trouble" rarely arose while he was giving interviews.) Finally, his little lips, pursed like the aperture on a balloon, muttered the reply across the table to me: "I told her, 'Not my cup of tea, Grace. But you do it if you want to, my dear. You do it, and find out what you can do.' "

Even after 15 years or so, the remark, as he reported it, still had the edge of a rebuke . . . the hurt tone that covers up anger at someone's ingratitude or disobedience.

But she went away – and she found out. She was plainer, dowdier and more self-willed than she'd ever appeared on the screen; and *The Country Girl* won her an Oscar – something no Hitchcock film had ever done for its leading lady. Yet it didn't undo the Hitchcock image of her, so much as unsettle her own confidence in what she wanted to do in her career. She was sure about what she *didn't* want to do. *Green Fire*, for one; but as MGM had consented to postpone it until she had finished *The Country Girl*, she had to make it. Then the refusal period of stardom began. *Quentin Durward* was turned down; one of Sir Walter Scott's heroines fleeing across country clutching her purse – No, thank you. A Western, then? It, too, was out. Westerns weren't places for ladies, unless they were in the saddle like Joan Crawford. Even saloon towns didn't promote an actress's stardom, unless they were Mae West or Marlene Dietrich.

When Hitchcock called with *To Catch a Thief*, it was like entering a great sheltering harbour once more. She played the "American Girl" again, this time abroad and with all the money in the world – but no man, at least until Cary Grant lands on his feet (and at hers) as a retired cat burglar.

Few scenes in any film at the time, between a star and his leading lady, have been so saturated in sexual innuendo as those between Grant and Grace Kelly in *To Catch a Thief*. For her seduction scene on the Côte d'azur, Hitchcock had her costumed entirely in white, and he personally hung a diamond and platinum necklace above the strapless gown. Grace Kelly in the film suspects it is her jewels that Grant is after; but Hitchcock sets up the dialogue between them in such a way that she is forever inciting Grant to "take" what she holds most precious, which is not necessarily (or customarily) a film heroine's necklace. "Give up – admit who you are. Even in this light, I can tell where your eyes are looking." – Close up of the necklace and of course her bosom – "Look . . . hold them . . . diamonds. The only thing in the world that you can't resist. Then tell me you don't know what I am talking about. Ever had a better offer in your whole life? One with everything." In innuendo, if not in words, it is an invitation to sex; instead of the man doing the seducing, it is he who is seduced. Hitchcock's most recent biographer, Donald Spoto, expressed surprise that such dialogue didn't provoke any outcry from the industry censors of the time; but the moralists let it by. Once again, the pleasure that Hitchcock took in presenting a woman as a sexual vixen had been safely indulged.

One wonders where the partnership of Kelly and Hitchcock would have led next, or whether they had any future left to fulfil after three highly successful movies together. Hadn't Grace Kelly been as "fulfilled" as she could be under his direction?

I met her first, briefly, at Cannes in 1955, where *To Catch a Thief* was being shown, and raised that question with her.

"Mr Hitchcock is the best craftsman I have ever worked with," she said.

"But aren't you always going to play essentially the same role when you appear in a film he has had written for himself to direct?"

"You think that after three pictures with me, he has fulfilled himself?"

"No . . ."

"Then what? You think I have?"

The expected answer was "Yes", but, fortunately, it didn't have to be pronounced, for before I could reply, she added, "I guess I'll have to take things as they come . . . You know, *che serà, serà.*"

Now the remake of *The Man Who Knew Too Much* hadn't started shooting at this time; it wasn't until I saw it a year or so later that I made the connection between that last remark of Grace Kelly's and Doris Day's "theme song" ("*Che serà, serà*/Whatever will be, will be") in the film. Had Hitchcock, I wondered, tried to press her into it before he had settled on Doris Day, and failed? But, anyhow, by the time *The Man Who Knew Too Much* had been released, in May 1956, Grace Kelly had voluntarily ended her film career and become Her Serene Highness Princess Grace of Monaco. *Che serà serà* indeed!

The Swan, her penultimate film, had already illustrated the uncanny way that art sometimes has of anticipating life. In this last involvement of Hollywood (to date, anyhow) in Ruritanian romance, she played a princess who is strongly tempted to marry her brother's handsome tutor, but decides instead to follow the call of duty and marry the prince who comes a-courting. The film hinted, just *hinted*, that maybe she might not live as happily ever after with the prince as she would have with the commoner. But this was surely Hollywood populism at work. After her farewell film, *High Society*, she married her real prince and there seemed no doubt of her contentment as an attentive consort, a faultless wife and a tireless arranger of this, that and every other event in Monaco's crowded calendar.

It wasn't until 1980 that I met Grace Kelly again. She had entered the authorship game, which is what I have to call it to distinguish it from the writer's trade. The difference is that one lends one's celebrity to the former; the latter, if one is lucky as well as skilful, makes one a celebrity. In this case she had collaborated with Gwen Robyns, an early and sympathetic biographer, in publishing *My Book of Flowers*. This was a series of essays that ranged lightly and informatively over all aspects of the floral world, mythical, medicinal, culinary and so on. Now ruling families are not usually prolific writers; the book was hardly likely to meet much regal competition on the sales counters. But it was felt that, without venturing too much into controversy, she might say a few words on the floral theme to a palace-approved journalist. The choice fell on me.

Princess Grace, as I must now call her, was not at all an enemy of the media. On the contrary; she realised its value and may be said to have exploited its curiosity, in the early years of her reign, anyhow, to put Monaco on the map and, more important, to suggest how she was putting Monegasque values back on the shelf. She had an excellent public-relations lady in Nadia Lacoste. The two worked well together. Probably, though, they erred in selecting a film critic to interview Her Serene Highness on this occasion. A gardening correspondent might not have done the job better; but he (or she) would have kept to the prescribed path. Gardeners dislike trespassers; so, I was to find, do princesses.

Princess Grace had just turned 51 and was coming up to her 25th year of marriage to Prince Rainier – long enough to have seen three children into the world (or that small portion of it that Monaco encompasses) and thus make the principality relatively safe from annexation by the grasping French. But was it long enough, I wondered on the aircraft going down to Nice, to make her nostalgic for the other realm of make-believe? She had already made one attempt to return to the screen. Hitchcock had offered her the role in *Marnie*, later played by Tippi Hedren. But the thought of their Prince's consort appearing on screen as a frigid petty thief had made ordinary Monegasques so alarmed that she hurriedly backed out. (It had also made the MGM lawyers alarmed, but that was on the grounds that Hitchcock might enjoy the unexpired portion of HSH's suspended contract with the MGM studio – to their loss.)

As I read the book to which she had now put her name, I hoped our conversation wouldn't be restricted to such topics as "Flowers in Food and Drink", "American Flowers in Europe" or even "Flowers in Ballet and Music."

So far as I could see, there was no chapter headed "Flowers in Films", which would have given me a conversational *entrée*. I began rehearsing little verbal ploys that I hoped might pull us away from the flowers and into the films, on the lines of: "I happened to pass through the Nice flower-market on the way here, Ma'am. You remember . . . where Cary Grant was once quite badly bruised when the extra playing the flower-lady overdid things and hit him over the head with a bunch of gladioli in *To Catch a Thief*." Or would she rise to the bait if I linked flower-beds with a corpse and reminded her of the unladylike conduct she and Thelma Ritter were about to get up to with spade or shovel in *Rear Window*?

However, the book did hold one small surprise: "Copyright Grace Grimaldi", the pré-title page read. Just that. A more assertive note than I'd anticipated. Was it to distinguish this "Grace Grimaldi" from "HSH Princess Grace", the one who didn't officially set her hand (or pen) to anything but Palace communiques or charitable announcements?

"Please present yourself at ten minutes to eleven o'clock at the gateway to the right of the Palace's main entrance", was her office's instruction in the letter awaiting me at the hotel.

The Palace of the Grimaldis isn't an imposing place, though these Genoese rulers span a surprising 750 years of European dynastic history and the place has, in the mixed fortunes of Monaco, been by turn a fortress, a military hospital and (under the French Revolution) a workhouse. The "Toy Town" battlements, stubby little tower and patches of raw stonework all testify to the fits and starts of construction through the ages. The charm of the place lies outside the Palace walls, in the winding streets of Le Rocher or Monaco-Ville, which is the Principality's medieval quarter.

But immediately I entered the Palace courtyard by the

designated gateway and had my credentials checked by white-uniformed sola-topee'd guardsmen, I found myself in an odd, unexpectedly homely world. Honda and Yamaha motor-bikes nestled tank-to-tank on the Palace cobblestones, all belonging to the servants who, it appeared, made a practice of going home for lunch down the road. The concierge was a grave, but friendly man; he became positively talkative on hearing I came from Northern Ireland – his own wife was an Ulster woman. The waiting-room was as intimate as a provincial doctor's in any French town where everyone knows everyone else and everyone else's ailments. Strangely, it hadn't a single flower in it, though two coloured prints turned out, on closer inspection, to be of the English sentimental-bucolic school: "The Cottager's Favourite" (country lass being wooed by rustic); and "The Cottager's Wealth" (farmer's wife tending pigs).

My arrival was announced by telephone – and at 11.00 a.m. on the dot the return call came and I was led upstairs to the morning room.

The Grimaldis' Palace might have been constructed for a Feydeau farce. It is incredible the number of doors, passage-ways and cupboard-size elevators one passes through or ascends by, requiring many *"par ici"*s and *"merci"*s from the grey-tunicked page escorting me. Finally, he led me right up to a pair of tall white doors. He tapped, then abruptly threw open one half and I entered – and almost bumped into Her Serene Highness herself advancing slightly too precipitately to meet me.

Grace Kelly was in close-up right away. No chance for either of us to survey the other in polite but guarded long-shot. To have even inclined one's head would have been like making some vaguely indecent gesture. She backed off. I backed off, too. We tried again and this time the approach came off much better – I could fancy a director calling "Cut" in tones of satisfaction, and the clapper-boy chalking up a new slate for the next scene.

"Mr Walker . . . the critic from London?" she said.

The words weren't entirely reassuring as they held bad memories for me. Years before, I had witnessed a scene in a restaurant further along the Côte d'azur, when Princess Grace had encountered one of her American countrymen, the film critic Rex Reed, attending the Cannes festival. He had not been one of her favourites in the (then relatively recent) days when she

125

had been making her last few movies. "Ah . . . the critic from New York," she had said. Whether any taunt was intended, I don't know – I think not. But the almost (but not quite) involuntary reply had been, "Ah . . . the princess from Philadelphia." The Princess's greeting was now like a slightly poisoned madeleine to me on hearing the same words again, even in the rather rarefied environment of the Palace, bringing back memories I'd rather not have had revived.

She gestured to me to perch myself on a tiny chair, while she took another one, about five feet away. Both chairs seemed constructed to sustain only momentary encounters. A coffee table in between us served as a buffer. The vase of flowers on it didn't look carefully enough arranged to be emblematic of the book we were supposed to discuss; on the other hand, I ignobly reflected, it might well conceal a tape-recorder. One of the princess's children had been behaving badly and I guessed she was nervous of the media at that moment, and perhaps regretted having to give an interview, or any kind, to a journalist. I really couldn't blame her.

The morning room might have been chosen for its very anonymity; it dashed any hope of seeing her against a more intimate and revealing background. Its token chairs, its very upright sofa, and its rank upon rank of family photographs (reasonably animate) and rows of paintings (historically dead) were all set against pale tints as if the walls had been expensively buttered. It made the room virtually interchangeable with all those reception rooms furnished for formal chores by Europe's other crowned heads. (Buckingham Palace, though, I must record, is both darker and dowdier.)

However, she looked what she had been and what she was: "Grace Grimaldi", maybe; but still recognisably Grace Kelly, copyright of Alfred Hitchcock. Her hair, champagne hued, was now pulled tighter on her head than Hitchcock would have liked, except maybe when it would have been necessary to strangle the heroine cleanly. It revealed all the more clearly the contours of a face that was plumper, more matronly, but hadn't fallen or sagged. Hitchcock's fetishistic pedantry was imaginable in the complementary matching of every item she was wearing. She had on a cream suit whose jacket she was using as a cape, draped over her shoulders, leaving her hands free to gesticulate when a point

126

needed emphasising – very often – or when words didn't come – not very often. There was a cream blouse tied at the neck by a matching foulard, both with a small Wedgwood-blue motif; a gold bracelet watch, the only jewellery visible; white shoes rimmed in navy. (But no white gloves.) Her American accent had lightened since we'd last talked.

The interview began exactly as if she had rehearsed it and had determined precisely the degree of candour she'd find it to her advantage to display about her book without yielding up any privacy she considered it essential to retain around her life. Philippe Junot, the divorced husband of Princess Caroline, was clearly not a subject that could be avoided; but he was skilfully and innocuously inserted into the conversation early on.

"M. Junot gave me one fascinating flower anecdote for the book. How Himmler had huge acreages of gladioli planted, right in the middle of the war, too, so as to provide supplies of Vitamin 'C' for the men at the front."

We both considered Himmler's dietetic *démarche* for a few seconds. Then – inspired! – I said, "That's the kind of bizarre detail that would have amused Hitchcock."

"He hated flowers. He wouldn't have been amused at all," was the reply.

Well at least I had managed to get him into the conversation. Encouraged, I pressed on up the studio path rather than the garden one. "Flowers are supposed to bring out a person's dormant characteristics. Which were yours – when you were making films, I mean?"

She clearly saw where this ruse was leading; but she relented, a little.

"If I've any talent, it's for concentration. You have no option – you have to develop that if you're part of a big noisy family, as I was. My Hollywood career only reinforced it. I used to insist on closed film sets. Any visitors at all broke the concentration. But Hitch insisted on it, too, of course. He'd stop work if a stranger appeared; it didn't have to be a stranger, even – I once heard him answer a front-office executive who'd asked him what he was waiting for before he got down to work: 'For you to go away.'

"He used against them the only weapon they understood – waste of time. Time was the most expensive item in Hollywood. Far more expensive than what any star earned."

127

"I'm told your book will earn you around £250,000," I said. "Will you be donating your royalties to charity?"

A pause. Embarrassment or surprise? I'd been told before my visit not to mention money – not on any account. But "royalties" weren't money, were they?

"I have my own charitable foundation here, you know . . . And we have a ballet school that needs all the support we can give it. As for what the book may earn, one doesn't talk about that."

Again, I really couldn't blame her; as an author, I'd have said the same myself. She sat quite still now, very neutral – exactly the sort of expression (or no-expression) her old mentor valued.

"I'm told you almost returned to the screen in the ballet film that Herb Ross directed, *The Turning Point*."

Her attitude sharpened ever so slightly. She probably wondered who had told me that. She may also have wondered whether I'd been told – as I had – that the reason she had turned down the role of the ballet student's mother in the film was because it involved an extra-marital relationship with the leading male character. It would have been a perfect comeback role for her; she would have been exactly the age for motherhood and for romance whether illicit or not. But yet again the constitutional propriety of being a Roman Catholic consort had denied her a desperately wished for opportunity to revive the freshness of her creative life. I began to see why dried flowers occupied so much of her time as a form of compensatory creativity.

"I really don't have much interest in films now," she said. It was as if, once tempted, she had repulsed the sin even more vigorously.

"But haven't you been a member of the board of Twentieth Century–Fox for several years now? Surely that means you want to retain your links with films?"

"Not necessarily with acting. Don't forget that Fox is more than a film company. It is a conglomerate. It owns whole resorts, like Aspen, the ski area, and hotels and leisure centres."

In other words, there was a "mutuality of interest" that transcended her first love, acting?

"If you care to put it that way."

"But didn't you once write a film script, on film-making in the Sixties – a satire?"

"It was never filmed," she said bluntly.

Well, supposing the right subject came along?

"What would be 'the right subject'?" she said cautiously.

"Well, a version of Proust's À *la Recherche,* say. Joseph Losey's still hoping to make it, you know. A story which needs players with 'presence', with roles for people accustomed to acting out the protocol of a society long past its natural term . . ."

Her lips tightened. *That* description, she thought, hardly applied to Monaco. My incautious remark provoked a sermonette.

The principality, she assured me, was not very different from places whose industries were heavier and dirtier than gambling. "We have all levels of society here, all in touch with each other . . . doctors, teachers, businessmen, street cleaners . . . Here we have no unemployment, none at all. You mustn't think we're unique. Why, recently, we even had a strike," she added, brightening triumphantly at this proof of normality.

"Really? What part of the economy did it hit?"

"The casino."

Of course! In other places, factories went on strike; in Monaco, the gaming tables. "How did it end?"

"His Serene Highness ended it. But one doesn't talk about that."

But she decided to drive home the point.

"When you've lived here for a time, it's like a family."

"How big is the Palace 'family'?"

"I couldn't really say. Not with any accuracy. You see, whole households with children live inside these walls with us. It may look small. It takes a lot of work."

"Well, how many gardeners do you need?"

"Not too many of them . . . about six, I think."

She made an attempt to revert to topics that were less burdened by statistics, indoors and out. We turned to the Garden Club of Monaco, which Princess Grace had started. "I was inspired by a phrase of Colette's – 'Monaco is the country where the only frontiers are flowers.' "

"True as far as it goes," I said, "which isn't very far."

"That's your impression?"

"That's my experience. I can remember nowhere else I've travelled to, not even in the Soviet Union, where I've been required to reveal so many personal details of my life as when I

129

checked into one of your new hotels. I had to fill in no fewer than three *cartes de sécurité*."

There was no warmth now in Her Serene Highness's looks. "Yes," she said, "I've been told we have more *gendarmes* here than New York has cops. If that's so, all I can say is New York needs more cops."

That settled that . . . Between us, with an effort, we got the talk back to flowers. They weren't simply to be enjoyed by rich people, she said. Small could not only be beautiful; it would be economical. She had made a special study of "the alternative kitchen", which is Nature's. Nature provided all kinds of concoctions like crystallised roses, violet-based *gelati*, even stinging nettles which, when stewed, were delicious – they tasted like spinach.

"Do you often serve them at the Palace here?"

She met me head-on: "No, but I often have herbal *tisanes* . . . for headaches."

She mentioned "our farm". The image of Versailles crept perceptibly closer.

"You mean Roc Agel?" I asked, referring to the summer estate up in the mountains behind Monaco to which the Grimaldi family retreated in August, once the Red Cross Ball, the last great binge of the season, was over. "I hear you have a whole menagerie of animals there. Does the Prince still borrow camels from the Monaco Zoo?"

" 'Borrow?' He doesn't need to borrow anything from the zoo," she replied with a touch of asperity. "He owns it."

It was clear to me that "serenity" and "patience" were two different virtues; she was running out of patience and now I feared even for her serenity. It seemed as if I couldn't say a thing right. It had perhaps been a bit mischievous of me not to fall in line and allow her to lead. But as I sat there in front of this stiffly proper woman, I could not help remembering the Grace Kelly of over 20 years before who had defined the "All-American Girl" and combined her appeal with the seductive image of the "Hitchcock Woman". When I'd asked her then how long she saw herself playing the latter role, I'd had no idea that one day she would be immured in a part that history had created, not Hitchcock, and for far, far longer than the cruel term of even the "slave contracts" of Hollywood. I felt a curious resentment, selfish no doubt, of the same kind (though not of the same degree) as I have felt whenever I have occasionally come across Greta Garbo, aged, bent but still formidably herself, on a New York avenue or in a Swiss mountain station. I thought of all the roles that *you* could have played, Grace Kelly, and you Greta Garbo, and all the revelations that time and maturing talent might have allowed us to witness in your performances. Garbo's act of abdication had been wilfully selfish; Grace Kelly's was voluntarily self-sacrificing. But the result was the same: the movies had left me the poorer in each case.

Having little to lose, I made one last effort and brazenly asked her if she missed making movies.

"Oh, come now; I made my last film, *High Society*, 25 years ago . . . What have I now left to give?"

No use pushing her any further – and no chance, anyhow. She rose. "I am afraid I must leave you now. One is always trying to catch up, and one never does. I assure you, I don't lack things to do."

The conversation froze into a second's formal leave-taking. Then, suddenly, quite out of character, she thawed and the only unprepared look I'd seen came into her face as she asked, almost anxiously, "You haven't forgotten anything?" It was one single note of domesticity in a fairly chilly 45 minutes.

A few years later, when I read Sarah Bradford's posthumous biography of Grace Kelly, I learned that one of her persistent fantasies had been that the day would come, for some reason or other, when she'd at last be able to be like anyone else and would decide to be a "bag lady". She'd wander through Paris, or wherever, collecting things people had left behind. She interpreted this daydream as signifying the strength of her desire to be regarded as "normal".

It was nearly midday when I got outside. The Palace servants were revving up their Japanese bikes in the courtyard, in readiness to commute to their homes for lunch. The crowd in the square in front of the apricot-coloured crenellated walls had grown denser since I had entered the building; the morning guard was about to be relieved by the afternoon picket. Bugles blared. Drums beat. Men in vanilla ice-cream uniforms re-possessed the red zigzagged sentry-boxes without a struggle.

Not many months later, I heard of Grace Kelly's fatal accident.

131

The car had came to grief on the very same hair-pin bend of the road that Hitchcock had made her drive down in the big open roadster in *To Catch a Thief* with Cary Grant beside her. Her driving, she'd said, had caused Grant to turn pale under his tan. Actually, she didn't enjoy doing the scene, for she hated driving. Hitchcock had maliciously played on her dislike of it, forcing her through several re-takes and then, once back in the studio, putting her through the sequence again, this time with rather poor and obvious back-projection. He could have filmed all of it in Hollywood, if he'd wanted. But "reality" to him was never so real as when he rearranged it.

The Palace remained in an extraordinary "spellbound" state in the days immediately following Princess Grace's accident. It puzzled many people, and still does, why those nearest her hardly dared admit, even to themselves, the extent of her injury and thus misled the rest of the world into believing that there was no cause for alarm – that "Princess Grace could not die". That, of course, is exactly the way one thinks of film stars.

NO NEED TO BRIBE A FILM FESTIVAL JURY; IT CAN DO THAT FOR ITSELF

It's strange how very few of those who are invited to sit on film festival juries ever get round to writing about their experience. But then evaluating the films tends to run a poor second to awarding the prizes; the two things are not at all the same.

I have served on festival juries in Cannes, Berlin, Chicago and Cairo and short of seizing power in a Latin American republic there can be few sweeter ways of tasting dictatorship in the world today. I admit that on each occasion I have come away feeling a worse man for the experience; which is not a contradiction. Power doesn't corrupt; not exactly. To rephrase Lord Acton's aphorism slightly more cynically, it is loss of power that corrupts absolutely. One minute, one's word is law. Then the verdict is delivered. The next, one is looking in vain for a place to sit at the awards supper. But for ten to fourteen days on the annual circuit that stretches from Avoriaz in January to Hawaii in December, and taking in the other two or three hundred film festivals happening somewhere in the world in the intervening months a jury member can be sure of being fêted, fretted over and fawned upon in a manner to which one's humdrum job as a day-in-day-out film critic hasn't accustomed one.

Bribery and corruption are supposedly the perennial perks attached to the job of juryman. In my experience, they are not so insidious as vanity and flattery. Yet sometimes they prove true. One sometimes *is* offered a straight bribe for a guaranteed vote. It happened to me and eight other jurors at one Cairo film festival.

A minor Middle-Eastern oil-state which had recently begun sending its 16mm productions to international film festivals made overtures to the jury to honour its latest film in return for £10,000. The sum was to be split equally between the nine of us. At least it was fairer than buying votes individually, for whatever the vendor thought one was worth – safer, too, as we would all

135

be implicated. But the Western sense of guilt isn't so easily mocked or pacified. No sooner had it been made than we felt obliged to report the offer to one of the official guardians of our integrity. "Ten thousand pounds!" this gentleman cried. "I hope you refused!" We did indeed, we said smugly. "They insult you," he went on. "I'm glad you turned it down. They'll have learnt their lesson. Ten thousand pounds . . . not nearly enough!"

Of course, there are "bribes" and "inducements", and the line between them is sometimes harder to draw than in that instance.

One major international festival used to reckon that everyone it invited to sit on its jury had to come all the way from Hollywood, by air, first class, return. It insisted on forwarding the amount to cover such expenses, even if one lived less than an hour's flying time from where the festival was held. This attractive flat rate is no longer available. I wonder why. Perhaps there were complaints from jury members who really had to come from Hollywood.

But as far as bribing individual jury members, the major-league festivals are relatively free from suspicion today. The lengths they go to in order to protect one's virtue can be far more irritating. One is chaperoned closely by the jury secretary; one has to sign into the screenings – certainly at Cannes – lest one's absence be questioned; even going to the loo during the projection of the movie requires a nice calculation of how long the necessity is likely to take – too long, and the film's producer, who seems to have his eyes (or his deputy's) fixed on the jury *loge*, may lodge a complaint, requiring the temporary absentee to sit through the whole film again.

I was once shooed away from a film company's luncheon in Cannes by none other than Robert Favre LeBret, the austere and dreaded festival president, who secreted himself inside the restaurant door precisely to protect his jurors from such possible lapses of protocol by the hosts (whom he regarded with suspicion) as a bank-note of large denomination wrapped up in the table napkin of influential guests.

But it would not only very foolish of a film company to try and buy an award for their film in advance; it would be quite unnecessary, too.

The truth is, you don't need to spend money on buying votes at a film festival. The work is sometimes done for you already by the way the event is set up in the first place. Most of the blandishments and pressures that determine how the prizes will go come from within the jury room itself, rather than as a result of irregular pressures from outside. The jurors usually do a good enough job of prearranging their own prize-giving without any prompting from hungry *papabili.*

From the minute the festival organisers begin to select the jury, generally six months before the event, to allow for drop-outs, the prize-winners begin to be selected.

I must qualify this with a *caveat.* I don't think it is ever possible for a festival to *guarantee* a prize to such and such a producer if he will put his film into the competition. Which, of course, doesn't stop filmmakers from trying. There have been quite a few instances at various festivals of those who expected to be among the winners being cruelly disappointed at the *palmarès* ceremony and making no secret of their belief that they was robbed. But this usually comes from expectations being pitched unnaturally – if understandably – high by the festival organisers who are loath to let a famous name believe he won't come away richer by a major prize if he permits them to screen his long awaited and much publicised new production. It is not an edifying sight when the votes are in and the expected name is absent. The late Glauber Rocha, the leading exponent of *cinema novo* in Brazil, was such a poor loser at one Venice festival that he pursued the jury with his vocal protests for several hundred yards along the Lido. It gained him attention, if not an award, and looked good on Brazilian television. Even the great Visconti, to whom, one would think, an award more or less mattered not at all, threw himself into a furious pet when *Death in Venice*, which had looked a certainty, was routed by Joseph Losey's *The Go-Between* at Cannes in 1971. He had to be (partially) mollified by a hastily minted award for his collective works, which included, no doubt, the particular one that had just lost.

Dirk Bogarde dryly recounts a vituperative run-in with the festival authorities when he served at Cannes as president of the jury in 1985. Not only had John Huston's *Under the Volcano* failed to win a prize, but Bogarde and his fellow jurors set their faces against even applying "The Visconti Palliative" of making

137

an official *hommage* to Huston. The festival had deemed one or other honour to be such a matter of course that it had had no reservations about encouraging Huston to come all the way to the South of France from the up-river compound that he occupied for most of the year in South America. *"Six thousand miles,"* the jurors were sternly reminded. How *could* they refuse an award or an honour in the circumstances? It was not seemly. It was not *honnête*. To which, according to Bogarde, an unnamed juror retorted: "Listen; you do *not* win the fucking *Palme d'or* for travelling."

True; but you *can* win it without much physical effort of any kind, provided the right jury mix has been achieved in advance.

Over the years, reports from behind the closed doors indicate that individual jurors tend to vote according to the expectations that led to their appointment. Knowing this, the films that a festival wants to see honoured can often be spoken for before the voting is recorded. There have been famous exceptions; but the general principle holds true.

A pro-Hollywood bias, a Left-wing inclination, a post-modernist sympathy or a youth-cult trendiness; it's a case of "pick 'n' mix" being adroitly related to the complexion of the entries. Both are usually prerogatives of the festival director(s). In the jury room, there are few surprises; the jurors get to know each other very, very well during the ten days they share the duties and the pleasures of jury service. Where surprises *are* experienced is among the accredited festival-goers, critics, *chroniqueurs*, producers, distributors, free-loaders, etc. For they will have been judging what they've seen on the screen and discussing its fitness for an award; very few of them will have been second-guessing the minds, attitudes and prejudices of the jurors who are actually deciding the day's winners and losers.

Odd things start to happen to jurors just as soon as they are convoked for the first time to meet each other and be inducted into the rituals of their craft. The first (and many more) of the rituals is to consume an inordinate amount of food and drink while trying to memorise the names of their fellow jurors: strange-sounding names that may belong to a far-off critic about whom they know little or an instant celebrity about whom they knew nothing until he or she became a "media personality" and thus eligible in the festival's eyes to pass judgment on Tarkovsky or Cavalier or Greenaway or Kwon-Taek Im.

It's a universal principle that jurors love power. But it's a human failing that they also want to be loved for themselves – a fact that has also mellowed many a long-serving despot. One way of being loved is plainly to give popular awards. Now it is the shrewd festival director who can hint that while currying favour is not the reason for them all coming together at Cannes, Berlin or Tokyo, nevertheless keeping as many as possible of the competitors and the audiences reasonably happy and contented is a noble alternative.

This desirable goal has been assisted in recent years by the highly fissionable nature of the main prizes. At one time the prizes used to be awarded to single films and solo stars; now they often tend to be *ex aequo* citations, shared between two or even more contenders. This may look fair enough; until one realises that a split award doesn't signify equality of achievement, so much as stalemate on the part of the jury.

It is appalling how swiftly and naturally jurors turn into politicians and start making bargains, horse-trading and even reneging on understandings or promises.

Even when there's no split vote, there's a rule of natural justice that is just as pernicious. It is that one prize, and one prize only, shall be given to each worthy film. A film that has already been awarded a prize for, say, direction, is extremely unlikely to be awarded another prize for, say, its star's acting. It has happened, yes; but usually it takes a juryroom mutiny for it to happen. Jurors don't have much inducement to turn into mutineers, since they are kept, or keep themselves, between films in an almost continuous state of indigestion, constipation or even, in some individual cases, intoxication.

The shrewd festival director picking his jury has additional precautions he can take. The *persona* whom such a director will find most *grata* is . . . another festival director. For one thing, directors from elsewhere know the ropes already. For another, they can be trusted not to rock the boat. Festival directors usually live well in the barren months between their own annual events. Quite a number of them are resigned to doing extra-curricular work at their colleagues' festivals, provided this encompasses a room (*de luxe*), board (*à la carte*), and of course first-class travel (*pour deux*). If Chekhov's "Eternal Student" were alive and well and living in contemporary times, he would probably be putting

139

in his days and nights trying to set up a film festival or, failing that, doing the rounds of other people's.

Next on the "acceptable" list are very distinguished film-makers. They make good jurymen provided they haven't yet begun to live off their past distinction, instead of their current box-office. It's even less desirable that they should have languished in limbo for any length of time while trying unavailingly to set up their next movie. If the garland of laurels they wore in their heyday has turned into a crown of thorns, they can become very nasty indeed and be tempted to use their power in the jury room to pay off old scores, real or imagined, against the individuals or film companies that have scorned or soured on them or, worse still, grabbed their glory.

Famous film stars are dodgy, too, for the same reasons, but they have several factors in their favour. One is, they *are* famous; and since a festival nowadays lives or dies by publicity, a few faces at least that lend a semblance of celebrity to the locality are welcomed like a series of divinities stopping momentarily at Eboli.

Another thing to be said for having a film star or two on the jury is the likelihood that they won't actually have been to see any movies for years. An exception, you'd think, should be made for the ones they themselves star in; but even that is doubtful, now that the stars are generally excused, for the most part, from any contractual obligation to support the publicity by attending the *première*. Only if they own percentages, net or, preferably, gross in their films, do most stars today feel any need to come out at night and shine at the event. Therefore they can be counted on to approach their work on the festival jury without any preconceived notion of what it is about, what's "in" and who's "out". This renders them susceptible to winks and nods, as broad or as subtle as the impressionable celebrity is used to picking up from his or her director (or publicist).

Film critics who get on to juries have of course seen plenty of movies – too many, maybe, for their own or the festival's good. But proffering an invitation to serve as a juror can very effectively de-fang the sharpest biting viper. Possibly for the first time in their lives, they are made to feel like film stars. They know what it is to be photographed, interviewed, recognised as important by their occupancy of a reserved *loge* and not simply a commonplace by-line, and they gain a reflected glamour from the real tinsel among their fellow jurors.

Someone who has suddenly had celebrity thrust on him or her is more than welcome to a festival director. A best-selling novelist, a Women's Movement activist, a "refusnik" poet, a dissident politician, even (God help us!) a television presenter; someone who has never made any visible or suspected contribution to cinema will be greeted as a great *coup*.

Such people bring their own goods with them, so to speak – fresh, topical, controversial or popular and, above all, easily identifiable by the mass-media covering the festival, who are grateful for the excuse that such non-specialists give them to forget about the films for a moment or two.

These non-specialist jurors are usually envied and disliked by the specialists; they are supposed to act as ballast, but frequently behave as if they were the precious cargo.

Women jurors are a danger area. Many a festival director has planted his foot firmly on it, only to discover a landmine where he thought there was fertile earth. There are various reasons (some of them dishonourable and even sexist) for selecting women to be on a festival jury. Women are seen as representing a) their own sex; b) the Women's Movement; c) glamour. In other words, they are viewed generically. "We need a woman; would Charlotte Rampling be free?" is a query I actually heard from a festival chief. No one has ever heard anyone say, "We need a man – let's try Klaus Maria-Brandauer."

It's a nice irony, however, that generic selection can sometimes be the undoing of a festival. For alliances made by gender, if a jury contains several women, prove extremely difficult to deal with, especially as the festival director is male, as he usually is. Thus Pauline Kael, critic of the *New Yorker*, and Marthe Keller, the Swiss actress, contributed to some unusually hotly contested jury sessions at Cannes in 1977. When the jury president, Roberto Rossellini, died suddenly a few weeks later, some cynics said, "No wonder".

Ingrid Bergman actually broke the jury's vow of silence in 1973, when she was president, in order to express the disgust engendered in her by *La Grande bouffe*, that marathon tale of self-immolation by gluttony, even before the film had been brought to official judgment.

Françoise Sagan turned round several months after she had served as president in 1979 and made public allegations of "pressure". The festival, in turn, riposted with its allegations of unpaid telephone bills. An unedifying *contretemps*.

Guglielmo Biraghi, the Rome film critic who also runs the Taormina festival and, more recently, the Venice event, met the feminist problem head-on one year at Taormina by picking an all-female jury. In this case, where the choice was left to women, and women alone, the result reflected a massive disunity almost from the first vote.

The most predictable jury members used to be card-carrying members of the Communist Party. You knew where *they* stood, which line *they* toed. At least, you used to; since the advent of *glasnost*, this old certitude has gone the way of many others. I met Elem Klimov, the Russian director, shortly after Gorbachev's cultural revolution had enabled this former "dissident" to seize power in the Soviet film unions and declare that reforms were on the way. "What kind of films can we expect to come from Russia in future then?" I asked him. "Bad ones," was his cynical reply. Reforming the ways doesn't necessarily imply refining the means. It was the same man, when president of the Cannes jury in 1987, who was rumoured to have swung his vote successfully against not one, but two of his own countrymen who had films he disapproved of entered in the festival. You can see how tricky it's become, having a Communist on the jury.

It used to be so easy. The Soviet juror was a reliable man; the fact that he had been let out of Russia at all, to serve on a tribunal made up generally of Western capitalist representatives, was proof of his own solid orthodoxy. He voted first for the Russian entry, then for the East bloc film, then for the film from the Western country with the strongest Communist Party. Nowadays, he's as likely to be found voting for the Hollywood candidate as the Manchurian.

More loosely labelled "radicals" are another matter entirely. They are notoriously volatile. All sorts of things set them sounding off. Not necessarily films. Let a police horse step on some demonstrator's toe in far away Milan and, by some seismic tremor of sympathy, the radical juror at Cannes, or wherever, threatens to resign so as to show his solidarity with the lamed one – and will probably try to take the rest of the jury out with him in a joint show of anti-fascist feeling.

142

No, it is not easy to assemble a film festival jury; but once you have done so, your problems, far from beginning, may actually be half over. The jury will do the work for you and, in the process, compromise itself without realising it.

I served as a member of the festival jury at Cannes in 1974. René Clair was the president that year. He was then 75; it was 50 years since he had directed his first film, *Paris qui dort*, and nine since he'd made his last, a Franco-Romanian co-production (always a bad sign) called *Les Fêtes galantes*. He wasn't depressed by his recent inactivity. He was a member of the Académie Française, that august group of self-elected defenders of the French linguistic faith which met every Thursday in an endless endeavour to define the constituent parts of the language and preserve its purity. The exercise had kept Clair's mind lively and his wit untarnished. We soon discovered a mutual appreciation of the linguistic absurdities that modern vernacular had introduced into international parlance.

Clair was a very small delicate man, not unlike a bird in the way he cocked his head as I talked to him, as if it assisted the acuteness of his hearing. He all but hopped along, too, ever on the look out for any detail of life or manners that accident scattered, like breadcrumbs, in front of him. As we walked down the once elegantly Edwardian sea-front named La Croisette, he looked up at one of the pompous ferro-concrete blocks of flats that were being erected on its gracefully curving crescent and quoted disdainfully from a billboard which advertised, *"Appartements de Grand Standing"*. The "Franglais" annoyed him terribly. *"Comment cela s'appelle en anglais?"* he asked me. "Apartments *de luxe*," I said helplessly, and from that instant we were friends, mutual victims of the indignities that great languages inflict on each other when they fall into inferior hands.

The other members of the jury were unusually sympathetic, too. Monica Vitti had to be more than a token woman; she disappeared off to Rome two days into our judging, to vote in the plebiscite for divorce (it was lost) and then, on her tardy return, had to have a crash course in viewing all the films she'd missed. After every screening, she signed the jury register, "Veni, vidi, Vitti."

Irwin Shaw was the American juror, even though he'd been

resident in Switzerland for many a tax-sheltered year. He was then enjoying a great comeback in popularity and solvency. His novel *Rich Man, Poor Man* had found a new audience as one of the earliest TV mini-series successes. "It's found its level," he used to say, without self-disparagement. Shaw needed his liquor to make the day shorter, or, perhaps bearable. When one got to know him better, he was a deeply melancholy man under the "Tough American" hide of the ex-GI who's settled in Europe on a writing grant. His indulgence in tennis and/or whisky frequently made him late for jury meetings. He'd have to be summoned by telephone whereupon he would pick up the receiver, and, without waiting to hear who was calling, answer guiltily, "Oui, j'arrive . . . j'arrive."

Then there was Jean-Loup Dabadie, one of the cleverest dialogue writers of the later New Wave, particularly of Claude Sautet's films; Kenne Fant, of Sweden, president of Svensk Filmindustri, but a novelist as well as the representative of corporate power; the French film critic Michel Soutter; his countryman Felix Labisse, a rather sad-looking artist who played the dormouse in our deliberations; and lastly a veteran Russian filmmaker who had turned up at Nice Airport in response to the invitation issued to a totally different Russian filmmaker who had apparently not been granted a permit to travel; he looked rather like Mischa Auer's double.

Ours was a main-line, solidly based European jury; even the American was an expatriate.

Our duties weren't onerous. If we found it inconvenient to attend an official screening, another one was set up in next to no time. But as I said, we were closely guarded against intruders and discouraged from fraternising with anyone with a vested interest in the results. The hardship really came from the numbers of luncheons and suppers that the jury was expected – indeed commanded – to attend. We didn't just have to sing for our supper; sometimes we had to grace two suppers a night with our presence. Our virginity was never in danger, however; the other people present generally had absolutely no interest in the films. Still, it was an unrivalled way to meet the mayor of Cannes, the city's chief of police, the prefect of the Alpes Maritimes and the bishop of the region. Facing these authoritarian figures seated at intervals round the same table, one felt a little like an extra in a Jean

Genet play. One half-expected them to throw off the trappings of office and assume their favourite film fantasies. But no, none of them, it seemed, ever went to the movies.

As jurors we got on well together; but the first cracks in our conviviality appeared the morning we were driven up to the Villa Yakimour. This elegant white residence stood on a hill-top overlooking Cannes and the Mediterranean. It was the home of the Begum Aga Khan, a former French beauty queen, now a graceful if Junoesque dowager, pleasingly frank in her opinions and even refreshingly laconic about her own status, present and future. "And did you see what is in store for me?" she asked me, when the small-talk had turned to Egypt, Abu Simbel and the white marble tomb topped by the single red rose in which her late husband, the Aga Khan, is interred, and which I had visited some months earlier. "Yes," I said, hesitantly, recalling the way that the carved inscription on the side of the tomb had petered out in an area of polished blank marble . . . where the Begum was to have her own interment recorded one day. " 'Here is my space' ", she said, quoting *Antony and Cleopatra*, with an amused lift of her eyebrows. How odd to enjoy the jet-set life-style and know one's "space" is already reserved in the tombs of Egypt.

The villa's remoteness from downtown Cannes – as well as its secure defences – made it an ideal location for the jury's secret deliberations. The Begum was in the custom of lending it every year for that purpose, entertaining everyone to lunch after she had had the results formally announced to her first, in courteous repayment of her hospitality.

The villa was indeed a beautiful place, sitting amid lawns that were enamelled with flowers of hyper-brightness. Being given relatively unrestricted access to it was one of the real privileges of jury service.

We met in the library, a room with a high-vaulted ceiling painted in scarlet and olive and having pleasant associations with a desert ruler's tented encampment. Appropriately, too, security had been built into the decor. "*Les fenêtres sont blindées*" ("The windows are bullet-proof"), Gilles Jacob, the festival's executive director, whispered to us with approval. (One gets to value such details when one runs a film festival.)

It was about 9.15 a.m. when we got down to voting for the winners, and we quickly hit difficulties.

145

Cannes makes it a rule to have an odd number of jurors; that way, one avoids hung decisions – such, anyhow, is the theory. In practice, it may not work. It didn't this time. Four of us voted straight off for Francis Ford Coppola's *The Conversation* and four for Pier-Paolo Pasolini's *One Thousand and One Nights*. René Clair refused to use his casting vote, being reluctant to incur the resentment of the losing faction so early on in our proceedings, and he called an adjournment.

This created intense and understandable vexation in Robert Favre LeBret and Gilles Jacob. Both of them were "sitting in" with us, bringing their "presence", if not actually their "persuasiveness" to bear on the deliberations. Now they saw us all troop out into the gardens for a breathing space and an informal exchange of opinions barely ten minutes after we had begun.

This is when festival directors see aeroplane schedules looming even more imminently than festival awards. If the jury cuts things too close, there may not be time to get the prizewinners to Cannes for that night's ceremony. In the old days, the stars, directors, and so on, lasted the whole festival through staying in state in Cannes. Nowadays, one gulp is enough for most celebrities, and only a guaranteed award or some other fail-safe honour will lure them back for the gala *clôture*. And here were we, the jury, impervious to such imperatives, insisting on serving art and merit, rather than the flight schedules of Air France.

We were all strolling along the terrace, engaged in earnest little confabs of one or two people, in French and English, when I was startled to hear our Russian juror saying, in his imperfect but assertive French, "All this is in our past." He was addressing the Begum Aga Khan, who had emerged from the salon to see if all was well with us and why we had quit the library. The Russian waved a hand around him, indicating beyond any doubt his disapproval of the luxury and privilege the rest of us had lately been admiring.

Not one bit put out by his compromising Marxism, Her Highness endowed him with a gracious smile. "I am glad to say, monsieur, it is still in my present."

As we walked and talked, it soon became clear that those of us whose native tongue was English, or who were fluent in it, that's to say Shaw, Fant, Dabadie and myself, were for Coppola; the Latins and the non-English speakers, namely Clair, Vitti and

Labisse, were for Pasolini – and of course this self-styled Communist filmmaker got the Russian's vote, too, though the man from Moscow could hardly have felt easy with the homo-eroticism of Pasolini's version of the Arabian Nights.

Shaw and I took René Clair aside and tried to bring him round to our way of thinking. Suddenly, both of us realised simultaneously that Clair simply hadn't comprehended one crucial line of dialogue in *The Conversation*. It is the remark that Gene Hackman's "Private Eye" picks up on his tape recorder early on in the film when he is shadowing the two young suspects. It makes him think they're plotting a murder. He only realises his mistake much later on in the film, on replaying the tape, when a different context lends the line a radically different emphasis; the man he had previously seen as a victim had now to be considered a potential killer. Since the French sub-title had been identical each time the line of dialogue had been spoken, the fatal nuance had failed to carry its meaning to Clair (and, I suspected, to others).

Immediately Shaw and I explained to Clair how the dialogue represented a cunning narrative twist. His face lit up. *"Mais c'est génial!"* he piped up, "It's genius!"

We went back indoors and took a second vote and this time Coppola won by one vote. Even then, a bargain had to be struck. It was agreed that if the jury made Coppola's film the *unanimous* winner of the *Palme d'or*, then the *Prix special du jury* (the second prize) should go *unanimously* to the Pasolini film. Even at this late stage, the Russian made an attempt, admittedly half-hearted, to win recognition for his country's effort, a version of Tom Sawyer shot on the Volga. It was so bad it would have been embarrassing even to mention it in conversation. Now we were seriously being asked to consider it for an award. We hardly knew what to say or where to look. Favre LeBret saved us the trouble, anyhow. His voice, harsh with contempt, cut through our paralysis: *"Nous serions des cons, voter pour un tel film."* ("We'd be dumb to vote for a film like that.") The Russian shrugged. In his heart, under his Party card, he no doubt agreed, he'd done his official best.

The rest of us pretended we hadn't heard Favre LeBret, while privately blessing him for his interjection.

After a self-congratulatory glass of the Begum's champagne, we passed on to the acting awards.

Gene Hackman was the obvious choice as the "Best Actor".

147

But since *The Conversation* had just been awarded the premier prize, it would be indecent to confer on it a second mark of distinction. Poor Hackman was a loser before a single vote was taken. Jack Nicholson was next in line for his hugely sympathetic performance in *The Last Detail*, as the Marines MP escorting a court-martialled young "grunt" to a term of incarceration and deciding to give the kid a "good time" en route to the stockade. But Nicholson's rival was Jean-Paul Belmondo in the title role of Alain Resnais' film *Stavisky*.

The discussion was briskly conducted. Nicholson came out the winner. What counted in his favour, I think, was his ebullient presence in Cannes. He is one of the few superstars who makes access to himself easy; he must have done two dozen interviews and kept a high public profile, too. (Of course, he was no stranger to Cannes; long before he became a star, he had come to "hustle" the early films he had made with Roger Corman and Monte Hellman on the Croisette.) The award to him simply confirmed that a star who "puts himself/herself around" commends herself/himself to jurors, who aren't impervious to fan worship, either.

But now it was glaringly obvious that "the French have to get *something*", as Irwin Shaw said, after the third glass of champagne. Resnais' lack of an award was an embarrassment to us; but then it had been so to the Cannes festival since 1968. In that year it was on the cards that his film *Je t'aime, Je t'aime* would have won except that the festival was ended abruptly and violently when Godard, Truffaut and other French film industry radicals showed their sympathy with the strikes that had paralysed the rest of France by pulling the curtains across the screen at the Palais des Festivals and causing Favre LeBret to cancel the event after ten days of strife.

Unfortunately for Resnais, a majority of our jury felt that *Stavisky* wasn't up to his best standards. Then someone (I have a feeling it was myself) recalled that Charles Boyer was in the film, playing a venal baron. Why not honour Boyer? Not just for his role in *Stavisky*, but for his "contribution to cinema *including* his role in *Stavisky*". This face-saving manoeuvre is known as an *hommage*. It is usually deployed, as it was this time, when the jury is stuck. Its use unsticks everyone like some magic solvent. We eagerly voted Boyer his *hommage* and glowed with humanity as well as hubris and had another glass of champagne. Later on, we were badly rattled when Boyer, correctly guessing our motivation, berated us for our impertinence and called it an insult to Resnais. He probably wouldn't have accepted the *hommage*; but a prize-winning film like *Stavisky* gets an invaluable publicity windfall when a clip of it (as well as a star in it) is seen on the French TV coverage of the Cannes *palmarès* on the very eve of its opening in dozens of Paris cinemas. Boyer was persuaded to go up and receive his *hommage*. He reserved a special scowl for us as he passed the jury box.

He was dead right, of course; we had behaved meanly to a great cinema personage by turning him into a token figure.

It was very soon realised that we hadn't much in the way of choice when we came to award the "Best Actress" prize. This isn't an unusual discovery at international film festivals. Male actors still dominate the screens in national cinemas; festivals simply replicate the imbalance. We decided to vote for Marie-Josée Nat in Michel Drach's wartime family "weepie", *Les Violons du Bal*. French honour was satisfied, though it's more doubtful if French art was served.

By now we were on our sixth glass of champagne. Intoxication of various kinds and degrees had set in. We were hell-bent on ennobling almost anything that moved on the screen. We had a couple of extra prizes we could award at our discretion – for technical achievement, and so on – and we couldn't wait to parcel them out.

Then it struck someone that Carlos Saura hadn't been honoured. There was a good reason for that. The Spanish director's entry, *La Prima Angelica (Cousin Angelica)*, hadn't been considered to be among his best films, and up to then no one had pushed very strongly for it. But now the name "Franco" was mentioned – and suddenly we all began to play politics.

It was "clearly" unthinkable for Saura to return home to "Fascist Spain" without a prize from Cannes to reinforce the Spanish cinema's fight against censorship and political represssion. Anyhow, he had been loyal to Cannes for many years. In spite of the "repression", at home, he seemed enviably prolific and seldom failed to have a film ready for selection. In a few moments, we had voted Saura a special jury prize and felt we had also done our bit to assist Spain's return to the democratic system.

149

We went on to give another special prize for technical artistry. And then, drunk with power, as well as with the contents of the Begum's cellar, we resolved on a final show of strength.

There was a general feeling that year, among the festival-goers, that Cannes had not been a vintage event. The standard of the official competition, it was claimed, should have been higher. (No doubt the festival chiefs agreed with this common criticism, and would have liked to be able to do something about it, too.) We decided to associate ourselves with this popular feeling; we would add a postscript to the awards deploring the unsatisfactory selection, thus confirming our independence of the festival authorities while giving them a reproving rap on the knuckles.

And we would have done so, had the "festival authorities" not forestalled us. They were probably used to the mutinous dementia that grips juries in the last stages of judgment. Leaning reproachfully across the table, they reminded us that we had already done far more than our duty. We had named three *additional* prizes; one for Boyer, one for Saura, one for technical artistry. Our generosity was commendable. The prizes were all worthy ones. But how could we now go on to deliver a general rebuke to the festival for the lack of opportunity it had given us to show our wisdom and discrimination by rewarding the deserving? It did not make sense.

A silence fell over us. We had been well and truly out-flanked. The censure motion was forgotten. We were spared further embarrassment by the appearance of the Begum's butler who announced, *"Madame . . . messieurs . . . Son Altesse vous invite à déjeuner."*

The Begum Aga Khan received us in the dining room and had the results formally communicated to her. The festival directors seemed well pleased with them. And indeed they should have been. In virtually every instance, the prizes had fallen out the way Cannes wanted them to do that year – and all without bullying or bribery. At the time, I was surprised at how well we had done. It had seemed then a bit like a mind-reading act on the stage. One was so gratified and bewildered by the accuracy of the illusionist's "reading" that one forgets one has involuntarily been led to agree with what was in *his* thoughts from the very first. All festivals do it; Cannes has brought it to a high art.

* * *

Things worked well at Cannes, of course, because we were a homogenous jury and reasonably free of cultural schisms. But when dissension breaks out on a festival jury, it means trouble for everyone.

A few years earlier, I had been on the jury at the Berlin Film Festival. At that time it was held in the month of June, which turned Berlin into a hot and airless city, instead of in icy February, as the world festival calendar now requires. The pressure at Berlin didn't come from the festival directors; it was applied by one jury member whose commitment to Jean-Luc Godard went well beyond critical and even rational support. This man kept up a continuous querulous refrain. If Godard didn't get a prize, how could this juror return home? If Godard didn't get a prize, what would people think of the Berlin Film Festival? If Godard didn't get a prize, would the rebellious youth who had forced Cannes to close in 1968 not be impelled to do the same in the streets of Berlin? If Godard didn't get a prize . . . and so on, for hours.

The lobbying was conducted with a persistence that was deaf to all objections. But it was self-defeating. The opposition to Godard only hardened. When we finally broke up, we'd decided our list of prize-winners – and Godard wasn't on it. Even after a few nightcaps at the Kempinski, we were sober enough to resist our fellow juror's last-ditch (as we imagined) plea to create a special prize for Godard.

We had to return after breakfast the next morning – the morning of the prize-giving – in order to "justify" our choices. The process of "justification" is a horrendous part of jury service in Berlin – or used to be, for I believe it's now been abandoned. No wonder. It was like sitting one's "A" level exams all over again. In part, it served a useful purpose. It was intended to help the trilingual translation of the reasons behind the prizes. The German, French and British jurors made themselves individually responsible for the citation that followed the announcement of each prize. But this meant that the three jurors not only had to compose an appropriate citation, they had also to reconcile its translation in all three languages and *then* submit the result for approval to the other jurors whose knowledge of English, French or German might be more than a little imperfect. It was a nightmare. It lasted all through a working lunch until well into the afternoon. I've since decided it was the festival's shrewd way

151

of seeing us off the premises, so exhausted that we couldn't muster any protest if we'd felt inclined, we were so glad to see the back of the job.

But on this occasion, anger erupted almost the moment we sat down. For Godard's tireless hustler, who had left Berlin by train before dawn and hence escaped our labours, had paid his respects to a number of jurors in the early hours of the morning and had pleaded with the more malleable ones to re-open the voting just as soon as we were convoked later in the day.

A political conscience, it seems, doesn't sleep as soundly as an artistic one. A couple of the jurors had woken up feeling that maybe Godard *had* been treated unjustly. It took nearly two hours to quell the incipient mutiny. It was achieved only when the majority of the jury threatened to stage a public walk-out at that night's ceremony if *any* attempt were made by the dissident jurors, by vote or voice, to pay tribute to Godard.

I am quite sure Godard would have loved the ruckus. As it turned out, he was denied the triumph of anarchy as well as a prize. The waverers backed down. Dr Alfred Bauer, at that time the festival director, mopped his brow with relief, and that night we had to endure several minutes of frustrated rage from the Marxist claques in the Zoo-Palast audience when they realised Godard wasn't going to be paid the homage traditionally his due.

All too soon, it would be the turn of Fassbinder whose name on a festival film *had* to be honoured by any jury that feared for its political credibility and, in some festival capitals, its physical safety.

On many occasions, Orson Welles accepted the call to *hommage* which was made at festivals great and small largely for the reason that, like Mount Everest, *he was there*. (The reason he was there, of course, was that he had been invited and it seemed to him a good idea to escape his creditors for a while and have his immediate living expenses taken care of.) Welles' appearance eventually became a slightly pathetic running joke with those of us who witnessed it often enough. But I consider his *hommages* a far more pardonable gesture by jurors than the political reflex which still prompts some of them to vote for Left-wing film-makers irrespective of the quality of the works in competition.

Ingmar Bergman, Woody Allen, Federico Fellini, David Lean and Stanley Kubrick are among some of the artists who never win prizes at film festivals. The reason is simple and honourable: they refuse to allow their films to be put into the competition. (Kubrick even refuses to *send* his new film.) I used to ask myself, What do they know that we don't? Then I began to serve on film festival juries – and found out.

WHAT MADE MARLON BRANDO STOP RUNNING AND FIND PEACE AT LAST

The thing I admire so much about Marlon Brando is his willingness – compulsion, if you want to call it that – to take risks. He has played parts in ways that few other actors would dare, and fewer still bring off.

Sometimes, indeed *often*, he has done so in pictures blatantly unworthy of him, in roles he should never have accepted in the first place. But then who said a genius has to possess good taste? Brando takes those risks less often today because he makes so few films. And I feel the poorer for it, cheated out of what I consider I have the right to expect.

I can't say that of many actors. In that catchphrase made famous by the *The Godfather*, I find myself wondering what offer you *would* have to make Marlon Brando these days that he couldn't refuse. A man who knows him well, Elliott Kastner, a producer who's worked with him several times, tells me that when you approach Brando to do a film, you have to adopt a certain tone of voice. Woe betide the producer who calls Brando and nervously murmurs a figure – Oh, let's say four million dollars, which is what he collected for about 12 minutes' work in *Superman*. When the star who's being propositioned hears in the supplicant's voice the note of fear that he knows he induces in many people in Hollywood, then the call is usually a wasted one.

Brando's long-term relationship with the movies has been one of creative belligerence. It's hardly reassuring to the moneymen when they read that he once said, "You have to upset yourself. Unless you do, you can't act." Brando's "upsets" have sometimes been on an epic scale. So have been the bills that eventually faced the filmmakers. One of his employers is said to have been left standing in tears, lamenting, "I don't think *any* artist should be so difficult. I think of Johann Sebastian Bach with all his kids, and still getting his work done."

Plenty of film stars have produced and/or directed their own .

movies; Brando is among the number. But that doesn't limit the extent to which he'll push his involvement. Whatever the movie he's in, Brando *imposes* himself on all of it. "He irradiates it" is how Bette Davis once put it to me – and Davis herself was no mean take-over artist. Considering all he's been through – considering all he's put others through – Marlon Brando is remembered in Hollywood as if he were a combination of Tamburlaine and St Sebastian, conqueror and martyr. He is a despot who inflicts pain and a masochist who needs to receive it and glory in it. Kenneth Tynan said of him, "He doesn't mind bruising his soul." But that, though true, doesn't catch half of it. Tynan should have revised his verdict to read, ". . . his body and soul."

Elsewhere, I've alluded to the star's predilection for painful epiphanies in his films, cruel self-torturing moments of revelation – as if the list of grievous bodily harm he incurs for his art somehow sanctions the spurious make-believe, rather on the principle of "I suffer, therefore I am." That's actually not uncommon in a macho society like Hollywood's. Not all the hurt Brando has received has been self-inflicted, however. He made enemies from the very moment he flew into Hollywood direct from Broadway in 1950 bearing a gift that was too rare, too individual to be welcome in a Dream Factory that at that date was still dedicated by the founding fathers to clanking out, with unrivalled technical efficiency, the serial entertainments based on the replication of unique personalities. Brando brought to Hollywood the first new style of acting to afflict the place since the coming of sound. He destabilised the Hollywood system by threatening to usurp the functions of director, producer and editor as he deployed "The Method" to research the primacy of his own self in front of the cameras as they turned: he refused to subordinate that "self" to the technical demands of "The Product". The Method, as Brando practised it, anyhow, was more than a style of acting. Had it just been a style, that would have been made welcome in the cage provided for it and he would have had all the creature comforts he needed pushed at him through the bars for the term of his natural life which, in Hollywood then, meant seven years – the term of the standard star contract. But Brando made the Method a means to an end; and left no one in doubt that it was he who would determine the end. This disrupted the work of filmmaking more than somewhat. It made directors feel threatened, it caused producers uncertainty and, perhaps most disruptive of all, it left film editors without the blueprint for the jigsaw of takes, shots and reactions that stars who simply "took direction" and didn't listen to the inward pilot of their souls had traditionally provided for them. Editors found that a Brando performance would only cut together in a certain way – his way.

Some directors, of course, welcomed this, but, significantly, they tended to be ones with roots in the theatre or an appreciation of stage acting: Zinnemann, Kazan and Mankiewicz, for example. Such men were imaginative iconoclasts by temperament. For them, it was magic to work with Brando, and his breach of the rules was an extension of their own contemplated or applied insubordination against their Hollywood overlords. They welcomed him as an accomplice, an accessory before the act of creation – not as a subverter of the system, which he wasn't: not yet.

Yet even from the front-rank directors he worked with, Brando kept his distance. Not all were of a mind to reach out to him, anyway. Zinnemann in particular stood off, exhilarated by the results of what he was filming, but taking care to let the star arrive at them his own way. He had the feeling that Brando didn't trust anyone even in those early days – maybe what he had heard of Hollywood had given him good grounds for that distrust – and therefore wouldn't or couldn't latch on to anyone for aid or comfort. The same director noted, wryly, how Brando's enormous and instantaneous success quickly changed the stance of his peers. For except for the stars, Hollywood actors tended to be diffident folk, not all that sure of their place in the hierarchy, somewhat apologetic about it, in fact. After the triumphs of Brando and Montgomery Clift, Actors Studio in New York began drawing an intake of Hollywood players, spending time there as participants or observers, and when they returned to the Coast it was noted by Zinnemann that they sported a strut in their stride.

Stella Adler, Brando's instructress in New York, taught him how to analyse a living character the way a forensic scientist dissected a dead one. Elia Kazan's private notebooks, published recently by the French critic Michel Ciment in his book on the director, reveal the astonishing lengths to which Kazan took his own analysis of the characters in the films and Broadway plays he directed, wrenching them away from their existence in the script until they become separate independent entities with pasts, presents and futures. With a star of a like mind, talent and methodology, no wonder the three movies Kazan made with Brando have the impact of the new order – which is fine in Hollywood, just so long as it makes money for the old order.

At first Brando assaulted Hollywood acting conventions by playing characters who were emotionally inarticulate and some-times physically incapacitated. But this was accidental, or, at least, simply the by-product of Hollywood's habit of impressing the actors it recruited from Broadway in the mould of the stage success that had caught the eye of the studios in the first place. In Brando's case, this meant *A Streetcar Named Desire* and Stanley Kowalski.

On meeting him for the first time in Hollywood, some directors like Zinnemann formed the impression that he was still playing Kowalski. It was as if "the act" simplified social relationships for him, keeping others at a distance.

But his success in *The Men* and *A Streetcar Named Desire* created an impression that the Method was suited only to the primal scream or the brutish reflex. Not true, of course; one of the greatest pleasures a film ever gave me was discovering Brando's performance as Mark Antony in Mankiewicz's *Julius Caesar*.

I was finishing my studies at the time at the University of Michigan, Ann Arbor, and trooped into the cinema near the campus fully expecting to share the already audible scepticism of fellow American students at the notion of Brando trailing a toga instead of a torn T-shirt. To my surprise, I saw and heard a Daniel outroar a whole den of Old Vic lions imported from England for the film. Brando took on James Mason; for heaven's sake, he even took on John Gielgud! And he won! The film showed us something in him we'd never seen up to then: his ability to absorb an alien discipline as well as throw a home-grown tantrum. I can never forget the speech he made as Antony on the Capitol's steps after Caesar's murder. The climax is thrill-ing – but it was the start that sent the hairs prickling on my lower neck. Brando was like a high diver testing the top board before launching himself off it. A little spring in the toes, a transmission of energy to prime the body, and *then*, the bound in the air, the impact of landing unexpectedly on that short single word "lend" – in "lend me your ears". Others had parsed the famous line conventionally, putting the emphasis on the *"Friends*, Romans . . ." But Brando didn't just speak – he listened. He heard the crowd – the Roman mob, impatient, intolerant, rendering him inaudible. Then he barked out the line, *"lend* me your ears" in a way that, 35 years later, at a Venice film festival, Joe Mankiewicz told me had made *him* hear Shakespeare differently, such a powerful kiss of life did Brando bestow on a line so well known it was practically dead with repetition over the centuries.

Later, back in England, I heard the film critic Paul Dehn lecturing at Stratford-upon-Avon and was enthralled that this compatriot of so many talents and unerring taste declared his own admiration for Brando in Julius Caesar, saying how "under the pressure exerted by the bent bow of Shakespeare's verse, the slack string of [Brando's] diction has been taken up, tightened and made straight, so that every word is a discernible and well-judged arrow . . ."

It was my guess – later confirmed to me by James Mason – that Brando had been modelling himself on Olivier, another actor in love with the verbal adrenalin that a high-soaring line of the Bard can send pumping through him if it is enunciated in a new and thrilling way. Yet Brando could also be amazingly colloquial and street-wise in ways that Olivier seldom attempted. Sometimes he that plays the king can't get near the commoner. Brando could – and did.

In *On the Waterfront*, the film that brought him his widest audience (and his first Oscar), in his early dialogue with Eva Marie Saint, you'd swear you were listening to the conversation of two plain people which has been recorded as they walk along the street by an eavesdropping "private eye". That kind of verbal verisimilitude, don't forget, was still fairly uncommon on the Hollywood screen in 1954 – not practised by the stars, anyhow, and almost certainly resisted by the sound recordists.

Hollywood praised Brando and put up with his unconventional ways as long as the movies he was in made money. Such has always been Hollywood's way; there are no rebels there who will be refused the privileges of the place provided they consent to pay the price that comes attached, which is to enrich their employers. Yet Brando never took to Hollywood, never truly settled in. He remained a "Why" actor in a "Who" society. And eventually the time and money consumed as he sought the answer *why* he should play a scene this way, and not that, began to throw expensive grit in the production machine and make those who ran it ask themselves *who* did he think he was. In those days – and it's still the mid-1950s we're speaking of, before most stars had been emboldened or been forced by studio cut-backs to seek their future employment as freelancers or independent producers – the studios possessed the financial and legal teeth to chew up a recalcitrant and costly talent at the first sign of a drop in his earning power. "I want to act; you want to sell me," Brando protested, the cry of discontented stars down the decades. The front office slapped a two million dollar law suit on him when he refused what he deemed to be unworthy pictures. He fought them, then capitulated and returned to work in even more demeaning ones. Thus the haughty retreat from *The Egyptian* ended in the abject surrender to *Désirée*.

Even in such a historical travesty, Brando was still fun to watch as the Emperor Napoleon, but now it was the fun associated with burlesque – and with something darker: self-contempt.

Bored stars can be dangerous people. They experiment. Sometimes if they are very big stars, they discover the extent to which people will submit to their eccentric whims, and this in turn becomes the measure of the self-disgust they begin to feel for wasting their talents on such ignoble experiments. It is an ugly and vicious spiral of descent – and dissent.

Brando could be remarkably sweet-tempered. In spite of his technical imperfections as a song-and-dance man in *Guys and Dolls*, he is far more likeable a character than Sinatra in the same musical. Brando's singing and hoofing, however imperfect, are extensions of his acting, the way Archie Rice's whole stage act in *The Entertainer* was an extension of Olivier's acting. Sinatra, on the other hand, is so practised a singer that he stands at a slight and distracting distance from his character. Likewise in *The Teahouse of the August Moon*, playing Sakini, the wily Japanese interpreter, Brando assumed a charm that not only suited the Oriental skin he was in, but for a time lightened the self-destructive load one had begun to see burdening him in his film career. He looked like he was enjoying himself. This was Peter Sellers' favourite Brando film. I watched it twice in Sellers' company and each time Sellers was in transports at the transformation Brando effected. Easy, looking back, to see what appealed to poor Peter. Brando was doing what Sellers himself was to discover he could do with Inspector Clouseau – seize and project through his comic imposture a characteristic of a nation that was completely foreign to him. Between the two stars (did they ever meet?) there was a mutuality of creative magic. On reflection, they didn't need to meet. The spark jumped between them.

My first encounter with Brando was in 1964. I wouldn't call it a "meeting". We never exchanged a handshake, not even a word; but it was, for me anyhow, probably more informative than if we had. For I caught Brando at work.

This is something that is almost impossible for an outsider to do nowadays. To begin with, he makes so few pictures; and now, of course, there is no way past the security cordon surrounding him when he does appear in a movie. I am still mildly surprised at the ease, even in 1964, with which an impulsive call to Twentieth Century-Fox's publicity department in Hollywood gained me quick access to the set of the film that Brando was then making for them. I remember I was met with an ingratiating handshake and an intimate "Alex" from a publicity man never encountered by me before (or since), who happened to be wearing a "Safari Club of Kenya" emblem on the breast pocket of his Very English navy flannel blazer. Later, I wondered what happened to him; something unpleasant, I suspect. But then if he really had been to Kenya, and not just to Abercrombie and Fitch's store on Wilshire Boulevard, he would have been aware of the risks run when one approaches big game or, in this case, Brando.

Despite a few hugely costly failures – including *One-Eyed Jacks*, in which he'd directed himself, and *Mutiny on the Bounty* – Brando was still the most prestigious of the protected species of stardom around the studios in the mid-1960s. He was working on the film that had begun production under the title *Morituri*. Some months later, no doubt after a studio-inspired poll had disclosed the paucity of Latin scholars who might be lured to a war-time espionage thriller of that title, it was premiered as

The Saboteur: Code Name "Morituri". One didn't need to know any Latin at all to predict that it was the film that was "about to die". And die it did, eclipsing any hope its Austrian director, Bernhard Wicki, might have entertained of a Hollywood career. Maybe it was already dawning on the people at Fox that what had started out as a prestige production with Brando, directed by an imported prize-winning European filmmaker, would be lucky to bring in any money, never mind be mistaken for art, so what harm could a little publicity do? Hence my welcome on the lot.

"He's playing a very interesting scene with someone I'm sure you already know," said my "Safari Club" guide, "– Trevor Howard". Already I began to smell blood on the wind. Trevor Howard had appeared, a bare three years but many battles earlier, in the remake of *Mutiny on the Bounty*, where he had played Captain Bligh to Brando's Mr Christian. Reports suggest that these characters' actual historical counterparts had parted company on warmer terms than Brando and Howard had done when they finished their scenes together. What, I wondered, had reunited them? Not just the money, I was honourable enough to suppose. Like prize-fighters, actors like them have a taste for the re-match. Each must surely have been fascinated by the other's performance in the *Bounty* movie – though that remark has to be qualified. In Howard's case, part of the fascination must have derived from disbelief in the foppish English accent that went with Brando's highly wayward interpretation of Mr Christian as a popinjay mincing his way through the King's English in a manner that should itself have invited a grammarian to lay on the rope's end. Exactly from what source he got this preposterous "voice", I don't know for certain, but I suspect he'd taken that old-time English stage-trouper Maurice Evans as his model. Evans at that time still personified Shakespeare for many Broadwayites and, even more, for playgoers in the sticks. It proved a bad model.

Ivan Foxwell, the British film producer who made *The Key* and *The Berlin Memorandum*, was making *Tiara Tahiti* in the same South Sea waters as the *Bounty* crew had just vacated and he happened on some of the day's rushes that had been printed for the latter film and then apparently abandoned when it shipped home to Hollywood. Curious for a preview of Brando's interpretation of Mr Christian, Foxwell had the rushes screened by his own unit – and within a few seconds all were convinced an elaborate prank was being played on them. Surely Brando wouldn't – couldn't – sound like *that* in the film! But he did. It was a rare example of his making a wrong choice rather than simply a poor copy. Four years later, for Gillo Pontecorvo, he made *Queimada!* (released in America as *Burn!*), and played Sir William Walker, the English Government agent sent out to destabilise Portuguese rule in the early colonial empire. And this time Brando's mastery of the English "Establishment" accent was total. Its provenance was also crystal clear in his mynah-bird imitation of that prince of diction, Richard Burton.

The tension was almost tangible when "Safari Club" led me onto the set of *Morituri*. Some high-powered baiting had taken place earlier in the day between Brando and Howard. Though they had a crucial scene to play together, they were presently making it very plain to everyone how "apart" they were in every other way. Brando had gathered his familiar court circle around him – secretary, dresser, make-up man, gofers. They stood in a huddle in the corner, looking as if they were all plotting another mutiny. Howard perched alone on a chair. But as soon as that hooded hawk's eye of his spotted me, he let out a loud whoop. "My old darling!!" he roared.

Now had we met in a London street, Howard and I would have admitted to knowing each other just well enough to exchange nods of recognition. I didn't really think his exuberant greeting had anything to do with the expatriate status we shared that day in Hollywood. Howard was simply annexing me, as a sort of "second", to support him in his corner of the ring. (I realised later that he was also, in a way, putting me under his protection by claiming me as a friend.) Having made Brando curious about this newcomer, Howard's one-upmanship then turned decidedly belligerent. "Just like *Mutiny on the Bounty*, my old love," he bellowed, though we were only a few feet apart. "He hasn't changed a bit – just like *Mutiny on the Bounty!*" Whereupon he shook his head vigorously from side to side and uttered sarcastic barks of laughter.

"Safari Club" smiled uncertainly. Clearly, he wasn't reading the signals right. He ought to have cut the visit short there and then. (Was it his first day in the job?) I could feel Brando glaring across the set at Howard and me. Seeing he'd hooked him, Howard now encircled my shoulders with a restraining arm and began making small talk in an undertone about my visit – except that it must have appeared to the enemy faction that he was making me privy to possibly dozens of malicious indiscretions about the film and his co-star.

Suddenly I felt a tug at my trouser leg. Looking up at me was a middle-aged man, barely waist high, but hugely pugnacious looking. "Hi, bud, where do you come from?" he asked in a Runyonesque croak. "Safari Club" told him I was from a newspaper in London, England, and the midget toddled back across the stage and reported to Brando. I expected to be strong-armed off the set immediately. But no executive action ensued. It seemed that Brando's concern was at lest I had come from Canada, since he and a newspaper interviewer had fallen out quite spectacularly on a recent visit there. I'd been taken as a putative "hit man" sent across the 49th parallel to even up the score.

The atmosphere on *Morituri* was already so edgy that the two high-tempered stars were being left severely on their own. No one wanted to provoke them and catch the backlash. Very little of the sequence had been shot that morning. Much of the shooting time had been devoted to re-thinking it. Much of that re-thinking had been done by Brando. What had been a relatively straightforward scene was now quite a complicated one. The set represented Brando's luxuriously furnished hideaway in the Himalayas. He was playing a sensitive German pacifist who had fled the European conflict and was now hoping to sit out the war in India with his music library and his art collection. "Fine set," "Safari Club" had already prompted. Yes, but as I seemed to identify several of the paintings on the walls as quite well-known ones whose customary habitat was in the national art collections of Europe, it appeared to me as if Brando's refugee aesthete had looted them *en route* to his exclusive Shangri-la. Trevor Howard played the man from British Intelligence who came calling to put the screw on Brando and force him back into war service and a more active role in the script than art appreciation. As written, the scene had been largely Howard's. He had virtually all the dialogue, hence ought to command most of the attention. Brando would have to retrieve what he could of it on reaction

166

shots. Or so the plan ought to have been. But Brando had decided that the scene could do with "improvement", and, as the story was told to me, I began to understand why Howard had vented his exasperation in a parody welcome when I unexpectedly appeared on the set – a visitor from a saner planet.

The first step Brando had taken to make things more "interesting" was to call for a trained dog. A large, lean and intelligent hound of Baskerville pedigree was procured from Canine Casting. Next, Brando demanded an Indian maidservant to be added to his domicile. A petite, pretty and sari-clad Asian girl was soon on her way over from Central Casting. But something else was still required to fit into the grand design that Brando had in mind. Ah, of course, music! A phonograph and a stack of 1930s records were rushed round from Twentieth Century-Fox's prop department. What was happening must have been obvious to Howard. What should have been his scene was being hijacked from right under his own sharp nose.

"Action!" called Bernhard Wicki, a stocky man with white hair and a look both watchful and detached, such as might have become a referee who was in the ring, but not part of the fight.

The shot was a "master" one, showing the cavernous room and its two inhabitants. As Howard launched into his dialogue, Brando and the hound simultaneously began a separate playlet, one tossing edible tidbits from a platter and the other snapping the gobbets out of the air like an actor who hasn't seen a square meal in days. As Howard hit his stride, the bead curtains were parted on cue and the Indian maid-servant sashayed down a few steps bearing a tray. "Vould you like some tea?" Brando asked in a German accent whose accuracy of intonation cut startlingly across the make-believe of the dialogue. As Howard ploughed gamely on into his speech, the girl made the tea ceremony into an alluring distraction, no doubt thanking Allah, or at whichever agency she worshipped, for the miraculous break that had summoned her from relative obscurity in a West Hollywood bungalow court to be here, *pouring tea for Marlon Brando*.

Finally, as Trevor Howard entered the home stretch of dialogue, to which nobody could now be paying the slightest attention what with all this pantomime going on around him, Brando again got his turn with a line. "Vould you like to hear some

167

music?'' he asked, and walking over to the phonograph he set a disc on the turntable. No needle was in the playing arm, so no Mozart was heard on the set to add to the other distractions. But this omission would be remedied when the music track was laid on the edited film and there was sure to be some seductive melody to overlay Trevor Howard's final run down.

What was happening was shameless sabotage. It was also a fascinating exercise in star-power. Brando, it appeared to me, was monopolising the interest with utter ruthlessness, playing a part that was parallel to though separate from the action. Yet his very disdain was giving the scene a tension that it simply wouldn't have possessed had it been played straight in an even-handed way. That much was clear.

It was equally clear, however, that this wasn't how Trevor Howard saw it. One sympathised with him. Word-perfect and with rasping tongue, as deadly in speech as a land-locked Bligh, he was otherwise quite paralysed by the attention-stealing mimicry Brando was putting on. He glowered as the take ended with Wicki calling ''Cut''. ''One more, please, gentlemen,'' the director decided. Brando didn't object; he seemed to be enjoying Howard's discomfiture.

''Action!'' And again Brando fed the dog – while Howard was talking – ordered his tea – while Howard was talking – and commanded music – while Howard was talking. Only this time it didn't quite go as planned.

''Vould you like to hear some music?'' Brando walked across to the phonograph and made great play of selecting a record. But in placing it on the turntable, he fumbled it – and the disc fell on the floor. Now Twentieth Century-Fox's propmen are perfectionists. As this was a period picture, they had supplied authentic old bakelite records. As the thick brittle disc hit the stone-flagged floor, it fragmented into a dozen pieces. ''Shit!'' said Brando. ''Cut!'' cried Wicki. Trevor Howard swivelled round, shot a glance of unholy glee at where he knew I was standing in the penumbra round the highly-lit set and cried, or rather crowed, ''Just like *Mutiny on the Bounty*, my old love . . . Just like *Mutiny on the Bounty*.'' Even ''Safari Club'' now heard the not-so-distant tom-toms beating for war. Through dry lips, he said to me, ''Maybe we'd better make ourselves scarce.'' The next minute we were on the other side of the vast sound-proofed door in the calm sunshine of Beverly Hills. Inside, no doubt, battle was being joined all over again.

Yet all this by-play wasn't simply a matter of actors' pride and rivalry. A close acquaintance of Brando's, to whom I once put the question, told me the actor's own opinion of his movie career. He summed it up as a mixture of "boredom and whore-dom". At some point, it had turned into a state of self-contempt – all those amazing gifts of his had been so lamely applied that there was now a positive joy, a malicious pleasure in misapplying them. Possibly the rhythm of filmmaking didn't fit Brando's metabolism, unless there was a director like Kazan who could inject his own imaginative vitamins into the star. Giving himself a fix of his own eccentric inventiveness sometimes worked temporary wonders; but all too often it has seemed to be dysfunctional.

Brando tires quickly. His self-absorption is profound, but it isn't matched in other matters by his attention span. "I get excited about something, but it never lasts more than seven minutes . . . That's my limit," he told Truman Capote in a famous interview in 1966, entitled "The Duke in his Domain". The effect of this interview was like lemon juice on the oyster that Brando had trustingly opened for the pearl-hunter. After it had appeared in self-convicting print, Brando closed up tight again – and has since kept his vow of silence, relaxing it only in the (rare) company of people who are not "in films", but in recent years shunning even them. When Brando talks nowadays, it's not for publication, but for those private sessions of psycho-analysis one hears he has gone in for, in random fashion, when the need or taste has taken him over the years. To outsiders, such therapy appears to have had the effect of reinforcing his angsts, rather than discharging him from them.

Sometimes his behaviour has enhanced his morbid glamour, as when he went in for simulating his own incineration in *Mutiny on the Bounty* or mortifying his flesh by being dragged along at the tail of a runaway horse in *One-Eyed Jacks*. Interestingly, the incidence of such masochistic scenes increased just as his slipping popularity was rendering him vulnerable to less self-satisfying forms of Hollywood torture, such as a diminishing box-office. This is often the cause of the "whoring" to which filmmaking

169

reduces some of the brightest and best when they have to go to work primarily because their star status or personal life-style demands it – or depends on it.

Brando started airing his refrain of always "feeling violated" around this time. He was in his 40s and might have been considered in the prime of his art, yet he was being forced to accept the studio contract system or risk suspension from acting anywhere and so forfeit all satisfaction. I imagine his festering resentment at the condition to which he was reduced in those years has influenced the distance he now keeps between himself and Hollywood – or indeed between himself and any world in which he's not in control. It may have directed him towards the causes he has promoted – civil rights, black power and especially the alleged genocide suffered by the American Indians and the theft of their patrimony. All are protest movements militantly critical of oppression, ethnic in the case of the Indians, but akin to artistic oppression in Brando's experience. A Hollywood actor, runs his protest, is much like an American Indian – a noble savage who's been turned into a dependent outcast. The movie industry, in his eyes, has been as guilty as any American government in selling out on the "treaties" it made with the tribes whose riches it thereby exploited. "We just excised the Indians from the human race," he once went on record as saying, which may be overstating the case, although if you were a star in Hollywood in the 1950s, with pride in your heritage and with your uniqueness to cherish and protect from predators, you might indeed feel just like that. Brando's acceptance of roles in some appalling films sometimes resembles a Redskin raid on the Palefaces. History justifies any atrocities that are committed.

I have often wondered how, if you were a producer, with a fat part you wanted Brando to play, you actually went about the business of holding a pow-wow with him. You couldn't just offer it over the garden fence, unless of course, as happened on one occasion, you yourself lived on the other side of the fence. Jack Nicholson did. He was Brando's neighbour on Mulholland Drive. One day he asked Brando if he'd like to make a quick couple of million bucks . . . which is partly how the pair of them got to star in *The Missouri Breaks*. Much good it did the film. In what was basically a "revenge Western", Brando surpassed all his previous experiments with the characters he was set to play and even appeared in Grandma Moses drag of poke bonnet and hobble skirt, all the more entertaining a disguise (for him, anyhow) in which to go bounty-hunting for the rustlers.

But although star may talk money unto star, the producers who actually do the paying have to have their message borne by lesser mortals known as agents. It was Steve Shagan who told me how he secured Brando's services for his film *The Formula* in 1981. Shagan is a writer and therefore somewhat saner than the run of Hollywood producers – which he was, too, on this occasion. His account of dealing with Brando deserves to go on the record. Not just as an example to be cited in the thick casebook devoted to the pathology of stardom; but because it offers a rare and authenticated insight into how star-power can transform itself into creative energy.

Among Shagan's earlier credits was the screenplay for *Save the Tiger*, which John Avildsen had directed and for which Jack Lemmon had won an Academy Award in 1973. Shagan and Avildsen knew that persuading Metro-Goldwyn-Mayer to finance *The Formula* depended on getting a star of Brando's magnitude – and they hoped to get Brando himself. The film was a contemporary thriller underpinned by documentary fact which confirmed that the German war machine had been kept running on synthetic fuel in the closing stages of the war. Where did "the formula" for the fuel go when peace once again made the world safe for businessmen? Shagan's guess was that it had disappeared into the vaults belonging to the international oil cartels. They buried it so as not to disturb the world markets – i.e., not shake their own profits' tree. It was Avildsen who had suggested there might be a part in the plot for Brando.

Now when trying to make a deal on a would-be film hit, it is always good strategy to "sell" it in terms of an already proven hit. What caught MGM's immediate curiosity was hearing the character destined by the makers to be played by Brando described as "a godfather". There was always room for another *Godfather*, wasn't there? Of course there was; even if, this time round, he wasn't a gangster who behaved like a businessman in the Mafia underworld, but a businessman who applied a gangster's philosophy to the corporate overworld. As the latter is the commonest self-image that Hollywood studio heads entertain of themselves and their empires, it was easy to make them identify

171

with the property. (All Hollywood movies are called "properties" until they find finance, whereupon they become "projects", subsequently going into production if their good luck holds, and becoming "major motion pictures".) Brando's reaction to the property was now crucial.

Shagan submitted the script through Brando's lawyer, one Kenneth Garey, who sounded optimistic when he called back a day or two later – at least Brando hadn't said no. An appointment brought Garey, Avildsen and Shagan to Brando's Mulholland Drive compound, which is sited on a bluff of well foliated scrubland overlooking Hollywood, ideal for contemplation of the infinite – in its philosophical or financial senses.

After the security systems had done their combined detective work and the Dobermanns had been restrained, the star emerged from his home and handed his visitors an exotic flower each. He had recently brought them back from the private islet he owned in the Pacific Ocean near Tahiti. Was a bloom in the hand worth a name on a contract? Who could tell? It was all part of the "Indian-like" attitude they sensed – gifts were to be exchanged before bargains were struck (or not). They got down to business, the star doing the interviewing. Why, he asked them, did they want to make *The Formula*?

"Because it says something about our times, and says it entertainingly," said Shagan. This apparently passed the first test; all stars like to be associated with themes of contemporary importance; all stars also like the audience to be still there at the end of the film. Emboldened, Shagan took his turn at the questioning. How did Brando see the character he was being invited to play?

Now Shagan and Avildsen had been primed in advance by other producers who had sat the exam and flunked the oral. Brando, they'd been told, possessed a sense of malicious fun, not totally separate from self-interest, in gauging the calibre of filmmakers who wanted him to work for them. He was accustomed to making proposals of such a flamboyant and outrageous nature that they'd have been laughable, if they didn't have the ulterior aim of probing the seriousness, and sometimes the sanity, of the producers sitting at the star's feet. There exists a story that when Brando had expressed willingness to play Superman's father in the first film in the saga that Alexander and Ilya Salkind produced it was on certain conditions – only if he could do it in a

172

green limelight and nude except for a bagel. A real bagel or a plastic one? asked the Salkinds. Their snide riposte (plus a multi-million dollar fee and a large slice of the box-office gross) softened up the star sufficiently for him to say yes. Whether he had in fact behaved like that on *Superman* or not is not certain; but Brando now actually answered that he saw the billionaire tycoon of *The Formula* living like a grandpappy figure in an adobe-style mud house, its rooftop bristling with communications satellites, while its owner pottered about the lettuce patch in the back yard cultivating his garden. Shagan decided that if this were bluff, he would meet it with bluntness. "I think you're describing the last scene in *The Godfather* crossed with your own home life in the Pacific."

Avildsen was just as forthright. Disagreeing with Brando, he said, "I see the guy as off the front cover of *Forbes* magazine." Realising that neither supplicant was so infirm of purpose that he would let the part be distorted out of recognition by a superstar's whim, Brando then got down to serious talking.

"We don't want a hod carrier," Shagan reminded him, "we want a creative presence." He later gave me his version of the star's reply. Brando told him, in effect, that simply "acting" a part wasn't a task he could contemplate doing any longer. "He said, 'I have to be impressionistic in my approach. I will respect the rules. I will speak your lines, in the main. But I will give them, and the part, an impressionistic touch here and there – to get the essence.'" The visitors' response was guarded; but they said that, basically, they trusted him – and they reported back to MGM that they had a "firm maybe" from Brando, which is "Hollywoodspeak" for a deal that will jell if the price is right. The fee Brando reportedly got was indeed lordly: two million dollars guaranteed minimum, paid to him in instalments of $250,000, by cheque, into his hand. He was also guaranteed 11.6 per cent of the gross, that's to say from the first dollar earned at the box-office. The money wasn't related to the length of time he'd be on the screen, or even to the quality of his performance. It was the (then) going rate for the enormous publicity that a star of Marlon Brando's magnitude would generate worldwide when it was announced he was going to be in *The Formula*. This, in turn, would pre-sell the film to exhibitors in various territories and, it was hoped, ultimately attract queues outside the cinemas they owned. It was, if you like, the key money that gives a film access to cinemas in every part of the world where the name of Brando is known – as well as to huge expanses of space in newspapers and magazines, and air time on radio and television, in the whole magma of mass media that diffuse, amplify and multiply the message: "*The Formula is a film starring Marlon Brando.*"

This is how Brando comes to possess a power that's separate from – and even superior to – the success or failure of any film he makes. Of course some of his films have been box-office flops. But his talismanic value has a long life in money terms and outlasts a flop or two . . . or three . . . or four . . . Even when producers know the score and should be wary of using him, they are frequently so nervous of another producer deciding to gamble again and pay the going price for Marlon Brando that the failure of his last film to perform well is consigned to any one of a number of possible causes. As the screenwriter William Goldman has said in his book of memoirs, *Adventures in the Screen Trade*, "In this business nobody knows anything." In the endemic uncertainty of Hollywood, Brando and his kind are the fixed points for hope and glory.

And what did Brando do for his fee this time? The answer is he recycled himself once again. First he went to his dentist to have an extra-broad upper dental plate fitted, one that would stretch his lips into the shape of a wide yet tight money-purse. Then he thinned the hair on his head into straggling locks that were tinted grey. He adopted a hearing aid of an old-fashioned kind, rimless "granny" glasses and what Shagan called a "fuddy-duddy" voice; and he wore the sort of mail-order suit where the belt holding up his trousers drops well below the waistcoat. His idea was to stress how something of the soil from which the tycoon wrenched his mineral wealth has stuck to the man's speech, dress and habits, though his brain retains the bite of an oil drill. His philosophy in the film sounded like that of the original Godfather, filtered through Harvard Business School: "You mustn't think of us as evil, rapacious little men, clinging desperately to our numbered Swiss accounts. . . . Power has the obligation to lead. If you nail me, you nail the American dream." As Hollywood is one of the chief suppliers of American Dreams, the speech contains a double indictment that would be very sympathetic to Brando. The speech was actually unconsciously prescient. I was reminded of it when much later, I read the remarks of the commencement speaker at the School of Business Administration at the University of California, Berkeley, in 1985, that were recalled in the *Los Angeles Times* in 1987: "Greed is all right, by the way. I want you to know that. I think greed is healthy. You can be greedy and still feel good about yourself." The speaker was Ivan F. Boesky, later the star of history's biggest insider-dealing scandal. Brando played a man who might have been Boeksy's pioneering mentor: a man who transformed true grit into true greed.

But true to quixotic form, Brando also slipped some special pleading of his own into the screenplay of *The Formula* – on behalf of frogs. Seeing a frog slip into his swimming pool one morning, the tycoon commands his butler to fish it out at once. Why? Because the pool is chlorinated. And how does he know that? Because one of his conglomerate companies manufactures chlorine. Thus the capitalist villain who shows his fellow men no mercy becomes an eco-saviour speaking in a paraphrase of Marlon Brando on behalf of the downtrodden, the outcasts, the squashable ones of the earth. These are the "impressionist" touches Brando provides – and your money buys. Provided, that is, you can afford him in the first place.

It's been almost ten years since his last movie, *Apocalypse Now*, and then he only just appeared, nearly concealed from sight by *chiaroscuro* camerawork that itself looked like the product of a compromise between appearing and not appearing. He had originally wished to be a disembodied voice in the Coppola film, turning his rotund reality into an intangible oracular presence. It might have been prudent for Coppola to accept that "impression", for what we did see of Brando was simply an obese looking bonze. Yet again there was the sub-text in the dialogue, the message he is trying to get through to us under the guise of his public statement. His dialogue with Martin Sheen, cast as the Pentagon's man sent to terminate Brando who is playing the rogue Intelligence officer turned maverick guerrilla, recalls nothing so much as the hostility that a rebellious superstar displays to the "messenger boy" despatched by a studio's front office to tax him with his expensive time-wasting ways.

His legend still does for Brando what many of his pictures have

175

failed to do if the box-office is the measure of bankability – that is, it keeps him a star. People know the name who spurn the movies. So it's perhaps no wonder that he is magnetised by roles that cast him as a Super Being unconstrained by the earthly laws that bind mere mortals. The hieratic pull possessed by a role is apparently what it takes these days to get him to the contract-signing stage. In *Superman*, he was seen in the Prologue for only a few minutes (but a few millions of dollars) as a "Presence" – a sort of God the Father seeing his infant Son off to Earth on a mission to reform mankind and ultimately save the world.

In the wasteland career of Brando's middle-age, there is one great performance. It is *not* the eponymous *Godfather*, which remains a marvellous assembly-line job, but little more once you've seen how the wheels go round. He remains an inanimate object moved by mechanism, rather than an organic creation. Olivier, another "Great Impersonator", as Gielgud once unkindly but not unjustly called him, might have managed the Godfather with similar brilliance. But what Olivier could not have managed, or at least cared to reveal so nakedly, was the carnal self-knowledge that Brando exposed in *Last Tango in Paris*. It needed the shameless revelation of autobiography accreting to his life's work in cinema as well as to his life to give the role its self-lacerating grandeur – more Delacroix in its terrible intensity than the deliquescent mutant of Francis Bacon that provided Bertolucci with his painterly cue in the credit titles.

I can never watch Brando in this film (which I've seen ten times at least, having been once compelled to view and re-view it to defend the film at the Old Bailey criminal courts against a pornography charge whose ironies and absurdities I've detailed in my book *Double Takes*) without experiencing acute discomfort as well as boundless admiration. Like Greta Garbo, another great recluse, Brando "comes out" on the screen with the otherwise unapproachable private self. At the same time, he gives me the feeling of being in the presence of an "intimate stranger", to borrow Richard Schickel's phrase from his book on contemporary celebrity, someone I recognise, who keeps telling me more and more about himself, but at the same time withholding any real closeness.

Recently, though, I was vouchsafed a glimpse of a Brando that I don't suppose more than a handful of people have ever come across – the star as family man. It was a Polaroid snapshot of him sitting cross-legged, an impish Buddha, smilingly lord-and-mastering it by the side of his sleeping Polynesian third wife Tarita. It wasn't a scene in Beverly Hills. There were more babies' diapers in sight than Gucci loafers; more buxom, dark-skinned women of comfortably middle-aged appearance – aunts, cousins, sisters-in-law? – than sun-spoilt starlets or Californian bimbos. The clutter in the room was convincingly thrown together as if by accident, not pre-arranged by some photographer from a glossy magazine. A holiday home? Perhaps; but even more likely, a motel cabin into which everything's been thankfully off-loaded out of the station wagon for at least one overnight stay on the comfort of a sprung mattress.

It was a happy snap. In one small room, a whole pagan rhapsody seemed to be going on. I could easily read into it a sense of Brando's gypsy disdain for the rule-keepers and time-servers, and his cheerful naïf embrace of the tribal simplicities of life in the Polynesian society where he now spends so much of his time. Tarita begat him a son, Tehotu, and a daughter called Tarita Cheyenne – a name that mellifluously blends the Polynesian and the Red Indian causes her father has dedicated himself to upholding. Tarita was 18 when he met her in Tahiti when making *Mutiny on the Bounty*. From second dishwasher at a hang-out called Les Tropiques, she found herself elevated by his whim into playing a Polynesian princess in the film. It apparently worried Brando not at all that he was even then married to another Polynesian, Movita, who, by an astonishing coincidence, had played Clark Gable's native soul-mate in the earlier *Bounty* film. Movita had given birth to Brando's son, Miko, and then to his first daughter, Rebecca. And to go one wife further back, Anna Kashfi, whom he married in 1957 and whose studio biography claimed was Indian, though others have alleged a Welsh strain, gave him his first son, Christian Devi. There have been other women in Brando's life – Nancy Kwan, France Nuyen prominent among them – who confirm the intense appeal that the small-bodied, dark, vivacious and probably rather child-like Asian or Eurasian female has for him. Anna Kashfi had the exotic aura of her putative origins on the subcontinent, though, as it turned out, little of the placidness of such latitudes. It is the Polynesian girl who is more amiable and adaptable to men and

their ways, a loving mother who regards children as bonuses, not
burdens. And to a man like Brando, it seems, children are more
precious than multi-million dollar contracts. After all, the child
who gurgles is nearer in spirit to the actor who mumbles – and in
both cases it's pure emotion coming through, for "the mumble is
the emotion", as Brando has answered when criticised for some
less than articulate performances.

Words kill emotions, he believes. Children who are bundles of
tactile love (some of the time, anyhow) seem more central to his
life now than playing parts without a heartbeat in them or winning those cold little gold statuettes that haven't come out of any
womb, but only out of Hollywood's great hollowness.

Why, then, should we be surprised if films hold no great seductive qualities for Marlon Brando? Nothing, anyhow, to match
the freedom he has found by becoming an outcast of the Tahitian
islands? True, he periodically returns to the mainland to check
his bank account – but even Crusoe had need of worldly provi-
sions. And *Paris Match* or its *paparazzi* outriders will catch him
at Papeete airport and record the spectacle of a colossus run to
flesh. Yet Brando's very corpulence expresses disdain for conventional stardom in every ounce of extra poundage it carries.
Most of the time, though, he's ensconced securely and privately
under the thatch of his 400-acre island domain of Tetiaroa, ironically part of what is called the Society Islands archipelago – a
headman who has found his tribe.

Do I still regret all that he has failed to perform for us, all the
parts he could have played, but hasn't? Selfishly, I do. But then I
remember that photograph. When Marlon Brando can fit so
genially into a home snapshot, he can be said to have discovered
something about life that he hasn't shared with the millions who
have seen him only on the big screen. He deserves to keep the
secret to himself. Just say that I have never seen him happier
looking. That must be our comfort – as well as the extent of our
loss.

THE GIRL
WHO BLEW
IN WITH THE
BOSTON
WINDS

Meeting most film stars off the set is usually disenchanting. (Meeting some on the set can be even worse: actually dull.) The meeting usually takes place in hotel suites or agents' offices – neither place conducive to truth and intimacy. Rare is the publicist who can fit the star to the background in a way that the ambience confers an interest on the interviewee and can even do him or her a favour. Even rarer is the accident that assists the interviewer and at the same time flatters his subject.

Both events happened to me one afternoon in early April at the Ritz-Carlton Hotel, Boston. It was just too early in the year to have melted the ugly grey furrows of frozen slush piled up by winter snows on the side of the street. Half-hearted snowflakes were still being whipped around the square. The light was leaving the sky already, and it was only just past midday. But more depressing still, it was an hour past the time Faye Dunaway should have been sitting there in the foyer, talking to me before we both went in for lunch.

I had twice been asked by the *maître d'hôtel*, very politely but, yes, with definite point in his voice the second time round, if he should keep the table for me. I was about to go over to him and tell him, more out of frustration, I admit, than politeness, to throw it open to the line of expectant clients waiting for a place. And then a woman blew in – or was blown in – off the street and plonked herself down opposite me. She looked a mess and I thought more wistfully than ever of the elegant and absent Dunaway. Her hair was in a tangle. The paper carrier bag said "shopping" and not "boutique". The raincoat looked like any old mac in a storm. Only the big cluster of rings on her left hand told you there was something about her more artfully arranged than her present disarray revealed. But already she was putting that right.

Before my very eyes, a transformation occurred – as meticulous

181

as it was unselfconscious. Indeed the attention it immediately began attracting from the men nearby – never mind the women – lent it a "performance" quality.

Quickly dipping into her shopping bag and retrieving a hairbrush, the woman flipped the long tangle of wind-matted locks smoothly into place around her cheekbones – and the face of a film star appeared. Now the people in the lobby were quite definitely looking our way. The Boston winds that can skin your cheek had brought a high-tempered glow to a face that was being warmed into a sultry flush by the indoor temperature. She half-rose and slipped her old raincoat off her angular shoulders and out from under her – and, yes, it was mink lined. Beneath it she wore a black velvety looking trouser suit, a close-fitting sweater the colour of a field mushroom's pinkish-brown flesh, a brown scarf with a minute gold pattern on it loosely knotted round her throat and a thin gold necklace. She tossed the raincoat onto the spare chair – I'll swear its workaday exterior had been remodelled often to sustain the glamour of the winter chrysalid from which Faye Dunaway had emerged. If she had come out of a cake instead of a coat (albeit a mink-lined one) she couldn't have attracted more attention. It was a perfect meeting.

The year was 1978. She hadn't yet played Joan Crawford in *Mommie Dearest*; it hadn't even been mentioned that she might. Yet looking back, I can well understand why Crawford, all unwittingly, should have once given her imprimatur of approval to the star who was one day going to impersonate her. "Of all actresses," Crawford had said, "to me only Faye Dunaway has the talent and the class and the courage it takes to make a real star."

Crawford may have sensed that Dunaway, like herself in an earlier era, exemplified the American girl who analyses life as it's happening to her and risks all on becoming the front-runner. "Courage" is what Crawford had; it is what Dunaway has – and she belongs to an even more risky world than Crawford did. The winnings may be greater now, but the gamble may mean losing all on one big bad picture, instead of simply going immediately into the next "programmer" that the studio has waiting for you and recouping your stardom. I cannot explain it, except by what I already knew of her – but being five minutes in Dunaway's company makes you aware that this woman is a compulsive risk-taker. "Give Faye enough rope and she will excel herself," said Arthur Penn, directing her in *Bonnie and Clyde*. He felt it, too; he got her to show it, and person and *persona* became one.

Inevitably, conversation turned to that 1967 landmark movie as we ordered our long-delayed, pre-lunch drinks in the foyer under the fretful eye of the *maître d'hôtel*.

To those who saw her and Warren Beatty not as public enemies but as surrogate avengers for the millions of little people hard hit by the poverty of the Depression, the view of Dunaway as the amoral moll posing on the car's running board in cheeky beret and maxiskirt, a pistol clutched in her left hand instead of a handbag, will always be *the* image of armed and feral womanhood – as indelibly printed on the romantic-erotic imagination as Dietrich in her silver topper and black suspenders lolling back provocatively on the cabaret stage in *The Blue Angel*. Dunaway, then 26, set an international trend in 1930s fashions for the next few years. And the film fired the starter's gun for the New American cinema that set its exponents (Coppola, Scorsese, Cimino, De Palma) off on the marathon of ever more explicit sex and violence which soon superseded the liberating permissiveness previously exploited by the European cinema of the 1960s.

Dunaway's impact was so instantaneous and inflammatory ("a sensual Erskine Caldwell backwoods beauty", *Time* called her) that many supposed *Bonnie and Clyde* to have been her very first film. "In fact, it was my third," she said to me. "Sam Spiegel had seen me working with Elia Kazan at Lincoln Center. Incidentally, it was Kazan who advised me to go into analysis – as a way of monitoring myself." She darted a glance at me, to make sure I took the point that acting technique and not mental therapy was the purpose behind her confessional sessions. "Well, Spiegel saw me, as I said, and cast me in that terrible Anthony Quinn thing called *The Happening*. Then Otto Preminger got his hands on me and put me in *Hurry Sundown* – and that did absolutely nothing for me, either, except add 20 pounds to my weight, out of worry. Actors need kindness; all I'll say about Preminger is that I didn't get it under him. To play Bonnie, I actually had to have sandbags tied to me when I exercised, to help me reduce. People talk about the nervous, strained look I had that worked so well in that film. It came from the crash diet I had to endure. I was dog tired and ravenous. You've no idea how interesting starvation makes you look.'' To get to make the film at all, she had to buy herself expensively out of her Preminger contract: an early sign of her enduring determination. ''It took me a while to feel proud of the way I played Bonnie. It was all too instinctive a performance. I have a lot of Bonnie in me. Both of us are Southern girls. Southern folk have an openness I admire, a *boldness*, though maybe I'm too naïve for my own good – too often approaching people in simple faith. You know, that 'kindness of strangers' thing. That's *very* Southern.'' Her eyes now darted out of the tall hotel windows across the square at the pillared State Center, seeing maybe the portico of a Deep South mansion, though this was only a stone's throw – or, on that day, a snowball's – from where Samuel Adams had penned the Declaration of Independence.

Like Joan Crawford, Dunaway emerged from a childhood where she had been simultaneously indulged by her mother and scarred by a broken home. Her father was a master-sergeant with the US Army; the restlessness she endlessly betrays is probably related to being carted around the Army bases as a child. The discipline that her father brought off the parade ground was applied to her, too, physically sometimes, though she absorbed and didn't fight it. As we talked she toyed with an outsized knitted beret of black wool that she'd whipped off her head on entering the hotel. A fingernail accidentally snagged a thread in it. ''Damn!'' she snapped, then clapped her hands at her own reaction to this mutinous detail in her apparel: ''There speaks the master-sergeant's daughter.''

Her parents separated when she was 13. The thrust of her escape from this upbringing is possibly what is still powering her career.

''Look,'' she said suddenly, ''let's go eat.'' I got up to move towards the restaurant. ''No . . . not here,'' she said, restless still after 20 minutes' attempt at settling. ''Somewhere else.'' I apologetically slipped the *maître d'hôtel* a $20 bill in mitigation (he probably made another by liberating the table to someone else, so I didn't feel too bad). Across Boston in a cab we went to City Hall and thence to Maison Robert, a French restaurant which she obviously patronised and felt to be a familiar parade-ground. She strode in confidently with the same ramrod stiffness I'd seen

184

Joan Crawford using, on and off the set, to make her own five-feet-five seem taller to the eye and the camera. We were seated at once. Again it struck me that she had arranged this scene with the care of a background chosen for a film. The decor was dark brown, to match her outfit. King-size anemones made points of bright stained-glass colour in crystal bowls. The room looked out on a graveyard containing the Union dead (and Mr Adams), cemetery stones like old molars in worn gums poking up from its turf and, as a surprising backdrop, a soaring modern brown-glass skyscraper with a bijou art-house cinema built into its ground-floor façade. It was showing Fellini's *Casanova*.

"Fellini's never off-duty," she said, employing once again the military locution. "He'd ask you, 'What did you have for lunch?' and then write a scene of you having whatever it was into the film he's making. You feel he's feeding on you, too." She speaks with a certainty that I guess has come from watching one of her early loves, Marcello Mastroianni, absorbing Fellini's life by artistic osmosis as he incarnated the director's *alter ego* in the films they made together.

Champagne cocktails were brought to us without our ordering them. Dunaway delved into her bag again and this time came up with a wooden swizzle stick to disperse the bubbles – "The Plaza-Athénée has the best ones."

"Oh Lord, hold my baby high", her mother had once written in a poem when Faye was an infant of three. After *Bonnie and Clyde*, her name stood very high indeed – above the titles of a batch of movies that should have consolidated her stardom. Should have, but didn't. "I guess I dropped the ball," she later said. Most of the ten she made up to 1974 – when *Chinatown* brought her an Academy Award nomination – were oddly disappointing, evidence of scripts picked in panic because better ones weren't immediately available and parts played as second-string interest to dominant male stars like Steve McQueen (*The Thomas Crown Affair*), Dustin Hoffman (*Little Big Man*) and George C.Scott (*Oklahoma Crude*). "It was a terribly 'political' period for women. But I go for the emotional experience, not the political commitment. Jane Fonda says the roles she plays must reflect American womanhood and be relevant to women's place in society. Bully for Jane! But I'm not a feminist, not politically anyhow. I identified with Bonnie's frustration – a girl who felt

185

her potential blocked – but I didn't see her in the political terms of the Depression. I didn't need to. The period made her 'political'."

For a few of her male co-stars she professes to retain fond memories and denies that they were ever rivals – "The top is a broad plateau: there's room for all of us." Warren Beatty: "We were like siblings without the jealousy." Dustin Hoffman: "He'd stand behind the camera, feeding me very personal lines for my reaction, private jokes or remembered moments we'd shared that he knew would create the mood and the expression we were after – nothing at all to do with lines in the script. Such is filmmaking!" Jack Nicholson: "A very levelling influence during *Chinatown*."

Chinatown returned the ball to Dunaway. What her femme fatale character, Evelyn Mulwray, had to hide – incestuous rape, it turned out – gave her a plausible cause for concealing her own nervous tensions, so that she never "stood easy" in any scene but radiated the guarded self-discipline that intensifies her sexual interest. The part tightened up her emotional muscles which, she admitted, get lax if she's not really interested in a role. The director, Roman Polanski, was another cause of the highly-strung quality that worked a marvel in the film. There were stories at the time of Polanski pulling her hair out, calling her "certifiable". All she would admit to, however, was the loss of one long hair – only one. It was a hair that had resisted taming. It would have distracted from her close-up. Polanski lost his temper and plucked it out of her head in a second of Polish pique – hence was built up the myth of a near-scalping. No hard feelings, now, though some years after our Boston meeting, when I mentioned Polanski's "troubles" with the US law which had made him a fugitive from justice, the response was cool. Polanski protesting his innocence in his published memoirs was one thing, she thought, but Polanski protesting his virtue . . .!

Dunaway is a curiously laminated personality: one side of her looking so controlled, so secure; the other side snatching, in grateful dependency, at whatever or whoever she fancies can steady her. A man isn't just a husband to her, I imagine; he needs to be a mentor. She would be too fierce a force for Woody Allen to tame; but she would probably benefit from the nourishing experience of what Allen calls "a tutorial relationship" between

186

a man and a woman. At my first meeting with her, she projected new-found confidence that she was going to settle down in Boston with her husband, Peter Wolf, the lead singer with rock group the J.Geils Band, and a man six years her junior. It struck me that he was scarcely the buffer zone she needed to put between herself and the blows that life delivered daily to someone of her hypertense nature. I'd read that she was "ruthless" in earlier attachments, but "restless" still seemed the truer word. "I'd grown up thinking divorce was inevitable . . . everything was temporary. My parents' break-up, I suppose, was to blame. Everything in my own life seems to fall apart with alarming regularity – perhaps I wish it on myself. Looking back, I can see that the people I had affairs with weren't necessarily the people I wanted to marry. But such adventures are necessary – so is commitment, I guess."

By the time *Network* had won her an Oscar, commitment to Peter Wolf had all but given out. Then one of those things happened that a professional screenwriter would never allow to get into the script.

In Hollywood, to cover the Academy Awards ceremonies, was the British photographer, Terry O'Neill. He took what has become the second most famous picture of her after Bonnie. He called it "The Morning After the Awards". It shows Faye Dunaway among the totems. It shows her both rewarded and sated, in lonely splendour, at the poolside of the Beverly Hills Hotel, the gold Oscar statuette on the table beside her, crumpled morning newspapers headlining her triumph at her feet. In her hand is a copy of a Walker Percy novel the title of which, *Love Among the Ruins*, accurately registers the fractured pattern of her emotional life. It says it all. Everything a semiologist could wish for in the way of the signifier and the signified is present: the solitary figure (stars are lonely people), the pool (the Hollywood pack's tribal watering-hole), the statuette (the iconic symbol), the abandoned newspapers (celebrity is short-lived) and the novel with its ominous title (stars are unhappy people).

Her divorce from Wolf followed – and, soon afterwards, her marriage to O'Neill.

Dunaway can play a hateful woman and still be a star; there aren't really many like that on the screen today when you do a head count. She did a thing in *Network* that is even rarer; she played the blind side of the character of Diana, the ruthless manipulator of the TV ratings, by letting filmgoers see what the woman herself was unaware of – how much she stood to lose by allowing her sex drive to be subsumed into the success ethic. For Diana, the ratings game was her sexual high; when they slumped, the sex kick went with them. "People actually advised me not to take the part – too cruel, too cold, too inhuman. But I knew all about the way the medium could be the mantrap. Remember Diana holding up her coffee cup at the morning conference – letting it chatter lightly against her teeth was my idea. That made her tension not only visible, but audible." Dunaway is continually faced by the need to avoid Diana's fate – work brings her the same precarious excitement. Marriage is desired, but might it not steady her too much? So is motherhood – which she now has – but it is dangerous too. She is one of those stars who lives by boldness – by challenges. Joan Crawford was another. I used to see it in Crawford, but alarmingly overdone, especially in her last years when the matriarchal persona transfigured every role she sought, or, more frequently, was forced to accept. Even in Crawford's last film, *Trog*, about a woman paleontologist who discovers a little prehistoric humanoid, she greedily seized on *the thing* for its mother-love potential, cuddling it like an adopted child.

Dunaway had just finished playing Joan Crawford when I next caught up with her. A changed woman, no; but a changed scene, yes. Now we met in a house on Chiswick Reach, on the borders of London and the bank of the Thames, a place where William Morris had once lived. She and her husband Terry O'Neill had rented the artist's house from the William Morris Society. She had wanted to buy it, which of course wasn't allowed. She was in love with England – and things English – in that semi-mythological way that requires you to see plain daily reality constantly recast in terms of romanticism. I can understand it; I myself never lose the vision of a New England in the autumn such as Hitchcock captured in *The Trouble with Harry* and, every time I go to Old Lyme or Saybrook, Connecticut, I expect to find a body in the woods with mismatched socks being covered by the drift of autumn leaves. The Thames at high tide periodically rose above the level of its banks and flowed across the road and into

Dunaway's hallway where there was a grating to let it drain away again. The house at times actually stood in the river! None of which impaired the sense of security she said England and married life and her newly born daughter gave her. I watched her stalk across the polished floorboards – we were sitting prudently in the upstairs living-room as a flood warning had been put out by the Thames Water Authority – and noted her pleated cream-silk skirt jack-knife round her long legs in lines of parade-ground sharpness when she seated herself. It struck me *she* was the sort of daughter whom Crawford should have had, in place of Christina. She said now that she wanted to simplify her life, by which I understood her to mean that she wanted more perfect control over it. Crawford had used the very same words on the very last occasion I saw her. Crawford's life then *had* been simplified by that curious state of dependency she'd entered into when her late husband's Pepsi-Cola company paid the bills without nourishing her ambitions – God knows why she should have had any ambitions left, but, being Joan Crawford, she had. She was ironing her own evening gown that afternoon – "I've given the maid the day off" was the excuse. Fortunately, as the maid couldn't have done a more perfect job of it, her expert work with the smoothing-iron made the excuse stand up.

Dunaway's portrait of Joan in *Mommie Dearest* was an act of dedication by one star to another, rather than an act of desecration. Dunaway's "Joan" was coloured by Faye's own background. Crawford's explosion of fury against her adopted children came, as Dunaway saw it, from the star's self-imposed discipline – her form of self-protection against Hollywood – that she thrust on her children in that terrible fashion with the wire coat hanger. "Horribly pardonable," said Faye Dunaway, "the recoil of a mother whose protectiveness is frustrated by the wilfulness of her daughter . . . Joan, the child of need, colliding with Christina, the adopted child of opulence." She could understand that, she said; but it clearly hadn't helped her resolve the contradiction in her own life between self-control and self-fulfilment.

Dunaway is a woman who is tempted and exhilarated by crisis. She has sought that creative state in her films, not always – indeed very seldom – with success. Often she has been deceived by the *idea* of the film into thinking it can be made into the content of the film – then she finds out it is not so and she's stuck with the result. *The Eyes of Laura Mars*, for example, in which she played a high-fashion photographer. But although the film was dressed to kill all right, it was she who ended up the victim in every sense. The remake of *The Wicked Lady* confirmed that period roles are not the best containers for her neurotic modernism. But being "period" wasn't its only drawback. Dunaway needs at least one big moment in a film when she "cracks" – loses her nerve, abandons herself to despair, then takes command, becomes herself again. It may last a second or two only, but it has got to be there. She bled beautifully, profusely, as the highwaywoman in *The Wicked Lady*, but her villainy needed to be vulnerable to something more piercing than a pistol ball. That chattering of the coffee-cup in *Network* when things aren't working out transmitted the high-tension panic far better.

Dunaway is at her most appealing when threatened. She becomes unpredictable, therefore dangerous. Like Mary Astor, fear works on her performance like an aphrodisiac. Her self-torment sharpens the edge of her sex appeal. If only they wrote scenarios today with the great gutsy romantic confidence of those hewers of scripts and drawers of drama who served Bette Davis and Joan Crawford and Rita Hayworth. Theirs were roles of the kind that Dunaway was born to take by storm and occupy by temperament and skill. She is a warrior queen who is a prisoner behind her own portcullis and has to be rescued from the fears that drove her there before she will give the signal for the drawbridge to be lowered. Unfortunately, they don't build castles in the movies any more.

Dunaway is one of the few stars who insists on seeing the rushes of her own work. "They are the proof of what you're doing. Seeing them, something clicks into place in me." She gives the feeling that she would like to move into the area of total control that Barbra Streisand inhabits, or tries to, when all those male chauvinists in Hollywood will let her. The technical aspects that most stars rarely preoccupy themselves with, Dunaway makes into something of a fetish. I have seen her grind her heel into the pavement in frustration, still recalling how she had worked up *just the right expression* for a horseback scene in *Doc* – Arthur Penn's 1971 film in which she played a nymphomaniac – only to find they were using a diffuser and the expression didn't even register. Part of Terry O'Neill's appeal to her had to be his superb technical knowledge of what works on film and what doesn't. Dunaway has to be convinced by others – and then convince herself – of the effect.

In *Chinatown*, Evelyn Mulwray ended up slumped over the wheel of an automobile, shot through one eye. "Don't worry – we can shoot you from the back," they told Dunaway. Not good enough; she knew how important it was to her character – to *her*. She got the make-up man to create a latex cast of an extra's eye, then drill a bullet hole through it. Truth lies in the eye of the victim. "Perfection, that's what one strives for – even if it's never achieved."

It was the master-sergeant's daughter speaking again.

PETER O'TOOLE MEETS HIMSELF, TWO FEET TALL AND BLUE-EYED, COMING BACK FROM A TRIP ABROAD

"What attracts our young lions is not the mundane, but the heroic." Thus Kenneth Tynan in 1963. He was rebutting a widely propagated belief that the new school of so-called "working-class realists" on both sides of the theatre footlights had territorial ambitions that were bounded by pubs, slums, factory chimneys and kitchen sinks. In the case of Peter O'Toole particularly, it was a shrewd observation. I only wish it had been fulfilled.

Tynan sensed the heroic dimension in that Celtic dandy. Now that I think of it, Tynan's own ambitions lay that way, too. The two men looked more like brothers than (sometime) adversaries. The play-actor and the critic were even remarkably similar dietary specimens. Both would have made good leads in The Dance of Death – by which I mean the Bergman ritual, not the Strindbergian one, though one could argue that they would also have been well cast in that misogynistic play, too. Both had anorectic looking bodies. You felt they had wires connecting their limbs and required the constant agitation of life to keep them standing up – otherwise, if left by themselves, they would collapse. The careers of both were to be interrupted – and Tynan's fatally truncated – by illness amounting at times to wilful self-neglect. The last time I saw O'Toole, he was wielding a cigarette holder like a lordly sceptre; the last time I saw Tynan, he had his lips clamped round a cigarette like a mother's nipple, and was gulping for every quarter-breath (if that) which was all his emphysema permitted him to draw. O'Toole on one occasion gave Tynan a painful physical beating (for some admittedly foolish prank he'd played on him, involving an invented IRA bomb scare) but, really, they seemed made to succour and support each other – not come to dusty blows.

Yet it was a pity that Tynan had so seldom the opportunity to witness O'Toole's heroic mainspring uncoiling itself in

195

performance and thus permitting the critic to celebrate it in print for posterity's illumination.

Unbelievably, O'Toole's name crops up four times only in the two best-known collections of Tynan's theatre criticism, *Curtains* (1951) and *Tynan Right and Left* (1967). The earliest mention already contains a *caveat* that goes a long way to explain the rarity of later references. When he saw O'Toole play the cynical Cockney private in *The Long and the Short and the Tall*, Tynan credited him with "technical authority". He predicted "greatness" for him, but he added the condition – "given discipline and purpose". It's a judgment that, in essentials, still stands; the pity is that the condition was so seldom honoured.

When the play got to the film studios, it was Laurence Harvey who took over the O'Toole role – to the growling resentment of half the young people in Bristol who had been to see O'Toole in it in that city's Old Vic. Laurence Harvey possessed "discipline and purpose", albeit of a lower order, and certainly a far narrower kind of calculation – Baltic, not Celtic. It is possible to say that O'Toole has been just too prodigally endowed ever to manipulate the lesser bundle of ways and means that took Harvey much further along the road to success than he deserved. There is truth in that, but not the whole truth. It's true, too, to say that, for many people, O'Toole carries around with him an odour of John Barrymore – of talents self-destructively squandered. But that, too, though just, is banal. According to one director, Ted Gershuny, O'Toole missed his moment. Burton became *the* international star with classical dimension; Connery became *the* superman with Bond's licence to kill; Caine became *the* international Cockney with cocksure sexiness; and there was no place for O'Toole. That's retrospectively acute, but it doesn't solve the mystery of the man's failure to climb to his own peak and plant his own heroic standard on it.

One feels about O'Toole, as one feels about others with great gifts and tragic flaws, that there is something innate that isn't wished for, so much as wished upon him. "Directing him," said one filmmaker to me, "is principally a task of containment." He has his Irish countrymen's quixotic notion that coming out of a fight the biggest smithereen is tantamount to winning it; it certainly has its compensations, if you don't mind the cuts and bruises. Though a natural actor, O'Toole is not an effortless one.

196

It is necessary to re-tune him, to take him down a key or two, before one feels comfortable with the tune that, at his best, he can turn into a prodigious solo. In movies, he has all too infrequently found that kind of director or producer who can give him "discipline and purpose". David Lean was one who could; Sam Spiegel was another. He had to knuckle under the autocracy of the one, the tyranny of the other.

Lean kicked up a sandstorm, literally and figuratively, straight into O'Toole's face after instructing him to keep his eyes open and not flinch in front of the Bedouin tribesmen annointing his character the charismatic "El Aurence". Lean and O'Toole are men who are both committed to a certain mystical myopia; they do not register the plain facts of life if there is a transcendental state to tempt their distant gaze, though their means of seizing the intangible are decidedly dissimilar. O'Toole seeks the stimulant: Lean, the purgative. Lean will put a mortal actor through the stages of madness, where he doubts his own wits, until the performance gains a kind of gratitude just from the dependency enforced on the player. Inquisitors in the grand days of soul-saving used to work the same sadistic salvation. Lean was there to shrive O'Toole's soul, just as the dreaded producer, Sam Spiegel, was on hand to scourge the body that O'Toole had delivered to him as per contract. In no subsequent film role did O'Toole manage to top Lawrence of Arabia – and, if he is to be believed, he never quite recovered from playing it, either.

He still rails against the light, after being compelled to submit to many months of blazing sun in Jordan. "My idea of heaven," he said afterwards, "is moving from one smoke-filled room to another." What that suggests, of course, is a series of Irish snugs, though, as Nicholas Wapshott has astutely observed, what O'Toole welcomes more than hard drinking is simply the *company* that goes with it. It is true that the distinction is a fine one – a fey one, too, on occasions. He was once said to have drained a full bottle of whisky in a minute flat, declaring it was an "Irish birthday", and then slept for 24 hours. "What's an 'Irish birthday'?" they asked him when he woke up. "Any day I choose to call one," was the reply. One hopes it was spoken with a groan.

O'Toole pole-vaulted to stardom in *Lawrence of Arabia*. That heady moment when you know you've gone over the bar a notch higher than anyone else was never again duplicated. *Becket*, by comparison, was a long-jump, the satisfaction coming from exceeding the mark set by Richard Burton. Their competitive cronyship at least made bearable a lot of what O'Toole called Anouilh's "blether". Of the two, O'Toole is by far the more sheerly entertaining performer. He can hold plays and players in affectionate disrespect. Burton, on the other hand, used continually to emphasise the solemnity of great literature. In my hearing, and O'Toole's, Burton would assert that it would be much, much better for him if he "threw up all this" and retired "to Oxford". Once, when Burton had saddled up his scholarly hobby-horse, I caught O'Toole's blue Irish eye, and he winked. "You mean, boyo, to *give* lectures," he asked, "or *take* them?" Of the two men, O'Toole was the more mesmerising to listen to, principally, I think, because his ear wasn't always so sharply cocked in self-entranced approval. Burton reminded me, in a way, of the curse laid on Bottom – that when the rude chap woke from sleep, he would fall in love with the first person on whom he set eyes. In Burton's case, it was with the first sound to reach his ears, which proved to be his own voice. He fashioned an instrument out of it that was too fine for everyday use.

So, to a lesser degree, did O'Toole. Theirs were both dramatic voices – theatrical in a now rather dated sense. "It makes you listen," said Ted Gershuny, "and listening is hard work." Listening is not for cinema audiences. Generally speaking, they prefer looking.

After *Becket*, O'Toole opened Britain's National Theatre in *Hamlet*, directed by Olivier. It was not the best of partnerships. Each can play the other's blind side mercilessly; the difference was that Olivier tends to avoid confrontations, preferring to freeze someone out, rather than expel him from the company. A look from Olivier can turn a person to stone, but he is a notoriously bad bully. He didn't apply the "discipline and purpose" to O'Toole that Tynan had prayed for. In any case, Hamlet didn't suit O'Toole's extrovert complexion – no more than Conrad's Lord Jim did in the Richard Brooks film. Passivity, to him, is an alien posture. If Jeremy Irons had been born early enough, he would have been the perfect Jim, the archetypal moral defaulter; O'Toole simply couldn't bear to lose the fight with his own conscience. And the public, which had gone to the film expecting a hero in the Lawrence mould, were left perplexed and resentful. It was his first serious set-back.

O'Toole wolfs down words with the same insatiable reflex as he sinks pints. He has a Victorian appetite for a text, demolishing it at a single sitting and rising from the table still looking hungry. This is one reason why he is an incomparable interpreter of Bernard Shaw – although I would still back Rex Harrison in the really caddish roles. Shaw's long-windedness suits O'Toole; he paces himself through the essay-length paragraphs like a long-distance runner. Burton had more music on his tongue than O'Toole, but he got out of breath in modern prose.

After the failure of *Lord Jim*, O'Toole began to get well and truly trapped by the popular, though exaggerated picture of himself as a hell-raiser. It's a fate that Celtic actors have to live with – some choose to live off it. By his nature, O'Toole is always happiest in the thick of the battle, which is one reason why, in a later debacle in *Macbeth* (Bryan Forbes's much bloodied 1984 production), he could no more bring himself to wash his hands of what other actors would have recognised as an unnervingly misbegotten spectacle than he could bear to wash one drop of blood *off* his hands. Either would have been capitulation – not his way.

His brawlings, however, have seemed to me to lack the meanness of the real true Irishman; they reminded me of how a stage Irishman would behave. And indeed although O'Toole was born in Connemara, he was reared throughout his formative boyhood years in Leeds – *in England*! His Irish manhood has been created with a pugnaciousness that looks as if it's intended as robust compensation for his un-Irish childhood.

What's New, Pussycat? was a determined attack on popular box-office. It succeeded, much to the surprise of its players, who were never sure from one day to the next what that spectacularly undisciplined film was driving at. Tynan's compass reading for O'Toole's career was being well and truly ignored. The film confirmed O'Toole's stardom, but at the cost of reinforcing his matinée-idol reputation as a ladykiller.

O'Toole and his agent Jules Buck set up a production company whose name, Keep Films, may refer to his legitimate aim of retaining as much as possible of his asking price in the post-*Pussycat* years. But if much was given him, much was forfeited

199

too. He travelled with a court, and in some pomp. Being his own boss often meant making his own choices; too many were bad ones.

Only brevity could have made bearable the whimsy of Shaw's *Great Catherine*. O'Toole's production stretched out a curtain-raiser to feature-film length. I recall Jeanne Moreau, as the eponymous Empress of Russia, telling O'Toole's stiff-necked English officer, whom she tames with her tickling, "The world is lookin' on." One felt like answering, "Yes, Ma'am, and yawnin'."

With Katharine Hepburn to keep her eye on him in *A Lion in Winter*, he had at least to share power. "A silly cuckoo," she called him. There was affection in her voice, but also determination that *she* wasn't going to get pushed out of the nest. Acting with Hepburn improved him – not so much out of recognition as back into it again. He was restored to the contender class, where he'd once been matched with Burton. Playing the same king, Henry II, years after the *Becket* affair, O'Toole showed he had put on weight, dramatic as well as physical; he had certainly put on enough beard. But the fungus usefully masked that too-pleased-with-himself complexion that he can all too easily confuse with being charming.

I think O'Toole should be regularly cast against type. He should be given things to do that require discipline – tasks that are the equivalent, in the more lenient criminal courts, of being sentenced to doing community service. Sometimes the lesser films he's made yield unexpected pleasures for these very reasons.

The need to act his age (and then beyond it) took priority over the temptation to flaunt his bravura persona in a film that's been unjustly forgotten: *Goodbye, Mr Chips*, the musical remake in the 1970s of the Robert Donat film of the 1930s. From that first oddly touching moment in class with Chips wondering lyrically to himself (and in tune), "Where did my childhood go/Was it so long ago?" the words drying up on his tongue as if he'd chalk dust in his throat, he was convincingly inside the old-maidish figure of the emotionally undernourished pedagogue. Make-up, too, seems to have a therapeutic effect on O'Toole. It fits in with his first love, which is the stage, in a way that few modern "all-film" film stars ever grow to accept or learn to use to advantage.

Robert Redford, for instance, would be killed stone dead if ever he put on more than a moustache. But O'Toole seems to wake up to the possibilities which hair dye, greasepaint and spirit gum can offer his long horsey features. Physically and vocally, his Mr Chips was all of a piece: the premature hunch that sedentary scholarship has imposed on his rakish figure; the utterance that's so characteristic of an ultra-cautious bachelor when he answers Petula Clark's invitation of a night out, "Looking forward to it immensely", as if he were pensively dictating a telegram; the shyness of the classicist showing her around the ruins of Pompeii as if she were his pupil and not his wife-to-be – it all falls into place as precisely as a sentence in a Latin text.

O'Toole's Mr Chips ended up a credible stoic of 85. And that is saying more than it sounds, since Terence Rattigan's screenplay contrived to make Chips both a headmaster *and* a widower on the self-same afternoon, courtesy of an enemy flying-bomb.

It can be argued that *Murphy's War* contradicts everything I've said about O'Toole losing his boisterous *persona* in a role: for in this *Bhoy's Own* story, a sort of *African Queen* set in South America and World War Two, O'Toole played the "mad Irishman". Not one dirty Dublin trick did he miss. He was all mock gab, low guile, damn-the-consequences devilment. But then the tale had to be played at 100 per cent proof, or it was simply adulterated adventure. O'Toole mustered a black Guinness-y relish; he gave a performance with a head of foam on it. And Peter Yates, who had disciplined McQueen in his time, made sure O'Toole walked the line – steady.

It is more than likely that an anachronistic star of O'Toole's unruly temperament needed a film studio behind him – and around him. The support and protection, as well as the constraints, of the old Hollywood "studio system" were generally beneficial to fostering long careers. They allowed for failure, too. Left to himself, with middle age approaching (and sometimes old age potentially and painfully visible), O'Toole acquired the look of a bygone object – somewhat like the Errol Flynn-ish Great Star of yesterday whom he played with such masochistic exuberance in *My Greatest Year*. His health was erratic; his level-headedness ignored in the gossip about his hot-headedness; above all, with a few exceptions, his films were disappointing in box-office terms. All things that made film companies shy away from a bad risk.

201

Ill-conceived projects like *The Ruling Class* damaged him even more. He played a Holy Innocent recycled into the contemporary image of a Jesus Freak whose schizoid saintliness is presumed to be both didactic and endearing. O'Toole acted with the energy of a man who has you flat on your back, one knee on your windpipe, while declaiming his fun-loving gospel in your eardrum.

Keep Films made the picture. To its distributors' pleas to cut its running time by a sizeable number of minutes, O'Toole was unyielding. Predictably – by all but him – it died. Its length of 154 minutes was the measure of his patience, but few other people's. *Man of La Mancha* surpassed it in only one respect: making it brought even O'Toole to the point of exhaustion.

When he returned to work, after a year off and several muted attempts at a comeback on the stage (*Uncle Vanya, The Apple Cart*), he disastrously let himself be promoted from a supporting role in Otto Preminger's *Rosebud* to its star lead. Thus he unintentionally ensured that he, too, as well as its flashily opportunistic director, would perish in a risible melodrama about the Palestine Liberation Organisation kidnapping a quintet of naked heiresses for a group ransom. O'Toole perhaps realised his mistake too late; he sauntered phlegmatically through the mess like an absent-minded Professor Higgins detachedly looking for five Eliza Doolittles.

Meeting O'Toole can be an unnerving experience, chiefly because of his unpredictable physical moods and a tendency, common to many of his histrionic tribe, to turn every minute into a performance.

Rosebud was entered in competition at the Cannes Film Festival in 1975, where, needless to say, it withered immediately and unrevivably in the scathing criticism of a community of journalists, not a few of whom were only too happy to settle the score with the erstwhile arrogant Preminger – though many, many more of them were saddened to see O'Toole taking the lead in such offensive rubbish at the height of the terrorist strikes at civilian targets all over Europe.

I had an appointment to see him immediately after the film; I was advised to cancel it.

Being also of an Irish turn of mind, however, I didn't. I had already decided on a head-on approach. That way, I hoped I'd be able to see the horns being lowered, the nostrils flaring, the hoofs pawing the sand, and (I hoped) be able to take evasive action in time.

O'Toole was behind locked doors in a suite at the Hotel Majestic. He obviously didn't need a messenger to bring him news of how his film had been received at the Press screening.

By unspoken agreement, it was decided we would skirt this disaster area and pitch the conversation on the neutral ground of generalities – except that "conversation" is a misnomer. It implies a two-way affair. What O'Toole gave me was a monologue, variations on a theme that he deliberately misinterpreted and then proceeded to distort in the manner of a man doing an audition, not offering an apology, not remotely. It was a splendid piece of impromptu cheek, uninterrupted by any necessity except occasionally wetting his tongue – which he did from one of several dozen bottles of Guinness gracing his Majestic drawing-room.

Occasionally I interrupted him – but it wasn't strictly necessary or easy. Just as pregnant women are said to eat for two, a loquacious O'Toole talks for two.

"Stars", I began, "are said to be over-reaching, overpaid, lazy, insecure and vain. Now would you say that's a fair judgment of yourself, Mr O'Toole?"

O'Toole dipped his lantern jaw below the foam-line of a tankard of Guinness, then came up for air.

" 'Ambitious', d'yew call me? Is that the word? Well, all I can say is 'Guilty, yer Honour'. Nobody's ever goin' to get to work on me with a knife and fork. If I'm to be carved up in this business, it's I that'll do the slicin'. But I've still got my biggest ambition ahead of me. Shall I tell you what it is? Do you fancy Kate Hepburn as Juno and me as the Paycock? I had a little chunter with Kate about doin' the film a few years ago, then some English director put the frighteners on her. Hitchcock filmed it in the Thirties, I suppose you know, and one night down in Totnes, O'Casey ran the fillum for me and Barry Fitzgerald. Jesus, Mary and Joseph, it was terrible!

"One thing you must do with Juno is get an edge on her tongue – you should hear the bold Kate's Dublin accent. The minute you string shamrocks over it, the play dies. It's the best Irish play ever I'll have you know."

"Better than the *Playboy*?" I asked.

203

"Augh, the *Playboy*'s a high-steppin' view of the Irish written by a West Brit. What Brendan called 'an effin' Protestant on a horse'."

"Well, how about 'overpaid'? Are you overpaid for what you do?" I chose the moment when O'Toole replenished his glass, knowing he wouldn't want to displace the liquid by too violent a reaction.

" 'Do I earn my keep?' you're askin'. Sure, don't I call my company Keep Films? Let me tell you something. Have you ever heard the sayin' 'remoteness of profits due'? A beautiful phrase, isn't it? Now hasn't it a beautiful sound? My God, these accountants are poets, *poets*! Do you know, it was *years* before I saw any profits from *Becket*. I do a picture for money, to please others, so I can do one occasionally to please meself. I earned a good whack for *A Lion in Winter*, enough to keep me goin' for five or six years. But d'you know all they paid me for *Lawrence*? A hundred quid a week – buttons for me and Omar. Actually, we'd have paid David Lean two hundred quid a week just to do it for him, though nowadays I feel it maybe could have been done better. David's a bit remote; maybe that's the trouble. *Lawrence* was his baby, more even than Sam Spiegel's. *Sam Spiegel!!!*"

As he uttered the name, O'Toole went into a paroxysm of mock shudders. He wobbled his way to the Guinness packing case, neck bobbing back and forth like a camel clip-clopping over waves of desert sand, poured himself a fresh draught with a marginally shaking hand, washed the name "Spiegel" off his lips and then resumed.

"Now what was the other thing you asked?"

"Are you lazy?"

"Correct! Do I like workin' at me own speed? you mean.

"I tell you, I'm an author's boy. Give me the movin' finger to do the writin' and I'll not call it back nor cancel out a line of it. Maybe I should have done. Often. With *The Ruling Class*, that was half the trouble – we ended up with too much script. But all good stuff! For *What's New, Pussycat?* we'd no script at all when we started. Peter Sellers and your man went into it knowing we'd have to improvise. Scared me stiff. Peter was the saving of me. He'd remember what he'd seen Freddie Frinton do at the seaside when he was a trouper and we'd improvise on that and Clive Donner would run round to the Plaza-Athénée with a tape-recorder and catch us at it, in full spate, and we'd have it typed out and show up at the studio before lunch, if we were able, and find Woody Allen had maybe improved on it and we'd start shooting it after lunch, if we were able. *Dee*-lightful hours they keep in these civilised countries like France! In America, you'd have to lug your carcase out of bed at dawn to get to work. You'd think they'd never heard of electricity in Hollywood – afraid it would grow dark before you started.

"Now about that other libellous remark you repeated: 'Do I got out on a limb?' "

"Actually, it was 'Are you insecure?' " I said. But not the slightest bit of notice was being taken of me.

"Well, I wouldn't have done *The Ruling Class* if I didn't like takin' chances, would I? It was a great play. It was like playin' all the parts in *Volpone*. Now *there*'s a play an' a half! If I was runnin' a drama factory – which God forbid! – I'd say to the students, "Play *Volpone*." Then I'd order them to do *King Lear* next, just for a rest. I tell you, my role in *The Ruling Class* was the most vital one I've ever played. I love a part that's leapin' an' fecund.

"Don't let them tell you that that picture was O'Toole's 'Jesus trip'. Not true. Nothing fantasy about it. Just heightened realism. Realism is what I prefer – yew know, stubbin' out your Gauloise on someone's flank."

"Are you vain . . . self-absorbed . . . narcissistic?" I cried, desperately swimming against the tide.

"You mean, 'Can I stand the sight of meself?' Well it's nice to subscribe to the view of us big stars lookin' in mirrors all day long. I used to do that when I was 16 an' living at the YMCA. I'm not 16 anymore an' I can't abide mirrors by me. When I'm filmin' I don't even watch the rushes – except when I'm also the producer. An' I hardly ever go an' see a film I've made. If it's bad, mendin' it's impossible. If it's good, all you think is could you do the same thing over again, only better. I had to leave half way through the Royal *première* of *Rosebud* back in London, I was so sure I was ruinin' it. To tell you the truth, I haven't seen the whole of it even yet.

"Do you know the most fascinatin' sight I've ever been given of myself?

"It was in Mexico. I'd been nibblin' away at the peyote. The imp in the bottle, they call it. And there I was, walkin' back to the motel I was billeted in at the time. And I became aware I wasn't alone. I thought it was a dog following me. I looked down and here was this little two-foot high Peter O'Toole, perfectly formed, walkin' an' hopping alongside me, lookin' up at me, givin' me the eye. Every hair was there, every line on my own face, even down to the colour of my eyes – which, as you know, are me fortune. It was like seein' myself for the very first time. Jesus, it was frightenin'!''

O'Toole's voice trailed off . . . He took another noisy sup of his Guinness, while those blue eyes assumed the expression he'd used when the bizarre shapelessness of Omar Sharif, all a-glimmer in the desert heat, started riding endlessly towards him out of the mirage.

Then slowly, he returned to the Hotel Majestic in Cannes. He focused on me, an earthbound critic in an armchair, and saw I wasn't a nomadic warrior on horseback. He let himself down with a sigh and a gentle bump.

"Now tell me," he said, "what was that first question you asked me?"

RANDOM THOUGHTS ON THE ENGLISHNESS (OR OTHERWISE) OF ENGLISH FILM ACTORS

One of the besetting sins of British cinema is the way its leading men are discouraged from growing up. By that I don't mean *ageing*, but simply looking, even *sounding* mature individuals marked by the world. Our leading men have a generational temptation to stay more or less suspended in handsome adolescence until they're well into advanced middle age – veritable Peter Pans of their profession.

American film producers are constantly telling me that Britain possesses the most capacious reservoir of acting talent in the English-speaking world, compared to which, New York is but a puddle and Los Angeles a spittle.

For most purposes, that may be true; but any advantage it gives us certainly isn't evident on the international screen. It's not simply Hollywood's cultural imperialism that makes its home produce sell abroad better than ours. Hollywood in any decade has a more *useful* repertory company of minor and major league stars. Its players fit themselves into the prevailing screen genres of the time and show a willingness to alter their appearance, accent, allure and even physique in order to do so. The milk-fed "Brat Packers" soon learn they've got to graduate out of campus comedies, reject the crush of the pre-teen fans and become contenders, trained by their talent agencies, conditioned by their own ambitions, in an altogether more heavyweight contest for the macho roles where the big money and the awards lie. Not so in Britain. Our theatres and films, our telly serials and acting schools, simply don't inculcate the same hard lesson – succeed or perish. Our promising screen newcomers aren't forced to grow up – and grow up quickly – into stars of the kind who show the wear and tear of the world on their faces as once the Deans and the Brandos did on their features (and not just on their T-shirts) as muscular personalities creating a ripple of manhood around them and so lending an interest to even the most perfunctory performance and sometimes even supplying the moral centre of the film.

British "brats" don't breed with the procreative variety of Mickey Rourke, Matthew Modine, Charlie Sheen, Emilio Esteves, Matt Dillon, Michael J. Fox, Tom Cruise, Sean Penn – just to name a few who are young and current or at least youthful and voguish. Even the lightweights – defined by the ambience of comedy in which their talents thrive best – like Tom Hanks, Matthew Broderick and Andrew McCarthy – have the drip feed of the television sit-coms to re-vitalise them between movies. Artificial blood, maybe, pumped into them only so long as the ratings show they're worth the weekly resuscitation. But then the genre films such kids star in don't run on much else besides youthful energy. But given the chance – and for all the sins that can be held against its exploitive ways, Hollywood is always giving someone somewhere the chance – this kind of sugar can be converted into muscle.

Perhaps we in Britain fail to breed the sort of boys who will be men because ours is a society that doesn't put a rewarding premium on proving your manhood, preferably by virile suffering, by accepting pain as well as by doling it out, the way that Dustin and Clint and Al and Jon and Jack and Mel and Burt and Charles – Charles Bronson, that is – can (or could) all do, whether they were on two feet or behind the wheel or in the saddle or simply up the blind alley or in the mean street. So different, all of them, from the *personae* (and even the names) of our own British-bred stars like Terence and Rupert and Hugh and Jeremy and Malcolm and Timothy (the pre-shrunk Timothy, that is, before he cast off Shakespeare and tried on the Bond-wear for superstar size). All of them are sensitive actors, intelligent performers, handsome boys. But their physicality – no other word for it, I regret to say, but that Actors Studio neologism – is a mite on the light side. Their accents are insular. Their charm no longer tips the scales when what's needed is the social attitude that goes with the look of the hard man, the cool customer, the self-reliant loner or whatever conviction the man-in-charge uses to enforce his presence in Hollywood films.

Our acting schools are nurseries of dramatic art; but Hollywood requires and rewards – and how it rewards! – the sort of experience that in Britain is generally to be acquired only in reform schools.

It's still surprising how relatively few of the recent crop of American film stars have bothered overmuch with drama-class training. If they have, if they've gained credits for stage experience at the campus drama school, in repertory or summer stock, in off-Broadway or even in on-Broadway shows, they don't list it prominently in their CVs. Once in Los Angeles, anyhow, their apprenticeship has to be to television, a form of factory production that makes the needs of the market-place its prime-time corner. The new intake quickly learn to shape themselves and whatever aptitude they possess to the satisfaction of the camera and the limited requirements of the role. The main aim is to suit the saleable social fashion in sex, violence, cuteness, success or other aggrandisement. They work directly on trends and traumas; their British opposite numbers, schooled more widely but also more gently, will still be studiously at work on texts and techniques.

Whatever revolution the last generation but one of British playwrights achieved in the theatre from the mid-1950s onwards, they rarely furnished potential young actors with roles of the sort in which the first generation of Method actors in America were annealed during the masochistic sessions of self-scrutiny to which Lee Strasberg insisted his pupils submit at Actors Studio in New York. Richard Dreyfuss has frequently deplored the fact that the American experience deprived him and his generation of such British-style indoctrination in the Classics: Strasberg emphasised the Self at the expense of Shakespeare. His pupils were urged to dig up their feelings and lay them out on display, but were deprived of the instruction in textual analysis and vocal delivery provided by the whole repertory of English Classical play-texts for British actors seeking to be weaned into stardom.

The Method pupils worked their way through the roustabout studs, bruised siblings, sadistic father-figures, masochistic mothers and butch gigolos of Williams, Miller, O'Neill, Inge and Odets. On the other hand, Pinter, Orton, Stoppard and the Shaffers, to name the modern models of our acting academies, were and are playwrights whose theatrical senses feed on cerebral masquerades, party games and ludic wordplay. Even the

211

humanism of Wesker and the self-flagellant exhibitionism of Osborne, for all the emotions they permitted their interpreters to let rip with, were channelled into verbal declaration unrooted in the treacherous proving grounds on which the interpreters of Mamet or Shepard today test their physical aptitudes. You felt that British actors were being encouraged to cover the first intimation of violence with at least seven veils of ambiguity, which Stanley Kowalski would have shredded as brutishly as he did Blanche DuBois' genteel pretensions. English actors let their powers go to their heads; Americans, to put it vulgarly, to their balls.

Life, to be sure, has often taken a hand in differentiating one breed from the other.

I smile when I come across Ian Fleming's comment in a letter to a friend to whom he reported he had heard that at long last they had found an actor to play James Bond. "Saltzman thinks he has found an absolute corker," he wrote (as his biographer, John Pearson, recorded it). "A 30-year-old Shakespearean actor, ex-Naval boxing champion, etc., etc., and even, he says, intelligent."

Now Sean Connery is indeed intelligent. He may even have acted Shakespeare, though exactly when and where his several biographers have not told us. (Could Harry Saltzman, co-producer with his partner Cubby Broccoli of the first nine Bond films, have thrown in that bit of information as a sly aside, a sop for Fleming's notorious snobbery?) Whether he did so or not, the side of 007 that showed up to phenomenal world-wide advantage was not the "Shakespearean actor", but that represented by the "ex-Navy boxing champion". Probably just as crucial in determining Connery's appeal was the period of "etc., etc." in his early manhood. Fleming's languid abbreviation encompassed (if only he'd known it) such early trades of Connery's as bricklayer, life guard, print-room cleaner and even coffin polisher. He had also been a bodybuilder and a male model, in both the unclad state (for art classes) and in the apparell'd one (for menswear). The effect of all this experience wasn't limited to keeping trim, however desirable that is for a leading man; I am sure the gym classes at the Royal Academy of Dramatic Arts already do that for their students. Such rough trades left Connery marked by life like those American stars of the 1960s and 1970s who appear to have modelled themselves on that all-round jack-of-all-trades Jack London. Garage mechanic, life guard, hash slinger, ski teacher, lumberjack, bartender, dock labourer, carny barker, bookie's runner, even correctional facility recidivist – such are some of the freewheeling vocations filled by top-flight Hollywood stars in those decades, temporarily at least, before matriculating to acting. There's never been a tradition in Britain of letting life groom you for stardom in the same rough and ready, hit and miss fashion. There may no longer be one in America; if so, more's the pity. Acting classes there have boomed with aerobics ones, both of them spin-offs of the "culture of narcissism", the peer-pressure preoccupation with appearances and the social and economic compulsion to project a saleable image of success. More and more in life as well as what, in the market-place hype, passes for art in Hollywood, is processed into a cosmetic product that the newest generation of stars can apply to every bit of themselves – and come out of the changing-room with as up-front an image as any of the male models in the pages of *Esquire* or *GQ* with whom they are in fact interchangeable. (Older stars are now put out to grass in Ralph Lauren ads.)

Yet for all its shortcomings, for all its vulnerability to hucksters and hype-merchants, American society still promotes an instinctual self-awareness that the British social climate does not. It may be an overgroomed one; but it's impressive. And it is often sensationally effective. It bestows on the American male star his classless stature – at least as far as most of the rest of the non-American English-speaking world is concerned – and his assertiveness which proclaims that life today, as most of us suffer it, is an uncertain business in which bone and muscle count as much as looks and breeding. A film industry that would only throw up school bullies obviously has its dangers, but it is more commercially viable and intrinsically fascinating than a cinema of head prefects or monitors.

The two British screen actors who "crossed over" and became international film stars acceptable to Americans without having to make a single concession in their appearances or accents were the two who were least representative of the British school of well-bred acting. I refer to Sean Connery and Michael Caine.

Caine, like Connery, had been a tradesman before becoming

an actor. He and Connery both came from traditionally independent-minded – all right, *bloody-minded* – sectors of British working-class life: respectively the Scots-Irish clannishness of an Edinburgh tenement from which Thomas Connery (as Sean had been christened) escaped into the relative freedom of the Royal Navy's below-deck pecking-order; and the masonic togetherness of the Smithfield meat market and East End milk rounds which Maurice Mickelwhite (as Michael had been born) got to know before being called up for the Korean War. Both stars came to thank such experience for the chip-on-the-shoulder self-assertiveness that made instant sense to any American watching them display it in the right film.

In their early days, just hearing them speak was like hearing a voice from the other side of the class barricades. Connery's Scots-Irish burr flushed the public-school vowels (as well as the ethos) out of Bond's system; Caine's guileful lower-class Cockney said, in effect as well as in as many words in the movie *Alfie*, "I'm giving nothing away – except a good time." Both projected male-chauvinist images that were highly acceptable on both sides of the Atlantic at that era – the mid 1960s. Note, please, that this was well before the Women's Movement began to gear up for counter-attack. I have a feeling that Caine would have run into Liberation flak if he'd made his *Alfie* impact a few years later. Viewed today, the film presents its eponymous Casanova in a particularly piggish light that makes it hard to appreciate how acceptable it was in those days for a man to refer to a woman as "it".

My own early relationship with Connery and Caine was, oddly enough, put under a strain by references I made to the way each of them spoke on the screen. To my ear, Caine playing an officer and a gentleman in the film *Zulu*, which preceded *Alfie* by almost a couple of years, didn't sound like either. This remark hasn't haunted me, but it did haunt him for the first few years of his already imminent stardom. My own sharp Ulster ear, attuned by upbringing to pick out even a person's religion from the way he or she talked, at first heard only the "Irish" in Connery's debut as 007. He took this to be affront to the "Scots" blend in his Bond. It's hard to think the precision of an accent could ever matter so much in the American pantheon of stars which these two Brits soon joined.

214

The *personae* that their films created around them became attached to the physical persons of Caine and Connery – and it is out of such a perceived fusion that a star is born. In the case of each of them, it was a *persona* well outside the traditions of polite and well-bred middle-class British film stardom. It stuck to them – and it made them.

Each of them was set on becoming and *staying* a film star. As far as I know they didn't ever hanker to conquer the stage. And the screen has established them, fused its own illusion with theirs, magnified their individual uniqueness and serial uniformity and generally made them so much a part of the collective imagination of filmgoers that it is virtually impossible to imagine them playing in a theatre. Their reality is far more anchored in the image than the flesh. The fact that neither man in the flesh looks exactly film-star material has not diminished the spell they exercise wherever they go in the world; that is indeed a very American kind of stardom that only a few famous British players have ever shared. "I'll make so many films," Caine vowed, "that I'll be a star before they find out I can't act." And he did; though now he can act, too, and act superbly. Connery was a hyperstar as long as he had his 007 licence to kill; without it, even in more nourishing roles, he was simply a superstar. But he took a typically Scots attitude – "Scots" rather than "Irish" this time – and decided to use the Bond roles that put him mainly on display in order to subsidise his need to take roles in other films that stretched him as an actor. "Bond" was the poor boy's bursary to "better" parts. Significantly, though, the parts have all been screen ones, like Caine's. In that, the pair of them are unrepentant "outsiders" who don't fit in with the British acting tradition that embrace stage *and* screen – the tradition that may make a great actor, but rarely makes a film star.

For a brief but influential spell in 1958, it looked as if Laurence Harvey would be an international star as big as Michael Caine would become in the next decade. Nowadays *Room At The Top* is preserved by Simone Signoret's performance in it as "the other woman" – she is its only character who looks lived in and suffering. But it shouldn't be forgotten (though with the passage of time, it has been) that Harvey's attempt at playing Yorkshire lad-on-the-make with a sly and nasal provincial accent was a

215

vocal revelation to British audiences at a time when stars were expected to speak like gentlemen and, generally, could still manage to do so. Harvey's career up to then comprised no fewer than 23 undistinguished performances in as many now all but forgotten films, but with *Room At the Top* he found a story of a changeling's opportunism much like his own life and he inhabited it the way a pickpocket's hand goes after its victim's wallet. He made it his, and for a time it made him, although, it must be added, the shrewder hand of James Woolf, one half of the Romulus production company that made the film and had Harvey under contract, steered him into later roles and rewards on the strength of his single exceptional success in this one.

Born Larushka Skikne in Lithuania, Harvey anglicised his first name, then borrowed the "Harvey" from the fashionable Knightsbridge department store, Harvey Nichols, that represented the luxuries of the good life to the boy who had reached London (three months at RADA) by way of South Africa. He must have understood the cynicism of John Braine's success-at-any-cost hero, if not his terminal remorse, with a steely autobiographical pang that is nearer the experience of hungry American stars than British ones.

Harvey was a good actor, technically speaking; he would have been a better one if he had been able to come to terms with his vanity. But he always saw himself as a romantic lead; he was never prepared to settle for being a leading character actor. Audiences sensed this narcissism and rejected him, until the desperation of Joe Lampton to get to the top temporarily overlaid it and in any case fitted the cruel ending of the film, if not quite the crocodile tear that was all Harvey could manage to squeeze out as the car swept him and the boss's daughter he'd married up to t'top at the fade-out.

Then Harvey did a remarkable thing. Hardly was he free of *Room At the Top* than he turned himself into a stringy, cheap, pushy Pop promoter in the film of Wolf Mankowitz's Soho-set musical, *Expresso Bongo*. Paul Dehn, himself a clever composer of lyrics and sketches for West End revues as well as a film critic with a mannered but cutting edge to his columns, wrote that Harvey had "extended his range beyond our (and probably his own) wildest dreams. His agent is in a back-alley class of its own – predatory, with sentimental overtones – and it is greatly

Scofield as
Bartleby (with
John McEnery): a
marvel of fine
shading in a one-
note character.

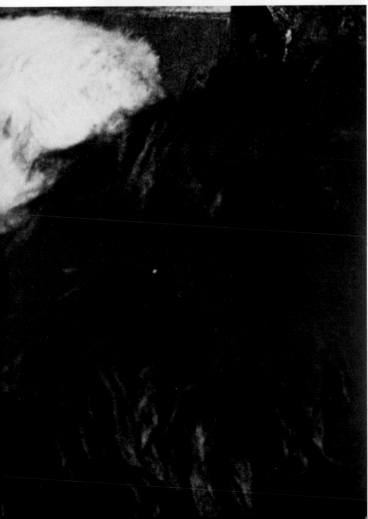

"His fur cloak sits
like a sack of coal
on his shoulders":
Paul Scofield's
King Lear in the
Peter Brook film
can stand toe-to-
toe with any of
Olivier's classical
roles.

Opposite Guinness as the scampish opportunist Denry Machin in *The Card*: one of his few out-and-out extroverts. **Above** Dancing a regimental reel in *Tunes of Glory*: the role-reversal as an up-from-the-ranks colonel was a skirl of triumph, too. **Left** One of Guinness's rare failures: Hitler was a devil who couldn't be humanized, though the technique was fascinating.

Above Dirk Bogarde (with Peggy Evans) as the spivvish young killer in *The Blue Lamp*: there was a "wide boy" before the "pin-up boy". **Below left** Enter *The Servant*: class malice gave Bogarde the chance to explore deeper kinks in human nature than earlier films provided. **Below right** The actor as author: David Tindle's painting of Bogarde in the spare setting of his Provencal farm, now part of memory and four books of autobiography (detail).

to the credit of Mr Mankowitz that Mr Harvey is able convincingly to interpret the part quite differently from Paul Scofield who played it (as convincingly) on the stage.

"Mr Scofield's agent was a cynical husk whom adversity had sucked dry of genuine idealism. Mr Harvey's is a man whom adversity recharges with false ideals." Dehn in those last words had taken uncommonly close measure of the nature of Harvey's own ambitions. "Every 'discovery' he makes," Dehn continued in the *News Chronicle*, "sets him electrically a-crackle with bogus generosity and synthetic enthusiasm." Exactly.

But his desire to exploit the chameleon talents he'd revealed he undoubtedly did possess wasn't able to resist his obsession with becoming an international film star. He left almost immediately for Hollywood to do some of the films that the astute James Woolf had lined up for him when he was "hot".

For the rest of his short life – he died of cancer at 45 – Harvey shuttled back and forth between Britain and America in parts large and small, but mostly indifferently played except for his Joe Lampton sequel *Life At the Top* and *The Manchurian Candidate* which required him to portray a "zombie" assassin. He succeeded socially where he failed professionally and became an adroit practitioner of the sort of opportunism that passes for resilience. It was a pity, for he had the "outline" of a star and desperately wanted to fill it in, but he had not been given the substance. At home really on neither side of the Atlantic, he always seemed to be applying for a passport to a favoured piece of territory called "Stardom" and to be always turned back at the border. Connery and Caine were sure of their nationality papers and found a propitious moment in Anglo-American cinema to start their travels between America and Britain. In Laurence Harvey one senses a displaced person who only occasionally found his role and restlessly spent time and talent in the pursuit of vanity. Unlike Connery and Caine, he didn't "travel" well; he simply commuted.

Trevor Howard was called the "old reliable" for so long in British films that it is hard to remember he was once the "young romantic" – and very much what Laurence Harvey aspired to become.

Had Howard been born a decade earlier – he was in fact born

in 1916 – it's possible he might have been as permanent a fixture in Hollywood's English colony as the cricket stumps that Niven, Colman, C. Aubrey Smith and the other Anglo Saxon expatriates had planted in the Bel Air earth and vowed to defend "for Lords and country" with the same patriotic certitude as the toasts they made in 1939 to "King and country". Howard in the late 1930s was handsome, angular, sensitive and English, like the less dreamy brother of his namesake Leslie (who was actually Hungarian by birth!), and his ability to bowl a line of dialogue against any star with the bat would have served him well in pre-war Hollywood and kept him among the studios' top-ranked leading men – a rank below Ronald Colman, perhaps, although *everyone* who was cut in that understated romantic style naturally deferred to Colman.

Had Howard been born slightly later than he was – between the two World Wars, say, instead of slap in the middle of the earlier one – he might have been a ready and able contender among the Tom Courtenays, Alan Bates, Albert Finneys and Tom Bells of the late 1950s theatre and early 1960s cinema. Howard could look as well soiled by proletarian life as any of these; and, as he showed when he moved from heroic roles to a bleaker sort of anti-hero, he proved he could do more than *look* soiled – he could actually go to seed. No one became a better exponent of the dissolution which is far more a spiritual malady than mere dissoluteness. He did Graham Greene signal service in that department. Marked by his own off-screen excesses – for in his time he was a womaniser and muted hellraiser – he could assimilate the burnt-out case far better than stars like Richard Burton who really were burnt out. "As Scobie," wrote *Time*'s then anonymous critic of his performance in *The Heart of the Matter*, in 1953, "[Howard] is pity in the flesh and, moreover, a spectator gets the sense that he is not one aspect of the hero in one scene, and another in another, but the whole man at every moment."

James Bond was waiting for Trevor Howard to play him had he been 20 years younger. The role of Alfie, he wouldn't have filled so well, for reasons that have to do with class as much as comedy. Yet he and Caine shared a link with their audiences that transcended their attractiveness to both men and women; each appealed to all the men who could remember the time they themselves, however reluctantly, had worn uniform. One of the surest ways into the affections or respect of cinema audiences is to play military men – and these two actors were uncommonly good at that. Howard had the parade ground on his tongue as well as in his upright carriage. Everyone who ever wore a uniform must have a memory of some officer or NCO like him. And in the same way, everyone who ever knew a "barrack-room lawyer" identifies with Michael Caine's revival of the spirit of "dumb insolence" whenever the higher ranks in and out of uniform have to be sardonically challenged and put in their place with a look, a word, a pause or, simply leaving the door open at the end of the interview.

Howard had always been more than a little feared by fellow actors and even by the stars of greater magnitude with whom he acted, for film is a funny thing, and it's almost as if the camera loves a bastard better than a hero. Howard was very good at playing bastards. Even film critics were sometimes wary of meeting him in the flesh. Not for any physical threat he represented, but because he was a notorious freebooter who didn't play by any rules and got a kick out of behaving unconventionally, even disgracefully. Good copy, yes – until turned against oneself.

I am occasionally haunted by memories of the two times I was was put on the spot by what I now suspect was his malicious impulsiveness. They're anecdotes that teach one the same lesson that his co-stars learned somewhere between the call of "Action" and the cry of "Cut". (I personally think Howard sometimes misheard "Cut" as "Out", and took it as his due that some sneaky trick of his in delivering his lines had had its intended effect in hitting the other player's unguarded wicket.)

The earlier incident occurred in 1970 when David Wickes, the TV producer, along with a camera team and myself (as writer-interviewer) in tow, were making a visitation to John Huston and David Lean, both then in the South-West of Ireland. Huston had received us in his Irish manor, the former abbey of St Cleran's, like the patriarch he was, not asking us to love him, but simply to admire him: a Great White Father trading beads of geniality with us respectful Redskins. Lean did not receive us at all. Correction: he did not receive *me*, though he patiently paraded everyone else in our party in front of his visionary's

gaze whenever he relaxed his contemplation of the seemingly endless schedule of making *Ryan's Daughter*, which was then entering
its second year. A phrase of mine in a review of *Dr Zhivago* had
been the fishbone that stuck in his gullet. Actually, it was a phrase
borrowed (with due acknowledgment) from John Grierson who
had originally used it about Von Sternberg – the one about directors who die turning into photographers. Lean declared himself
officially "dead" as far as I was concerned and refused to let me
interview him – an act for which I respected him, rather than the
contrary, particularly as I simply wrote out the questions I would
have asked him sitting off-camera, and my producer then put
them to him in my place, thus satisfying the honour of both sides.

Getting some of the *Ryan's Daughter* players to talk of their
experience of shooting the film over so many months in Ireland
was a harder business than we had reckoned on. I had a feeling that
their tempers had not been improved by the perfectionism Lean
imposed on them. Later on, seeing the film, I doubted if some of
their performances had, either. Howard was in a predictably ratty
mood. I don't think he guessed that his role as the village priest was
going to take the acting honours (though John Mills, as the village
idiot, a showier part, took the acting Oscar). About David Lean,
though, he was the soul of discretion and propriety. He declined to
say more than a few non-committal words. "Have you seen Bob
yet?" he growled. "He'll talk." No, I said, I hadn't approached
Robert Mitchum, who was playing the part of the village schoolteacher, a stoic of passionate parts. I'd heard Mitchum was, well,
not very approachable. "Bloody nonsense!" Howard roared like
a cannon firing at the Light Brigade. "He'd *love* to see you."

An instinct told me there was mischief in the making, but I
wasn't quite sure what. Howard forced me into a tiny car he had
rented and we drove at a chicken-killing pace along a rocky causeway to a flintstone house as ominously isolated as any Hollywood
mansion on a *film noir* set. Atlantic waves beat against its granite
pediment and threw spray against its windows. We braked sharply
and noisily in front of its solid door. Howard jumped out and
marched up to the entrance and began thumping the knocker up
and down. The door was opened by a huge figure in white trousers
with a white T-shirt bulging over his Popeye-like biceps. The
bodyguard.

"Bob's asleep, Trev," he said, looking down at us. "Well, wake him up," Howard bellowed. "Tell him I've a friend here who insists on meeting him." – "I don't think that's wise, Trev." Howard marched into the hallway and called up the stairs, "Bob! . . . Bob! . . . BOB!!!" There was a minute's silence as we stood there, Howard, the bodyguard and I, as if we were all waiting for a long-distance echo to come back to us.

Then with awesome deliberateness, folding a black kimono – or, more accurately, yukata bath-robe – around him, and looking like the Minotaur on day-release from the maze, Robert Mitchum heaved into sight at the top of the stairs. Silently, he marched straight downstairs. Silently, he marched straight across the hallway. Silently, he marched straight up to us – no, *not us*, straight up to *me*; out of the corner of my eye, I noticed Howard had drawn back. What Mitchum's intention was, I hardly had time to speculate. But his bodyguard clearly didn't need the time.

He knew him and jumped to a speedier conclusion than even Trevor Howard had. In fact he jumped physically in between Mitchum and myself, barring his boss's way with one forearm and sending me spinning out the front door with a swift thrust of the other while he kicked the door shut with his foot – all without missing a beat.

"Hmm, 'fraid we came at a bad time," Howard said as we drove back across the causeway that now seemed to me the bridge of life. I shot him a sideways look. Was there a shade of disappointment that the encounter he'd promoted to relieve a dull day in Dingle Bay had not taken place quite as planned? Maybe; but there was also innocence in that boozed old face. "Bob must have been at the bottle again," he said. I remembered that Howard belonged to the generation that poured its spare energy into the glass. But I somehow doubted if, on this occasion, Robert Mitchum had been up to that.

The other occasion when Howard's benevolence was exercised in my direction occurred at a particularly unexciting San Sebastian Film Festival. In the middle of a soporific Press conference that even he could not kick-start into life, he suddenly decided to play the Ancient Mariner. He singled me out of that phlegmatic crowd, and holding the rest of the critics with a glittering eye, expatiated not on the shortcomings I'd no doubt exhibited over the years whenever his career came under review but – *worse!* – on the shining virtues that he alleged I, above all other critics anywhere, had displayed ever since the name of Trevor Howard had featured in a film column. I was immediately damned by the justifiably contemptuous looks of fellow critics, one of whom asked Howard, "Are you speaking ironically?" – "No, no, no dear boy," Howard bellowed; and off he went again on his paean of hyperbole until I made myself scarce, banished by the blistering bonhomie of which he is a cruel master.

To several generations of filmgoers, of course, Howard had always been *the* romantic Englishman – his reputation as such sealed by one film as securely as any *object* placed in a time capsule for posterity, to be opened eventually and wondered at. That film is *Brief Encounter*.

To do him justice, Harward was reputed to groan at the mere mention of it – "as if I never made another bloody picture in my life!" he said to me. I have to sympathise.

Brief Encounter is still seen by millions as the quintessentially English love-story, which I suppose it is, if guilt, not passion, is taken to be its true concern; mutual misery, not romance its real texture; respectability, not sexual fulfilment its craven compromise. I squirm whenever I see even clips of it on television. The oddly forgotten fact is that the audience attending the film's sneak preview at a theatre in Rochester's dockland (Cineguild, its production company, was Rochester-based) greeted it in part with derisive laughter. It wasn't until West End critics saw the film at their Press show that it began accumulating its legendary properties as *the* middle-class English romance of all time. Film critics themselves in those days were middle-class to a man (saving the presence of Miss Powell, Miss Lejeune and Miss E. Arnot Robinson); and "romance", as Noël Coward conceived it for the one-act playlet on which the film script came to be based, was defined at a safe state of friendship, like the one between himself and Gertrude Lawrence, in which the ego of each was an additional contraceptive device.

Brief Encounter gave the English middle-class two of its most durable role-models in "Alec" and "Laura", or, rather, Trevor Howard and Celia Johnson, for few can name the "names" of the characters they played, (a question surely made for "Trivial Pursuit" and its quiz cards).

Even at the peak of sexual permissiveness in the 1970s, *Brief*

Encounter seemed to console middle-class people in Britain instead of convulsing them with mirth like that no doubt uncouth audience of working-class cynics who, according to Howard's biographer, Vivienne Knight, actually yelled, "Ain't he ever goin' to 'ave it orf wiv 'er?'' at the preview.

But then, of course, a society like that of the early 1970s that's guzzled its way to sexual satiety does tend to hanker after the exciting old emotions that the screen hasn't shown – has hardly dared *name* – in ages. Emotions like "shame" and "conscience" and "remorse" (very rare) and especially "the struggle to be sensible", as it used to be called. Nowadays, with rape all too commonplace an attraction and filmmakers blowing their minds to devise new ways and places in which to show it happening, entire generations have grown up without a chance to witness the exciting struggle of the flesh that people like Trevor Howard and Celia Johnson had to undergo in *Brief Encounter* in order to remain "sensible". Liberated folk from the mid-1960s to the late 1980s have hardly had a chance to empathise with a married woman on the screen who tells her lover, "Self-respect matters . . . and decency . . . I can't go on any longer"; or, for that matter, with the lover who, instead of immediately throwing his beloved flat on her back and screwing her, replies, "We can't do such violence to our hearts and minds".

Brief Encounter is the middle-class conscience wallowing in a tub of sinful bathsalts, but coming out to dry off (with eyes averted from the mirror, of course) and resume the respectable apparel of tailored skirt or buttoned-up suit.

Coming just as the war was ending, in 1945, the film offered absolution for folk of Laura's or Alec's age, in or out of uniform, who had "let their standards drop" and wanted to repent before peace compelled a return to respectability. Howard and Johnson played characters whose marriages were closed ones – no counsellor or therapist existed in 1945 to suggest to them a little affair on the side would be acceptable in order to keep their respective households steady. Laura got let out of her suburban home to change her library book on Thursday, the day Alec did his hospital clinic; she took the "down" train back, he the "up" one five minutes later. They were the Romeo and Juliet of Milford Junction, kept apart not by a family feud but a railway timetable. Clever Mr Coward knew that carnal knowledge doesn't have as long a shelf-life as middle-class guilt. So we got continual exchanges like, "Do you feel guilty?" . . . "Are you angry?" . . . "Am I boring you?" . . . "Will you forgive me?" Once you notice it, almost every line of dialogue in the film, whether spoken by "him" or by "her", sounds as if it is couched in tones of abject apology and uneasy puritanism. When Alec's friend who's lent him his flat returns to interrupt him (Alec has naturally delayed the moment of consummation by complaining about the damp firewood while Laura hasn't even got round to taking her hat off), he provokes the most priggish scene in perhaps the entire history of British cinema. The closest that Trevor Howard and Celia Johnson get to actual immodesty is the boating accident on the lake in a London park which compels him to strip off – his socks, anyhow, which are then dried out in the boatman's shed. The nearest Laura comes to visualising the delights of sinfulness, should she and Alec decide to elope together, is her daydream of both of them standing at the rail of a cruise liner or underneath Pacific palms. It's as if the road to infidelity led not to bed, but to Thomas Cook's.

It's worth recalling that there have been a couple of attempts to resuscitate the characters that Howard and Celia Johnson immortalised – a word I regret to have to use, but there it is.

The first comeback planned for them was bungled. It was a movie made for American television in 1974 in which the guilty lovers were played by Richard Burton and Sophia Loren. With an initial mistake as fatal as that – how could those two look guilty about anything? – no further errors were needed to compound the catastrophe.

Finding contemporary stars to play pre-permissive people is obviously troublesome. Meryl Streep and Robert De Niro were the couple cast together in Ulu Grosbard's film, *Falling in Love*, in 1984, still set in middle-class commuterland (American this time, Long Island sub-division) regulated by the goings and comings of the trains to and from New York. The stars of this updated and transplanted version of the plot toned themselves down so thoroughly in order to play Ordinary People that for many filmgoers they ceased to be stars. Their casting promised 100 watt bulbs, but the illumination they shed was nearer 20 watt. Their attempts at adultery apparently failed because they were so ordinary – just as Howard's and Celia Johnson's failed because they were so guilty. The penance this time round, however, was lighter. Whereas Howard had received the harsh moral sentence of being packed off to run a GP's practice in still dark Africa, De Niro was simply sent off to purge his sin by building skyscrapers in Houston. The women suffered more. Instead of being returned to an understanding and forgiving husband, as Celia Johnson had been, thereby allowing middle-class housewives of those days to enjoy the daydream of adultery but not be jerked awake by its penalties, Meryl Streep's punishment, 40 years later, was to miss the train bearing her lover away from her embrace to the architectural commissions of rich Texans. Other times, other timetables.

There has been no real successor to Celia Johnson. It is not simply the rarity value of actresses who can convey an exciting hint of an upper-class cold in the head while her presence puts one in mind of an illicit affair in the bed. The problem is finding English stars today who can play ladies or, rather, creating the role of an English lady for a star to fill. Solve that problem, and the screen will once again blush with decent English shame.

Amazingly, Trevor Howard made some 70 films between *Brief Encounter* and his death, aged 71, in 1988; yet that one film remains the measure of what was considered "the best" British cinema for the past three decades – it's still cited by British Council officers abroad in summing up the virtues of the homeland for foreigners. Howard's sensitivity gave its watermark to other and better performances, but none more popular. He could roar his way through a role if it called for it, like his Lord Cardigan in *The Charge of the Light Brigade*, somehow suggesting apoplexy as being the permanent condition of the aristocracy. And in a totally different (and otherwise negligible) French film, Henri Verneuil's *Les Amants du Tage*, one of Howard's cross-Channel ventures, he traded on his "Englishness" by playing a Scotland Yard man trailing two Continental lovers played by Daniel Gelin and Françoise Arnoul. It's not just a war of nerves he wages against them; it is a vile bombardment of "Franglais" accents and vowels, not muttered apologetically, but crowed out loud, with head thrown back, like an English mockery of Chanticleer, the Gallic cockerel.

But it was Howard's tenderness that sometimes struck a

225

braver note than many another British screen actor would dare emit. "There is no actor like him for suggesting the heartbreak behind the bleak, the unwavering look," Dilys Powell wrote about his performance in *Manuela*. He had a quality of repose which lets thought through and that's rare on any screen. Thought that's independent of action is generally an undesired distraction in a film – "physicality" is what plays at the box-office.

The only screen actor of the contemporary generation who has that kind of pensiveness is Jeremy Irons, and he has had to pay dearly for it. People simply don't know how very hard it is for actors simply to "react", to seem to do nothing, but just stand there, and still be interesting and involving.

Irons had the nerve to go the length in *Brideshead Revisited*, the resoluteness to play an essentially passive foil to the follies of the age – the age being inter-war England – until, as drink, drugs or homosexuality picked off the rest of the cast, he was left the melancholoy inheritor of what time preserves as well as erodes. Reticence such as Irons possesses is a very English quality and invaluable for films that have to encompass a long span of story in a short running-time. He brought the same advantage to the French film *Swann in Love*, in which Peter Brook's screenplay managed to convey, through his handling of one segment of time, Proust's search for all of it. Irons had to play a Frenchman, which was daring considering how touchy the French are at any attempt to expropriate their literary *gloire*. But it wasn't so foolhardy in historical terms, since the fashionable Frenchman of Proust's time had the English gentleman as his pattern-plate. Irons's performance was the smoothest of Channel crossings in the course of which his discrimination made romantic snobbery more absorbing to watch than unbridled passion. He fitted his English-tailored clothes with the ease of the born Anglophile – he put on the emotion with the garments. He cupped his monocle in place like a jeweller placing a gem in its setting. His elongated form – a physical determinant he shares with the two Howards, Leslie and Trevor – expressed its owner's social status as well as his sexual posture, whether he was stretching up and tinkling the chandelier lustres with his fingertips as his valet slipped a stiff evening shirt over his head or, in the love scences, winding himself like an eel around his mistress's body.

Unexpectedly, the same social antennae could also make Irons a plausible Pole when he appeared in Jerzy Skolimowsky's *Moonlighting*, playing the expatriate involuntarily left high and dry in London by the Solidarity uprising back home in Gdansk and undecided whether safeguarding his honour or his commercial profit as a "moonlighting" builder is the better response. Indecisiveness is the interface where Irons's Englishness is seen at its best. "Shall I . . . shan't I?" is the two-way stretch that brings him to pitch, like someone on an inquisitor's rack. He would have been better served in *The Mission* had he played a priest who lost his political faith and fell in with his spiritual superior's commands; instead, he played the opposite role and gave an impression of the will being stronger than the faith – a misjudgment. Irons has a streak of a Conrad hero in his professional make-up; he was born to play Lord Jim, and should do so, were anyone foolhardy enough to risk remaking the novel after Richard Brooks and Peter O'Toole had finished practising on it.

Terence Stamp's disappearance from the English-speaking screen in the latter part of the 1960s has been our loss as well as his. His withdrawal after a phenomenally acclaimed debut parallels Malcolm McDowell's. McDowell went West (to Hollywood); Stamp went East (to India). Both were lost to the mainstream British film industry in a way that Albert Finney might have been lost had he stayed up the Amazon, or in adjacent latitudes, after he had gone globetrotting following his tremendous successes in *Saturday Night and Sunday Morning* and *Tom Jones*. Finney was fortunately reclaimed for the stage (and the occasional ventures now into film roles). Stamp and McDowell, despite initial stage flirtations, got into bed with films and have stayed put there.

Both of them were male beauties made into sensational overnight stars: Stamp in *Billy Budd*, converting Melville's unactable symbol of goodness and simplicity into a flesh-and-blood character; McDowell in *If . . .*, making the most perfectly timed landing in world cinema, never mind British, as the rebel schoolboy with his regenerative rallying-call to the young and disaffected who were manning the barricades everywhere in 1968.

Both instant stars, they had glittering futures projected for them which their speedy follow-up roles seemed to confirm. Both had the best directors: Stamp acted under Wyler (*The Collector*), Losey (*Modesty Blaise*), and Schlesinger (*Far From the Madding Crowd*); McDowell also under Losey (*Figures in a Landscape*), Kubrick (*A Clockwork Orange*) and (again) Lindsay Anderson (*O Lucky Man!*). And then, in their separate ways and in a key phrase of the era, they "dropped out".

In Stamp's case, a disastrous Hollywood Western (*Blue*) didn't help his advancement, but could have been written off as the mistake that many a gifted boy makes when contracts are thrust at him. However, the hallucinogenic butt-end of the 1960s and the pull of Indian mysticism turned him into "Our Man in Nirvana", and the even more insidious attractions of the Franco-Italian movie world (*Histoires extraordinaires*, *Teorema*, *Amo non amo*) introduced him to an existence where social life and ciné-life reinforce each other's most enervating qualities.

McDowell nowadays makes only a rare return trip from Hollywood, most notably when summoned by his old mentor Lindsay Anderson in whose *Britannia Hospital* he once again personified the savagely mistreated innocent through whose misfortunes this sardonic Savonarola of a filmmaker chides British society. It is rather like a belated example of "Lend-Lease" to see McDowell in a British film nowadays. Grey-haired and much older looking than his age, he generally turns up in Hollywood productions playing such improbable figures as the literary agent Max Perkins in *Cripple Creek* or a high-tech villain in the urban cop-opera, *Blue Thunder*.

Stamp was as Cockney a lad as McDowell was a Yorkshire one, and in their early years, anyhow, the same hardness was detectable beneath their good looks and on the sharp tongue that each of them used to good effect in the Sunday supplement interviews. But although Stamp could play a young tearaway in *Term of Trial* as sneeringly real as any schoolyard vandal, he retained an other-worldliness which the interviews and the intermittent roles in the films of Fellini and Pasolini entrenched without deepening. Recently he showed up in a British film, *The Hit*, as a supergrass getting his comeuppance – a Euroversion of *The Killers*. Yet here, too, the mystique of the character's non-involvement, even when his own execution is imminent, suggested how attractive Stamp still finds it to use that passport of an other-worldly personality in his dealings with the here-and-now of earning a living. The character's doomed *chutzpah*, believing himself to be master of everyone else's fate when his own is about to be decided for him, suggested a Stamp who was retracing his own mystical philosophy. Some roles are palimpsests of their stars' own experience.

Recently, he has appeared in American films like *Legal Eagles* and, more unexpectedly, in *Wall Street* playing parts (an art dealer, a high-risk corporate raider) where "Englishness" is deemed to be an incisive adjunct to villainy in much the same way as it used to be to decadence when the depiction of Ancient Rome in Hollywood's Biblical epics called for British actors whose crisp articulation sowed the vowels and consonants of corruption in the marble halls of emperors, leaving it to the American stars to supply the homely honesty of a Stateside accent in the stables of Bethlehem or on the crosses of Calvary.

At least Terence Stamp has returned to us physically after all his trips abroad, though that needs qualifying. In his sparely furnished set of rooms in Albany – that Piccadilly Shangri-la he first glimpsed on a trip "up West" as a teenager and which he prospered enough to be able to buy a privileged and reclusive address in later on – he sits and turns himself into a sharper, metropolitan Dirk Bogarde (another memory-struck recluse), as he writes his projected three-volume autobiography. The first volume appeared in 1987 under the engaging title *Stamp Album*, detailing a hero-ridden boyhood in the East End with charm and acuteness. I shall be particularly interested when he gets to the 1960s and the patrons of his worldly success.

Michael York is another actor who personifies "Englishness" at home and abroad, though generally nowadays he is more abroad than at home.

Endowed with the same kind of clear-cut crystal good looks as Stamp and McDowell, but, unlike them, looking younger than his age, he is the happier survivor of the same lure of the "good life" that filmmaking can bring in its wake when it is pursued in those agreeable latitudes favoured by high society and low taxation. York has been able to sell himself most successfully to movies and mini-series assembled out of the well enough known if not actually world-famous names of a parcel of countries in a way that makes the whole more attractive than the parts. York lends considerable lustre to the cluster of names on which the money is raised. And thus his wanderlust and his realistic evaluation of where the work is to be found have conspired to furnish him with an enviable existence as a Euroactor, a *comédien sans frontières*, ideally adapted to both the Common Market and the Jet Set.

Like the useful bachelor at dinner parties, he always seems ready and willing to go wherever a script calls him. He works best as a dashing but not aggressive junior romantic, good manners supplementing good looks, public school in accent and custom-tailored in appearance – every bit a credit to us and an example of how an actor's aspirations can take care of an actor's life. One is quite as likely to run into him between films as actually in them, on the treadmill of the film festival (as guest or juror), at the gala ball or the charity dinner (Monte Carlo and AIDS), at the couturier's collection, the private view, the first night or the important sale in the right auction house. He has shown that at a certain age and for a certain range of parts, Englishness is always in demand.

York came out of the National Youth Theatre; and "national" and "youth" are his perennial attributes, predominant in some of his most popular and a few of his best films. He stood in for Christopher Isherwood – "Herr Issyvoo", of *Goodbye to Berlin* metamorphosed into *Cabaret* – far better than Laurence Harvey did in *I Am a Camera*, fresh-faced, vulnerable, puppyish and getting our sympathy because he doesn't play for it. He was a blond, blue-blooded student in the Losey-Pinter film of *Accident*, where he showed he had perfected the aristocratic manner of drinking – which is all or nothing and, if the former, ends face down in the dinner plate. In *Seven Days in Japan*, he was – God save us – a Prince Charles figure crossed with Lt. Pinkerton and, in his Naval whites, so sweet I am surprised they did not eat him.

But to my mind – possibly to his, for he is a realist – he has done nothing better than *England Made Me*, Peter Duffell's 1971 version of the Greene novel about the moral un-making of a young public schoolboy. Glib and plausible, callow and callous, deceitful and smooth enough to get away with anything, he assembled all the public-school vices into a memorable portrait

230

of a weakling. For all his romantic dash – which netted him D'Artagnan in two (admittedly English) films – York is a miniaturist when given the chance, pre-eminently self-revealing in small touches, in the character's basic cheapness, for instance, as he shuffles a tip for the telephone girl so as to leave much less than is expected; or his patronising acceptance of a job from Peter Finch's financier as if it was he who was conferring a favour, not being offered a living. York can look life in the face and lie to it with a smile in the film. In England, that is called charm.

Paul Scofield, unlike the peripatetic Michael York, has made his natural home on the national screen; unfortunately he's not often to be seen in residence. The respect he commands is enormous; he's believed to weigh the moral rectitude of playing any part he is offered by the film producers more than the salary. I don't know if this accounts for the paucity of roles he's played – in 30 years, hardly half-a-dozen screen appearances and some of them a puzzle, to say the least. What *did* he see in playing "Zharkov of the KGB" in *Scorpio*, a film directed by Michael Winner? (Are they related?) Certainly it was no fault of his that the producers of the film version of *Staircase* preferred Rex Harrison to re-create the haughtily comic "queen" that Scofield had played on stage. One would even have sacrificed Laurence Harvey's surprise package of spivvish energy in *Expresso Bongo*, already mentioned, just to have a record of Scofield in the role. Anyhow, he didn't do it – and "didn't" is the word that rings hollowly down the list of British films we might have hoped to see from him over the past three decades.

Physical mishap cruelly and painfully took him out of a film, *The Shooting Party*, after he'd intimated he *would* do it. A shooting brake overturned during the first day or two's filming and James Mason replaced him. Fortunate for Mason; it was his last role, that of a landed agent – the part all English actors of pedigree look born to play on or off screen – and he turned it into a cunning study, astutely populist yet inflexibly privileged, a sort of Harold Macmillan among the squirearchy, and a worthy requiem for Mason's own up-and-down-and-up-again career. Would Scofield have played it drier, more *bien pensant* than merely benevolent? We shall never know.

231

For gravitas and moral authority, Scofield is the man to count on. He must always have looked old in an inwardly weathered way even if he has now, with the passage of the years, been whittled down to the minimalist essence of a Giacometti sculpture. When Tynan called Peter O'Toole a *"debutant"*, he had already labelled Paul Scofield "our senior *jeune premier"*. The erratic pattern of the British cinema's stop-go production fortunes doesn't facilitate star-building in the Hollywood manner. In the latter case, mere exposure attracts attention and, by a law of averages that insists you must do something right sometime, may bring the fateful lift-off to stardom. Had Scofield sought or accepted more film roles than he has, the exposure of his moral grain might have gained him fame as the British Spencer Tracy – and if this sounds to some an *infra dig* compliment, then it's precisely the snobbish reflex of that kind that has deprived our cinema of talents like Scofield's.

"Where in Britain is the automatic choice for Lear?" Tynan asked in 1957, this being his current touchstone of great acting, defined as "acting with presence, assurance, power". Five years later Scofield was fit for the role in Peter Brook's production at Stratford-upon-Avon. But not until 1971, in the film of *King Lear*, for which Brook had to turn to Denmark to get co-financing, did Scofield do it on the screen. Arguably (we shall never know, of course) 20 years in waiting made his screen Lear the greater creation and, anyhow, it is the only evidence to match against stage memory. I certainly place it toe-to-toe with any of Olivier's classical roles and find it not half-an-inch less. Seizing on the Danish winter, with its mercury-toned sky and Edvard Munch-black seascapes, Brook lowered the ceiling on Shakespeare's play, forcing the characters to stoop beneath the weight of predestinate events. A castle's corridors resembled mineshafts, and when Lear is seen first, his fur cape sits like a sack of coal on his shoulders. Clothes swaddle his courtiers like winter chrysalids. Lear himself is a self-made figure, both Frankenstein and Frankenstein's monster; he achieves pathos through imprisonment in a body like a sarcophagus. The skin on his face looks like folds of leather, but when anger at his daughter's ingratitude inflates those cheeks, they crack with turbulent poetry. And Scofield's voice . . .! An old man's voice thin as threadbare linen at the start, it crackles with angry static as it explores the wild mindscape of his brainstorm before relapsing timidly, tenderly, into a brief sweet sanity and recognition of his own true child. "You will never see such another Lear," Tynan wrote of Scofield on stage; but it's the cinema that supplies the evidence to confirm the truth of that judgment.

I should have thought that simple self-interest would have impelled Scofield towards the permanence that the screen confers on acting as great as his, even if the opportunity to *be* as great is rarer on screen than on stage and vulnerable to all sorts of "intermediaries" in the way stage acting is not. He doesn't seem dependent on screen material to the extent lesser actors are. Watch him in that dry little one-joke British comedy *Bartleby*, based on Melville's story about "a man who isn't there" in any but the corporeal sense. Someone knowing nothing else about Scofield and seeing him for the first time would be overjoyed at the fine shading he gives to Bartleby's harassed boss, reacting to John McEnery's metaphysical self-extinction like a bemused member of the Samaritans counselling service for would-be suicides. Such a person would look forward to seeing this actor again, and quickly. Yet he would have had to wait and wait . . . and then feel let down by *Scorpio* – as Scofield himself may have been. "I've got the stamp of the classical actor," he said, after an earlier brief excursion into commercialism, "and I don't know whether the film people want that."

I've mentioned Spencer Tracy, who was the screen actor's actor in a way that Scofield is still the stage actor's, and I recall Stanley Kramer's comment that "[Tracy] thought and listened better than anyone in motion picture history." Scofield, too, makes you hear the thought – and that voice really makes you listen. Tracy had hankered to be a priest long before he became an actor and he used to admit that the role he felt most comfortable playing was one with a priest's collar round it. And if pressed, and in a reasonable mood (for, like Scofield, I suspect, he was a man who didn't like explaining) he'd add that a priest had a feeling about him of an "intermediary" – between God and man, I suppose he meant, as that's presumably what a priest's work is about. That is what the actor in Tracy did best – and the actor in Scofield, too. His words well up from an inner certainty that's beyond questioning and connect with us as if we're the only people on his moral horizon. Actors tell me they like playing scenes with Scofield – "He corrects my excesses," said one of them; "he helps me play down." Tracy was honoured in his trade for that, too.

But there is at least one great difference between them. Tracy came to represent the "Moral Majority", in the days before that phrase was a pejorative appelation. But Scofield's is a solo certitude not intended to gather votes so much as risk martyrdom, if necessary. He found Sir Thomas More in the Robert Bolt – Fred Zinnemann film, *A Man for All Seasons*, the perfect channel for that. I admire him in it, however, rather more than I like him. Part of this is my Protestant distancing from a thesis drama whose special pleading shelters behind the drama of a beheading. More of our traditional freedoms flow from a king who severed connections with Rome, even if it also involved severing Sir Thomas's head. But Scofield's playing is impressive, gifted with a suffering stubbornness, like a pine tree that many axes have tried to chop down. As he's "felled" by historical necessity, he exposes to view the many rings of worldly attachment – family, wealth, dignity and power – that it will hurt him to sacrifice in order to keep his soul intact. It's hard to pull off such a double trick – but Scofield manages it. When he ascends the beheading dais, it's with the sense of a man climbing the ladder to God and Salvation, yet simultaneously slipping down the snake of State necessity to his death.

Has Scofield been too scrupulous? Would I admire him even more had he been more yielding when film roles were offered him? Perhaps so; but by appearing so infrequently in movies, he's ensured that each appearance he does make has the aura of an almost moral event. I only wish there had been more "events". I've heard quite a few of our best directors say, at one time or another, "Send for Scofield." The pity is they should have had to send for a man who ought to have been at their door, clamouring.

International fame has come to Alec Guinness twice in a hardworking lifetime; on the second coming, it brought money with it. I wonder which he finds more comfortable to live with. Knowing him, I would think neither.

But of course we don't really know Guinness despite the 40 of his 75 years that he's been on the cinema screen. Even to put such a question to him would make me slightly uncomfortable and him intolerably so, though he wouldn't show it. He never betrays the distress that close encounters with the media cause him. He is too polite ever to cause a scene, though one notices that, under pressure, that drawl of his, that mellifluous elision of words into a linear equitone, grows deeper. The face remains bland as an aerial balloon, but the voice is his ballast and its tone is signalling that he's desperate for somewhere to land, to touch earth, just to take his bearings by himself, privately, after some importunate critic has huffed and puffed all round him and blown him off his premeditated course with mention of fame or money – such a question!

Sometimes he finds that quiet circumstances give him the upper hand in rude encounters, and then his glee is transcendent. I happened to be hurrying down Piccadilly one day in 1975 and this man with a small white semicircle of beard emerged from Hatchard's bookshop. I didn't recognise Guinness until I was a few steps past him. I whirled round, meaning to shout my excuses at his back – and found him standing there, smiling, meticulously measuring the time-lapse between the fuse of my belated recognition being lit and hearing my explosion of apology.

"Why the beard, Sir Alec?"

"Oh, for an American film I'm doing . . . a small part . . . a small beard."

The film was *Star Wars* and the part was that of the mystical Presence Obe Wan-Kenobi. At that time neither of us knew what riches Guinness was going to strike with it. Indeed no one did. I remembered I'd first heard the title about a year before at 20th Century-Fox's studios in Century City, Los Angeles. Jay Kanter, the new head of production, was reeling off to me a roster of movies that he hoped (for he was a modest man) would pull Fox to the top of the heap again. "*Alex and the Gypsy* . . . *The Duchess and the Dirtwater Fox* . . . *War Wizards*, that's Ralph Bakshi's new animated movie . . . *Star Wars*, which George Lucas has brought over from Universal. We'll have to do something about the title, of course. Can't have two movies on the slate with '*War*' in their titles."

Star Wars came out, unaltered, and proved to the rest of Hollywood that the box-office which had been thought finite for all

235

movies – and terminal for some – was actually as limitless as Outer Space.

Guinness's bit part in it – for that was all that Obe Wan-Kenobi amounted to, a role so stationary as almost to be a talking statue – made his name and fame known to millions and millions of young people and gave him a minor fortune into the bargain. Thanks to Lucas's generosity in sharing percentage points in the profits, Guinness probably gained a life-long annuity of more thousands of dollars than all of the fees he had earned in all of the films he had made. For a quiet man like Alec Guinness, that, as he would say, is much too much – like a jackpot spilling over your shoes when you've slipped in a shy quarter, just for form's sake.

For Guinness, the exercise of his art compels disguise. Kenneth Tynan, in an early extended essay on him, labelled Guinness – or, rather, lumbered him – with the description of "a man without a face". If Guinness were ever wanted on a murder charge, Tynan alleged, the varying descriptions of him given to the police would lead to multiple arrests. Amusing – but not quite true even at the time.

The Guinness face, looking younger than its 32-year-owner then was, first attracted attention when he appeared undisguised on the screen in David Lean's *Great Expectations* in 1946, playing Herbert Pocket, the archetypal "best friend". Typical of him to pick this "jolly good chum . . . two steps behind the hero" sort of role; or, if *he* didn't pick it – if instead, Lean picked it for him – at least he'd played it by his own choice in the stage adaptation he'd made of the same novel in 1939. Was the choice of a novel whose hero has his hidden and transfiguring parentage sprung on him also significant to a man who, as he has recently told us, has not yet solved the riddle of who his own father was? The only other film Guinness has made which owes its existence to his own literary adaptation is *The Horse's Mouth*. He played Gully Jimson, an artist as anarchic and embarrassingly public as his portrayer is private and reticent. The film is mentioned, once, in the index of his memoirs, *Blessings in Disguise*, but a scrupulous search of the page in question draws a blank in a book distinguished by its many tantalising blanks.

The young Guinness gave what may well be his sweetest performance – in the nicest sense – in *Great Expectations*. His Herbert

Pocket is such a transparently nice chap, you can practically feel
he's not wearing make-up. Guinness uses a trippingly metropolitan tongue to endow him with fluent decency as he keeps watch
and ward over his socially uncultivated young friend, Pip –
played by John Mills – rendering him the sort of service that a
pocket freshener renders the breath, making him wholesome in
civilised company.

Yet when Guinness next appeared in a film directed by David
Lean – "I owe him my film career," he was to write grandly, but
rather flatly – his verbal make-up had acquired the additional
weight and substance of physical disguise. His Fagin in *Oliver
Twist* is virtually the last full-blooded pejoratively Jewish villain
to be shown on the screen in a major production. Time hasn't
proved this disguise to be a blessing. When the New York Society
of Film Critics was honouring Guinness in 1987, their guest
requested them not to show any excerpt from this particular film
lest it caused offence to Jews. This reticent diplomacy was later
surpassed the same year at the dinner held in his honour at
Cannes by the British film community and attended by the
Prince and Princess of Wales. He then asked that *no* excerpts at
all from his films be shown. Yet, as Fagin, it must be said as
objectively as is possible for this Gentile critic that he holds the
balance well. Guinness doesn't turn him into either a loveable
Semitic rascal or a victim of anti-Semitic prejudice. A connoisseur of art (fine and popular), Guinness took his cue from
Cruickshank, the Dickens illustrator whose own taste ran to
caricature with a recognisable human outline. Guinness turned
Fagin into a "natural", an actor-*manqué*, whose tongue licks
the words he lisps the better to savour the flavour they leave
on it.

If the portrayal doesn't please Guinness very much now, I
think the reason isn't the allegations of ethnic offensiveness. I
think the reason is that it reveals, too obviously, the skills he
used to break into the role the way a cracksman breaks into a
safe. His fingerprints are all over it. He hasn't been able to wipe
them off after he's fished out the valuables within and laid them
out for our inspection.

Fagin, for all Guinness's virtuosity, is waxworks stuff. Animate waxworks, I grant you, but piling on too much excrescence
for a man who was to conclude that his own face was mask

enough. Morever, it incited a feeling at the time that Guinness might – just possibly *might* – be an impersonator. A brilliant one, admittedly, but a compliment that can too easily be used as a jibe. Olivier, as I've mentioned, has had it flung at him in his time, too. No, not *flung*, but placed delicately on one corner of his portrait frame like an art dealer's red dot that signifies "Sold" . . . passed into someone else's hands with no further possibility of alteration. Ideally, the essence of art should not be separable from the artist himself; we should still see *him* in the feelings he expresses than have him completely overwhelmed by a stranger's likeness.

In spite of himself, Guinness's skill at self-concealment became his biggest selling point in the cinema of the late 1940s. That he played eight parts in *Kind Hearts and Coronets* was due to simple logic rather than overweening ambition. The original idea had been to find eight players resembling each other closely enough to play all the members of the ducal d'Ascoyne family whom Dennis Price knocks off, one by one, on his unstoppable progress towards the title. When that notion had to be dropped, Guinness was offered his choice of playing any three of the d'Ascoynes. "If three, why not eight?" he replied in his quiet, reasonable way. It was an unassuming introduction to an assumption in the true sense and on the grandiose scale. It seems to me that the d'Ascoyne multiple-portrait gallery hasn't retained its prankish *élan* any too well over the years. Guinness hardly needed to bring several members of it to life; they were there simply to be put to death, disposed of before they could do more than strike a pose. The famous composite photograph of him in all the parts is striking not because one man could be so many different people, but because it makes him seem to be in so many different places at once.

It is easy, though, to tell which d'Ascoyne was Guinness's family favourite.

For a short time after leaving school, Guinness worked as copywriter in an advertising agency. He's always loved words – commercial as well as literary. The *Kind Hearts and Coronets* script is one of the most literate of its period; it's at its civilised best in the use of dialogue. And as Canon d'Ascoyne, the one member of the family in Holy Orders, Guinness rolled words around his tongue the way other men do their cellar wines.

Meeting Dennis Price togged out as a bishop – no less! – Guinness goes into his eulogy of the local ecclesiastical architecture and sounds for all the world like a connoisseur savouring the bouquet of a church.

Guinness and Ealing were good for each other. The intimate frame the studio put around his comic sensibility benefited it, though now it's fashionable to belittle its "Little England" appeal. But that, too, couldn't have been unwelcome to Guinness. In an earlier age he might have been a rival to Pepys or John Evelyn. He has the diarist's penchant for the small, the domestic, the parochial. Perhaps more Evelyn than Pepys, on second thought; he has no taste for the prurient. When he played Abel Drugger in *The Alchemist*, he was commended – by Tynan, of course – for possessing "the art of public solitude". True; but I saw that Ben Jonson production, too, and as I remember it, his was also the art of private observation. Guinness is a great looker-on; his memoirs testify to his powers of witness. I wonder if he keeps a pillow book and enters such occurrences as Edith Sitwell's luncheon at the Sesame and Imperial Pioneer Ladies' Club with its notable *dérangement* caused by the house fly that got behind the blind. A scene that sounds straight out of *Kind Hearts and Coronets*; indeed a scene that should have been in it, with Guinness in drag playing Dame Edith, surely a d'Ascoyne cousin once removed.

But Ealing didn't go in much for the Peerage and cast him in humbler, meeker, commoner roles, generally as an innocent, though seldom as an incompetent, a law-abiding chap whose fantasies are rolled up as inconspicuously as his brolly – until he opens them with a snap and begins robbing the Bank of England or inventing the un-wear-outable suit. They look quaint now, those comedies. At the time they summed up the sort of Englishness that exported well, along with other items that tourists visiting this country seized on with cries of approbation as quality goods to take home. Guinness's Englishness was important to such films. His "Denry Machin" in the film version of Arnold Bennett's *The Card*, about a scampish opportunist scrambling up the ladder of provincial success, is among his liveliest creations and one of the few out-and-out extroverts he played at this or any later period. But it wasn't tied into the Englishness that was Ealing and has tended to be unfairly forgotten.

239

Sir Michael Balcon, Ealing's head (and headmaster), was a man whose excitable loyalty to the studio he loved occasionally betrayed him into minor indiscretions. Once he told me how he used to grind his teeth in fretful impotence as he emptied the bag of New York critics' reviews of a new Ealing film onto his desk, because he knew in advance that, if Guinness were in the film, "they'd all call it 'an Alec Guinness movie!' It's *not!* It's an *Ealing* one!" Talking to Balcon about Guinness, one got the impression of a talent that, though vastly admired, wasn't ever quite part of the cricket team that Balcon was forever assembling and shuffling in his mind as he ran the studios. Guinness plays for England – all right; yet he seemed to Balcon to belong to a foreign club that was not forever Ealing. In fact Guinness was under contract to Rank who had simply granted Balcon loan-out privileges – since Rank distributed the Ealing productions. This meant that Balcon was always having to *persuade* Guinness that he was right for such-and-such a part. Guinness, said Balcon, never admitted to feeling comfortable in a role. It never struck Balcon that this might be like a hair shirt on a doubting priest – the constant fretting that the garment induced was all part of the pledge that had been made to God. Balcon told me he put it down to insecurity on Guinness's part, but I'd put it down to unworthiness in the purest sense. Guinness is a worrier, an interior one. He finds it easier to speak to God than to an earthly critic. Unlike Olivier, he doesn't invite (much less enjoy) making his pain manifest. His extreme outward serenity is simply the curtain that's drawn before he steps into the confessional with the priest cocking an attentive ear at the grille but otherwise keeping out of sight.

As Guinness's fame has expanded, the publicity has made it harder and harder for him to keep himself to himself. "I am never quite sure he wanted to be [an international star]," Balcon wrote in his memoirs. Well I, for one, am quite sure he didn't – not then anyhow.

Guinness's life ambition was to be found on the stage – a *safer* place than the screen. However, the Ealing films were safe, too, in another sense. They were low on romantic appeal and altogether devoid of sex appeal. This is one of their most English features – and that suited Guinness. A *sexy* Guinness was all but unimaginable then; indeed his single shot at girl-chasing in an

Ealing film – in *The Captain's Paradise* where his skipper kept a wife in one port and a mistress in another – was his one Ealing flop. Looked at today, the film seems as if it would have been far more suited to the talents of Peter Sellers, who *could* be sexy and who – God knows! – wanted to be thought sexy.

Guinness and Sellers appeared together in one film only – *The Ladykillers* – where Sellers was one of the gang of grotesques assembled by Guinness in the disguise of a string quintet so as to deceive the little old lady under whose unsuspecting benevolence they are plotting a payroll robbery. This time Guinness had splurged on the make-up box like a man who has broken his diet and gorged himself on fudge. He'd acquired a cadaverous look, red-rimmed eyes, Calagari-like hair and rodent teeth out of *Nosferatu*, as well as a creepy voice which may have evolved out of the constraints imposed on his tongue by the horrific dentures he was wearing. Sellers would quite soon be hailed as "the next Alec Guinness" on account of *his* skill in assuming visual and vocal camouflage; but this time his own make-up was meagre and when I later asked him how he'd felt acting with Guinness, he said without a second's pause, "Emerald with jealousy". I should think such *grotesquerie* had already lost its charm for Guinness. The film, anyhow, rates only a single mention in his memoirs in which it is misspelled in the text and mis-titled in the index.

Guinness had had a wonderful schooling at Ealing. It had made his face – or his faces – known worldwide without his having to show it – or them – outside England. It had allowed him to play all the variations between the gentlemanly and the ghoulish. But there really wasn't much room left for roving wider – for where his fancy might take him, might not be where Balcon wanted to follow. It was time to leave school and matriculate to higher studies.

The animus of a comic actor seems invariably to turn him against comedy in his search for his common humanity. Again a comparison of Guinness with Sellers is inescapable. Once Sellers had tasted international success on a scale whose flamboyance would have revolted Guinness, he too would be smitten by the need to exchange his "fun face" for a "no face". The irony was repeated in their respective careers. Sellers began with what Guinness washed his hands of – or, rather, washed off his

241

face – namely comic make-up. And he ended his career playing exactly the sort of role in *Being There* that Guinness coveted – that of a man who "wasn't there" in the sense that people saw in him only what they wanted to see. Sellers in a sense was Guinness's worldlier brother, enjoying the good things of life that his more austere sibling put behind him for the higher rewards of the spirit. I never look at *The Ladykillers* but I feel a pang of sadness shoot through me as I watch two consummate clowns pass by each other in their scenes and go their separate ways. Sellers used to make a point of saying in interview after interview that he had so many *personae* he didn't know who he really was – Hmmm. The point probably wasn't lost on Guinness who, as I've mentioned, really didn't know who he was, or at least, who his father had been. That shared irony apart, their two styles of comedy, though superficially alike because of similar kinds of movies each appeared in, were actually distinct and different. It's doubtful if Guinness had a mind to improvise those surreal comic riffs that Sellers' unbridled brilliance created; while Sellers could never have orchestrated those middle tones of normality that Guinness composed into such a human symphony. Sellers had an urge towards chaos: Guinness, towards calm. Sellers had the attention span of a cockroach: Guinness, the meditation span of sainthood. All through his sadly truncated life, Sellers kept an envious eye on Guinness. Whenever Guinness had a new film out in Britain and Sellers was abroad, in Rome or Paris or Zurich, I'd get a late-night phone call and it would be Sellers leading the conversation round to asking me how Guinness's movie was – how it *really* was.

It's amusing to speculate how Sellers would have played some of the great Guinness roles. I can see him as Gully Jimson all right, for both actors found pathos in the comedy of a man whose unruly art – like Sellers's if not like Guinness's – goes on upsetting his life. With his reservoir of anarchy spilling out of the Goon Show, Sellers might have made a marginally more comic, manic and sordid figure of the painter as an anti-bourgeois flail than Guinness managed – though Guinness's satisfaction might not have come from his performance at all, but from the Oscar nomination his own screenplay earned him.

But what would Sellers have done with "Col. Nicholson" of

the River Kwai? Years later, Sellers would still lament his own
fame hadn't come early enough for him to be a contender in the
casting. He never ceased to "float" the military commander
Orde Wingate as the part he yearned to play. But he continually
envied the fictional licence Guinness's "mad" colonel enjoyed
in his delusional, unrealistic way of looking at things, which of
course was especially attractive to film stars like Sellers.

It was a measure of the distance Guinness put between himself
and Ealing that he could now play a man of Nicholson's
swagger-stick authority whose madness derives from his mis-
placed military virtues. It's no secret that David Lean had
wanted Noël Coward and, failing him, Charles Laughton to play
the part. One can see the flyness in casting Coward as yet
another Mountbatten-ish hero, such as he had played in *In
Which We Serve,* and then adding to his stiff upper lip a tragi-
comic degree of moral myopia. Laughton, too, would have been
good casting for the military masochist. Coward later regretted
not having done the film; Laughton, in poor health, didn't want
to take on Lean *and* South-East Asia.

Guinness offered initial resistance – How do you humanise a
martinet? he reportedly asked. Then he found the answer as
soon as he began. One wonders if his director's notorious
inflexibility infected Guinness with the vital contagious fanat-
icism; if so, that wasn't all he got from Lean. The star had
proved his worth as a comic precision tool in the "little pictures"
Ealing made. *Kwai* didn't compel him to enlarge his effects; it
simply enlarged the setting in which he displayed them – and
made him and it, epic.

Guinness actually underplays the man's mania, considering its
enormity in terms of vainglory and the aid and comfort he is
rendering the Japanese enemy in building the bridge as a monu-
ment to his own career. Guinness brought an English insight to
the part, perceiving Nicholson not just as a prisoner of war, but
as a prisoner of his rank, of his class, of that strait-jacket of
"officer and gentleman" which became Guinness like a bespoke
suit. His fantasy of building a bridge worthy of himself and his
class, even if it *is* going to help the Japanese invade India, is an
eccentricity of the same kind, if not on the same scale, as Ealing
had accustomed him to and he played it in the same key: funny
and yet terrifying, because so seemingly sane and correct.

243

In his monograph on Guinness, published five years before *Kwai*, Tynan accurately divined his gift for playing characters who are "nine-tenths concealed . . . whose fascination lies in not how they look, but how their minds work". Guinness can indeed suggest innerness; his stillness of manner is the kind that compels one to keep an ear cocked for the answering sound a conversational pebble makes if dropped into the scene he is playing. It's a feature that has become truer and truer of him. His Father Brown, in 1963, is an illuminated book; his George Smiley, in *Tinker, Tailor, Soldier, Spy* in 1979, almost a closed one.

This bland spymaster based on Sir Maurice Oldfield, a sometime head of MI6, gave Guinness's career its third wind. *Kwai* had made him an international film star; Smiley now made him an international TV star.

Though I admire the subtlety with which he trims Smiley's inner wick, illuminating him at times with that dim religious light which is most sympathetic to Guinness himself, I do miss the body language of his earlier roles. It is like watching the progressive disappearance from our ken of an *unsmiling* Cheshire cat – there's not even a grin left at the end.

Perversely, I admire Guinness for some of his inexplicable failures – inexplicable only in the sense that he should never have taken the role in the first place. For example, his Adolf Hitler. If it made him uneasy to humanise a martinet at the time of *Kwai*, then what did humanising the antichrist do to him at the time of *Hitler: The Last Ten Days*? The film was an oddity to begin with. Based on the final days spent by the Führer holed up in the Berlin bunker, it was written and directed by an Italian and shot in Britain, where it was banned by a Jewish cinema tycoon to whom the mere suggestion of a *human* Hitler was obnoxious.

Guinness apparently adopted the same trick playing the Führer as he'd done with Gully Jimson, not coarsening his voice so much as "hoarsening" it. He also used those pale Guinness eyes the way he had when playing the fanatical Ross in Rattigan's story of Lawrence of Arabia, another mystic with a *führerprinzip*. But even Guinness couldn't humanise Hitler; some foreign devils simply don't translate into English. One is left with only the technique to admire: something of a rarity in a "late" Guinness performance. He deepens his voice. He peaks his rages into hysterical explosions, as if he were placing each one like a bomb under his generals in revenge for the bomb one of them placed under him, and flattening them against the bunker walls. The smug satisfaction is present, too; the voice is all the time speaking "for the record" – his secretary's pencil is forever poised over the notebook, recording Her Master's Voice. Guinness strips the man to show his psychic scars. Years afterwards, I still treasure the early shifty look he throws under the map table where a subordinate has set down an attache case that recalls the primed one. His shuffling walk; his hunched, sedentary, constipated posture; the right arm stealing round to clamp the trembling left one firm; the preening *bons mots* over the cream tea as the Russian cannons rumble 50 feet above . . . I should not be surprised if Guinness were asked (no doubt to his apprehension) where he found his "inspiration" and replied, "The Mad Hatter's tea party". No matter that the accents of RADA occasionally infiltrate the inflections of the Reich – it is a remarkable interpretation. But one still asks why he did it.

Maybe the answer is, the Führer *interested* him. Even a Hitler must be brought to judgment and the High Catholic Guinness may have felt the temptation to inhabit the body so as to glimpse the soul that all men have, even the Führer.

There are times when even Guinness falls onto automatic pilot, when the tedium of a part persists in seeping through his voice in too mannered, too measured a tempo. Olivier in similar circumstances will fight back and even camp up the part, like a guest whose obligation to be on his best behaviour has been cancelled out by the boredom of the party. Guinness, though, remains the perfect gentleman, trying to rise above it. Sometimes one would prefer him to give way and have fun at his host's expense. He was once visited by an importunate newspaper reporter just as he was about to leave his home for Mass. "I welcomed him with a certain amount of dismay, I suspect," he admitted. That, I suspect, is how he reconciles himself to a role that's turning out a dud. After he's played it, when the film has been made and viewed by him "with a certain amount of dismay", it's a slightly different story. *Then* he can often kill with a compliment – which, in his visitors' book, is another kind of negative welcome. "Meticulous" is a word that slips acidly off his tongue after some frustrating experience with a film director.

245

What nearly always pulls him through the drudgery, though, is the perfect pitch his ear has retained for scenes that have no other merit save the way he reads them. The Guinness voice is a blade, so well tempered as not to be felt until its deadly work is done and he has slipped it under the guard of more imperious players in the scene with him. In *Our Man in Havana*, for instance. By all the rules, the scene where Noël Coward is recruiting him in the gentlemen's lavatory ought to have belonged to Coward. It turned into Guinness's simply by virtue of his modesty, his aptitude for making the "Little Man" an irritant to his overweening recruiting officer. He held his pitch – he triumphed in a minor key over Coward's trumpetings.

Yet in his very next film, *Tunes of Glory*, it was a major note he sounded, a skirl of triumph as an up-from-the-ranks colonel of a Scottish regiment who swears hard, drinks harder and is the darlin' of his men. He actually switched roles with John Mills who was set to play the "ranker", but settled for his opposite number from Sandhurst. Some actors, by no means the unserious ones, seek such role-reversals rather as other actors, all too often the un-serious ones, accept films in foreign latitudes because the work gets them a free passage to some attractive location. But Guinness was no "tourist" playing this Glaswegian "Jock". His vulgar "pitch" was the inner essence of the man just as his drunken roll was his outer symptom, each perfectly judged and sustained. It was a performance with an admission of breakdown always trembling on Guinness's lips. And when the man's collapse came, at the rehearsal for his rival's burial, he, typically, doesn't put it into words but, instead, lets his wandering mind weirdly stiffen his pacing gait into the tempo of the funeral march.

That mental breakdown is indeed a forte with him was most recently confirmed in *Little Dorrit*. He plays the heroine's father, the shiftless gentleman sponger who's lived half his life in the hive of the Marshalsea prison, like a King Drone off the labours of his children, until a sudden accession to wealth brings society flocking to his banquet table for his elder daughter's sumptuous wedding. It is an astonishing scene, one of the few in any film to make a viewer uneasy, feeling that the director has forgotten to cry "Cut" and Guinness is holding his wordless posture at the table like a man holding his breath below the surface in a water tank. Pride may come before a fall; in this case, dementia does – and Guinness makes its silent onset queasily observable. When he finally rises to his feet and the old lag in him bids the throng of titled grandees "Welcome to the Marshalsea", we have seen madness settle.

I am sorry if, with all these antecedents, Guinness's much praised assumption of that most English of crypto-characters, George Smiley, fails to impress me. It has the feel of a pension about it, not an incentive. With the layers that age allows to build up on one's face, a heaviness has been pulled over that inner life of Guinness like a thick felt curtain. His illumination no longer shines through. I really and truly don't think there's enough to the part, as written, to interest him. He still ticks, all right – but now he reminds me of a dignified grandfather clock mounted on castors. "The clock struck one/The mouse ran down . . ." or, in this case, the mole.

Guinness would always be happier in Graham Greene's church than le Carré's congregation; there is more there to hold him in awe and apprehension. A spy hunt hasn't the same intensity as a spiritual journey; exposure has not the same finiteness as salvation.

For Alec Guinness is a very spiritual man. Unlike a Scofield, though, he doesn't withdraw from the world. He waits in the wings, patiently, between performances. But he doesn't let time pass him by; he simply counts it out with that regularity that the monastic orders bestowed on the lay world when they established the clock to measure the working and worshipping day.

He is a "star" who would prefer to be simply a "name". His bias is towards humility and he belongs in a world which cruelly takes advantage of what it interprets as submissiveness. He has taken the measure of the movies and decided it will be a case of "the films in my life", rather than "my life in films". His Englishness in this respect is total; he seldom fails to give full measure – you feel he asks forgiveness if he falls below what we demand.

Though he has the comforts of his family, his religion, his love of literature and music, one feels Guinness is happiest strolling in the private wing of his interior world. We visitors can only tour the estate from the outside, sticking our heads through the railings or our noses against the window panes, and should he see us he will probably be careful to wave politely to us like a noble Lord acknowledging the curious encroachers who nevertheless make the upkeep of his stately home possible. Don't disturb him further; let us tiptoe on to Mr Bogarde's place.

Dirk Bogarde is not a man who lets one get to know him – "You haven't cracked me yet," he once snapped at Russell Harty in a television interview. He has had a lot to put up with, certainly. Popularity, for one thing, *vulgar popularity*. I can well understand the self-control he needed – fortunately he is magnificent at that – when ordinary folk recognised "Dr Simon Sparrow". Admittedly he was 33 when he first played the ingenuous young intern of St Swithin's in the Rank Organisation's 1954 film, *Doctor in the House*, which developed into the studio's most popular series. A doctor, it's said, is what every mother wants her boy to be – or her daughter to marry. A great many mothers and daughters must have fallen in love with Bogarde in that film and the three other *Doctor* comedies. And why not indeed? He was sensitive yet manly looking, with spaniel eyes and one eyebrow that could be cranked up a notch to convey sardonic feelings, and that slightly lopsided smile that saved – *just* saved – the face from looking too blandly masculine. A less intelligent man would have been happy with his local fame. Bogarde was not. A working lifetime as the screen's eternally eligible MD palled before his desire for better parts, better directors, better pictures – what, in fact, most actors think they deserve. The difference is, this actor got them. The way he got them confirms how talent will out and – dare I say it? – breeding, too.

Bogarde went into the theatre at the end of the war, in which he had served as an officer and then done "military policeman" duty in the Far East. He was an overnight success in a West End play, *Power Without Glory*, whereupon Noël Coward advised him, "Never go into the cinema . . . and never compromise." Both of the Master's commandments were broken almost at once. He quit the stage and signed a movie contract – and for at least half his career increasingly resented the compromises that the commercial cinema forced him to make.

Many people who recall those years in the late 1940s think of Bogarde as the Rank Organisation's pin-up boy. That just shows how people forget. His beginnings were rather more interesting and ambivalent. He made his first mark – though not his first film – playing a working-class delinquent in *The Blue Lamp* who callously gunned down the actor who later became the most celebrated and best loved fictional bobby in the British police force – P.C. Jack Warner, also known (indeed better known) as Dixon of Dock Green. A "punk", as the sort of post-war "spiv" Bogarde played would be called today, was hardly the kind of role that middle-class filmgoers warmed to at that period, when the police were still regarded as protectors of their values and, more important, their property. This young tearaway didn't even look as if he belonged to the *decent* criminals, the bad 'uns of the old brigade, who of course never shot policemen. Bogarde's anti-social act was all the more disturbing because he conferred on his criminal a sleazy glamour – sexy, too, using a gun as if it were a phallic object to fascinate and terrify his girlfriend. That was a very novel use to which to put a weapon in the polite annals of the British crime picture.

I sometimes ask myself where Bogarde's career would have taken him had he been able to exploit that early vein of erotic cruelty in, say, the French style that Delon or Belmondo did at a later date on a different screen. But the British filmmaking establishment shied away from the glamour of violence. They were in the main middle-class men catering to the tastes and prejudices of their class. They quickly raised Jack Warner from the dead to play the benign copper on radio and TV for the rest of his natural life – and just as quickly they shut down Bogarde's enterprising eroticism. When next he played outlaws, in films like *Hunted* and *The Gentle Gunman*, they were lawless all right, but also safely sexless. He was effectively neutered, left with his charm intact but nothing more dangerous.

Even the publicity build-up Rank gave him in those days was totally sexless. He was forever being pictured as a country-life lover, half film star and half landed gent. There he was in his Buckinghamshire mansion; in jodhpurs; in the saddle; frolicking on the lawn with his mastiff; looking hospitably out of his mullioned study windows; propping up his Bentley – the master in his domain. Fan magazines emphasised the comfortable bachelorhood of it all. Soft furnishings provided the ambience of stardom, rather than companionable females. "The guest bedroom he has designed in pink, cream and grey," said one magazine writer. "For his study, he chose man-sized armchairs."

It wasn't, of course, the whole truth, but the four volumes of memoirs that Bogarde has published in recent years indicate that there was a lot of the truth in it. Even then he was using the earth to shelter him. It is an image that has created a lot of his popularity. For the English nourish what remains of their own rural fantasies – even though it is about as little as remains of their own rural England – with well edited *Country Life* reports from people who have actually found their niche or their nest. Actors are peculiarly prone by temperament and opportunity to turn into landed gents. The Old English theatre has a strong tradition of country-house settings which may well have inclined the generation of actors who played the parts behind the footlights to live them out in real life behind the manor gates, climbing into their country tweeds once the make-up was off or popping off in the old Bentley down to the little shop they keep supplied with market produce, thereby turning fantasy into life-style and doing so very comfortably, thank you.

Bogarde's embrace of the grass-roots, however, has a more mordant quality. There's an ominous image in the first volume of his memoirs, *A Postillion Struck by Lightning*. I sometimes wonder if we were meant to take it as a metaphor for the life that the book and its companion volumes relate. On reflection, I don't think so; I don't think the author was even aware of it until his reviewers made him so. A pet tortoise has been lost by young Dirk and his little sister. Eventually, at the end of summer, it turns up again trapped inside a hole in the meadow – or, at least, its shell turns up. That's all that remains of it after the intrusive ants have eaten out the soft meat of the unprotected belly. I'd guess that it was this sort of lesson, learned early, that Bogarde never allowed himself to forget. Don't stick your head out of your carapace or expose yourself in such a way that the inquisitive world can devour you.

An episode that was more sinister followed this one in Bogarde's early life. Once again it was an example of captivity's unsettling consequences. As an adolescent in Glasgow, he had the innocent misfortune to be picked up in a fleapit cinema by a man who claimed to know "exactly how mummies were bandaged". Bogarde allowed himself to be taken back to this individual's lodgings where the arcane skill of the Ancient Egyptians was demonstrated on the nude mute boy.

But such misadventures seem to have been translated later into the protective arrangements for secure and comfortable living – *natural* living, like a natural diet. A domicile in the English countryside may even have had its considerable appeal enhanced by the fact that the Van Den Bogaerdes had come over from the Netherlands only a generation before and Dirk had been raised in that same lush swathe of Thameside country that had given rise to the "wild wood" fantasies of Kenneth Grahame. It was, in short, the Little England ideal of film stardom, already mentioned elsewhere, with its attachments to tradition, good taste and good breeding – in a word, to decency. (It struck me later, much later, when Bogarde began switching houses and counties, that it may also have had some practical attachment to taxes; in those days they lay heavily on even relatively modest incomes and a home represented a capital asset that could be sold for a very leniently taxed profit. If that were so, it was legitimate enough, and the pleasure in possessing an estate needn't necessarily lead to the lust to be an estate agent.)

Decency was enshrined by Bogarde on the screen in roughly three forms.

One was the heroic tradition, already set by Robert Donat, Leslie Howard and Laurence Olivier, to name a few. It was based on patriotism, gallantry, self-sacrifice: Bogarde in the 1958 remake of *A Tale of Two Cities*, for instance. You couldn't really believe his Sydney Carton had ever been a wastrel, he was such a nicely spoken young man, but he went to the guillotine with a touching piece of dictation on his lips. Second was the tradition of the romantic lover. This was a safely low-powered affair, a matter of selfless sincerity rather than anything more lustful: *The Wind Cannot Read*, for example. And finally there was the comic tradition of the *Doctor* series that kept Bogarde decent while indecencies – admittedly of a more genteel kind than the working-class ribaldry of the *Carry On* comedies – were being perpetrated all round him in St Swithin's. Bedside charm, in short, not bedpan impertinence was what was asked of him. He obliged.

It's maybe no accident that all the films named above were made by the same team of Betty Box (producer) and Ralph

Thomas (director), a parentally inclined couple whose instinct for the bourgeois box-office rarely let them down or pushed them into taking risks.

But there was a limit to the sensitivity that even Bogarde could put into playing cardboard lovers, comic cut-outs and pop-up heroes. That limit seemed to have been reached when he made *The Doctor's Dilemma* at the end of the 1950s. This was the Shaw play, though many of his fans imagined it was the fifth film in the *Doctor* series. They stayed away in droves on discovering it wasn't. Tired of "manufacturing seaside rock", as he put it, Bogarde jumped at an opportunity to go to Hollywood – and found, on getting to the Coast, that it was simply a different kind of rock.

He was cast as Franz Liszt in *Song Without End*, which, after a decent interval – about ten years – he confessed to being a fiasco, so bad that "I had to *beg* my agent to get me the role of the villain in *HMS Defiant* after [*Song Without End*] was shown." One winning aspect of Bogarde is his candour about flops.

Now he deliberately – indeed, it would appear, desperately – tried to break the mould he'd been poured into by Rank. His contract was running out, and advancing years would have put an end to his eternal juvenile appeal. But he didn't wait for either eventuality. In the film *Victim*, he played what I regret to say most of us in those days called "a queer" – and at a stroke his fan club dropped away like barnacles released from a shapely hull. Those that got the point (and didn't like it) were multiplied by those that missed the point – in large parts of England before the Homosexual Enlightenment, a reference to being "queer" simply implied feeling "poorly". Not that the point of the film was all that sharply controversial, though Bogarde is still ferocious in his insistence that it was ahead of its time and had a beneficial effect on homosexual law reform. I think this tenacious defence of it reflects his own state of mind at the time rather than any strong virtue preserved in a film that wishes to advocate "coming out", but turns tail, so to speak, before facing the consequences of it. A small step for homosexual reform, perhaps: a giant leap for Bogarde the contract artist. If *he* "came out" in any sense, it was for independence.

I first met Bogarde to sit down and talk to for longer than the customary Rank press luncheon of those days – which, Heaven knows, was often long enough – when he began his association with Joseph Losey.

If I were a film-school student preparing a thesis, I would propose a study of these two strongly driven and interrelated individuals. In many not too obvious ways, they resembled each other. Losey came to Britain a refugee and a victim of the post-McCarthy blacklisting of Hollywood talents; Borgarde was already increasingly alienated from cinema conventions that he found creatively stifling. They were both "outcasts", in a manner of speaking: one by doctrinaire conviction, the other by rebellious volition. Losey came of good Oregon stock, was well-travelled and professed to be profoundly radicalised. He must have been as novel a creative partner for Bogarde as he became an abrasive mentor. The English class system fascinated Losey; after all, wasn't his Communism dedicated to destroying such systems? Bogarde was English and yet not-English; he was by no means a political radical, yet he was ripe for rebellion against the system that had kept him – and kept him quite well, considering what contract stars were paid in those years. Both men liked a life surrounded by good taste and creature comforts: Losey disdained it publicly but adopted it privately, while Bogarde lived it publicly and yet took care not to exploit it vulgarly. Losey was more complex than any filmmaker Bogarde had met up to then, and he, in turn, felt that Bogarde yearned to play more complex parts than other directors had offered him up to then. The result was *The Servant*.

The theme of *The Servant* was perfectly adapted to the respective talents of Bogarde and Losey. Bogarde could sink his customary identification marks unrecognisably into the class malice of Barrett the manservant, in whose hands James Fox's lazy, spoilt young master comes apart like a family heirloom that has outlived its usefulness. And Losey could indulge his fascination with English mid-to-upper class manners and the smart life of Chelsea (into which he installed himself soon afterwards in a house in Royal Avenue almost opposite the one whose exterior figured in *The Servant*) with the comfortable alibi of being a saboteur out to subvert it. Harold Pinter's screenplay – his first – added a richer and darker set of psychological hints at the kinks in human nature than the Rank Organisation would then have thought it proper to let one of its cherished stars act on.

Losey, moreover, was a martinet of a type not very often encountered in a British film studio. He challenged, contradicted, disdained . . . His lip curled with a not unfriendly jibe almost every time I ran into him. He did his best to needle. It was as if he was always pessimistically expecting the worst and trying to forestall it by precipitating some cause for dissension: he sheltered from big disasters under little quarrels. Being of a divisive frame of mind myself, I rather liked sparking off him.

Bogarde, too, is sardonic and subtle. His autobiography cleverly creates an impression of ingratiating intimacy, but this conceals more than it reveals. Losey had a secret life, too; I have glimpsed it in between the many tantalisingly blacked-out passages of the dossiers kept on him by the Federal Bureau of Investigation which are obtainable under the Freedom of Information Act. They matched, Dirk and Joe. Losey must have been like a manifestation of Dirk's prayers: Bogarde, like a realisation of Joe's needs.

Bogarde looked as if he were playing a foreigner in *The Servant* – the role was so alien to the pedigree that Rank had given him. Oily hair, fishy eyes, face like porridge gone cold and stiff and a regional accent that was North country in origin but "below stairs" in destination. The man's attitude said "servant", his ambience whispered "parasite". It was as if all those years Bogarde had spent posing against his own photogenic bachelor backgrounds had been turned inside out, so that instead of the indolent owner of privilege and property he now stood out as the envious, arrogant, sly intruder, not quite belonging, not quite possessing, but manipulating and morally suborning young James Fox's phlegmatic trust in his supposedly safe little world of privilege.

Robin Maugham's *novella* had been about the way that the upper-class English are in thrall to their servants; and the way that servants who were "completely dependent on their employers for home and wages, can be ordered to work at any time, and whose environment can be shattered by a broken teapot or a spurt of temper". What's so remarkable about the film is the way Pinter gives this concept flesh. Barrett appears in only four or five of the small book's 69 pages and for the rest of the time is a powerful but indirectly reported "presence". The way

Bogarde inhabited that flesh, it was as if he had been cruising the prospects for years without finding his desired opening. Losey let Bogarde in through the door.

The topicality of certain political scandals helped the film. The suicidal melodrama of the John Profumo – Stephen Ward affair which exposed the casual debaucheries and public hypocrisies of the governing classes had eroded confidence in "our betters", and *The Servant* quickly came to be seen as a metaphor for a system of privilege that had outlived its usefulness and deserved to be destroyed.

The film brought Bogarde prestige, prizes and – best of all – satisfaction at being accepted as a serious actor. "We were singing that evening before we ever got to the cinema," he wrote to me on November 16, 1963, a couple of days after the *première*. Unfortunately, there was one thing the film didn't bring – money. It was only a fair commercial success. Despite the acclaim, it made it no easier for Losey or Bogarde to find finance for other "serious" films. Painfully, they scraped together mean little budgets for *King and Country* and *Accident* and a more generous one for that piece of Sixties "Throwaway Pop", *Modesty Blaise*. Bogarde also worked for John Schlesinger (*Darling*) and Jack Clayton (*Our Mother's House*), and paid the rent with formula films made on the tail-ends of expiring contracts.

The trouble was that he had come of artistic age in the "Swinging Sixties", which made it hard for someone of his chronological age group to find the prize parts in a British film industry increasingly financed by American money and devoted to selling Pop (the Beatles), youth (Finney, Courtenay, Julie Christie, David Warner) and the ferment of fashion, novelty and sexual liberation to American audiences.

Bogarde's determination not to compromise lasted until the bills fell due, which was not too long. He took the plunge and went to Italy to shoot commercials for sun glasses. And it was in Italy that he met Luchino Visconti and fell under his imperious magnetism – and, I suspect, a little under his arch-snobbery, too.

Visconti represented the European tradition of the *grand seigneur*. His fortune actually came from castor oil, much valued in a gourmand economy like Italy's. The Visconti ancestral title, Duke of Modrone, was genuine enough, however. Visconti and Losey might have been cousins a few times removed by an emigrant ancestor. Both of them played human politics with people while professing an allegiance to party politics of the Left wing. They were "patrons" as well as artists: able to adapt, inspire and encourage as well as inclined to be cruel, dismissive and utterly autocratic. If Losey trailed his outlaw status to add to his allure, Visconti looked as if he had stepped out of Proust's more sinister ranks of the minor nobility. If M. de Charlus had been a filmmaker, he would have been much like Visconti.

An actor finding that England couldn't supply him with steady work of quality was naturally attracted by Visconti's professional standing, his cultural assurance and his aristocratic style of life. Of course it was a wrench for Bogarde to sell up his cherished Sussex home – typically casting a disparaging eye on the "jewelled hand" of the vulgar woman who was buying it – and move himself and what he ruefully admitted was "the best dud collection of 18th century pictures in private hands" to the mainland of Europe. First he went to Rome. Then when the Italians rooked him *twice* over – instead of the permissible once – he settled in the Provencal farmhouse of his memoirs. In the next few years he made two films with Visconti, *The Damned* and *Death in Venice*, the second of which is generally reckoned one of Visconti's best and Bogarde's finest.

He and Visconti shared something else that passed in their eyes for a virtue: a revulsion against the vulgar moneymen who were unfortunately needed to "make movies happen". This generally meant the Americans. Bogarde's cavalier treatment by Hollywood has left a sour taste in many passages of his memoirs; Visconti was actively anti-American, but on a much more lordly scale. According to Bogarde, he would rail against "the wicked people at Warner Brothers" who cut his budgets and made filmmaking impossible, all the while sitting in his splendid *palazzo* in Milan, surrounded by liveried flunkeys and rare Picassos of the early period. He would never dream of firing a servant or selling a picture in order to make some domestic economies or prime the cash flow to get the movie under way. Having the best of both worlds is a childish fantasy; it's one that film people are well equipped to turn into reality. Visconti usually did so in the grand manner, and to be part of the court circle, watching it happen, had its fascination.

Bogarde wrote later that his relationship to this man was like that of a pupil to Plato or Socrates. But even such teachers of philosophy play their favourites. In *The Damned*, the balance of interest was early and decisively tilted towards another "pupil", young Helmut Berger, whose bravura performance as the sexually decadent scion of the armaments dynasty eclipsed Bogarde's role, which Visconti subsequently reduced in length. Berger, perhaps unsurprisingly, doesn't rate a mention in Bogarde's second volume of memoirs, aptly entitled *Snakes and Ladders*.

But there appear to have been no harsh words, only regretful ones. Visconti's spell remained potent. So did his promises . . . promises.

Visconti's hooded eyes, which were a large part of his visual menace, were sharp enough to see that Bogarde was at his best playing weak men. When Bogarde protestingly reminded him of the raunchy father he had played in *Our Mother's House* or the *professeur moyen sensuel* he had played in *Accident*, Losey's film of rivalry in love among the Oxbridge dons, Visconti merely shrugged and told him he possessed a big range of weaknesses.

He was right, of course. Weakness is what English actors play well, second to no other nation, provided they are good actors in the first place. Visconti was strong, definitely not weak; he was a duke and definitely "un-Gerrard's Cross", Bogarde decided. He hung on. Better domination by Visconti than indifference in England.

Part of the risk of working with Visconti, however, involved joining his court, competing for favours, suffering oneself to being patient with his imperial whims. To his credit, Bogarde avoided that kind of entrapment; perhaps he saw the risks with the detachment of the observant novelist he was nourishing in himself, if not yet ready to put to the test. Or perhaps he'd already seen what happens when masters and servants fail to keep their respective places.

His material rewards on any of the Visconti films were not large – under $50,000 for *Death in Venice*. It was the spell of working abroad, and for such a man, that must have been compensation. He could remain English (he has still no ease in any foreign language, though this is not necessarily viewed as a drawback by Englishmen) while keeping England at a proper distance from him. He was like the adopted *Inglese*.

Death in Venice was something he and Visconti were well equipped to understand – and perhaps they came to understand each other in the process. Thomas Mann's story of an artist's career trickling away into the sands of sterility had had its parallel, on a more commonplace level, in Bogarde's feelings about his own career. And Visconti knew how art needed the refreshment of the senses.

Von Aschenbach, the character played by Bogarde, is a man who has held his sensual nature in check for the sake of the purity of his muse; ultimately, it leads to his paralysis and extinction, though not before he has surrendered to his senses and to the *idea*, if not the physical reality, of the beautiful boy he keeps on glimpsing on the Venetian Lido.

This was, *mutatis mutandis*, the theme of the film *Victim* all over again; this time the man is the frustrated pursuer and death claims him rather than the cool, uninvolved boy whose rare, tiny smile is midway between invitation and mockery.

The encounter between these two takes place in looks and longing only; it is the aching gap between them that Visconti emphasises as Von Aschenbach's camera-eye trails the boy along the beach or across the hotel terrace. This kind of *rapport* is ideally suited to the talents of an actor who has learnt how to make the camera love him. Bogarde's best acting was always done straight to camera. Unlike the run of Pinewood actors, he assiduously cultivated the studio photographers and absorbed their generous tutelage even if the chance to apply the lessons were few and far between in his contract pictures. But now he could let every movement transmit an almost telepathic signal. He suggested a universe of physical trepidation when Von Aschenbach spots a male playmate planting a kiss on his own beloved boy's cheek and thus forcing the carnal side of passion in front of his unwelcome sight. Von Aschenbach is possessive in desire, not action, and Bogarde is skilled at just this kind of moral hanging-back.

It is the "weakness" Visconti lauded him for. Consequently, when he makes up his mind to act on his impulses, it is like a clash of cymbals amidst Mahler's sombre musical accompaniment. In a superb stroke, Visconti's command brings Bogarde to his feet as the motor-launch that's carrying him away from Venice passes out from under the Ponte del Rialto into a crescent of sunlight that strikes his forehead just as he issues the order to the boatman to return to the Lido, to his beloved boy and to his fate. An outward journey conducted like a dirge turns into a bold swagger, all shame dispersed.

Bogarde has written and often spoken of how the make-up, smeared callously on his face by the make-up man to give it the semblance of a dandy's death mask, turned out to be toxic and cost him a layer of skin. But the mortification was worth it as he dies by degrees in our sight. "The time left to us is like hour-glass sand – to our eyes, it appears that it runs out only at the end." Bogarde follows that trickle of life from first to last shot in the film until the vessel that holds it collapses, empty and abandoned.

To read Bogarde's last volume of memoirs, *Backcloth*, is to re-experience that same feeling, as death enters the narrative in a major role and begins the "gathering in" of friends and lovers.

Until I accidentally came across *Death in Venice* being shown on a late-night TV channel in a hotel room in The Hague, I hadn't quite realised how little dialogue there was in it and how unneccessary words were to Bogarde's performance: I understood every scene of it without penetrating the Dutch dubbing. The film is an opera almost without words in which Bogarde's great contribution is his presence. A cruel irony prevented his competing for the "Best Actor" award at Cannes when the film was entered there in 1971 – for the version was the dubbed Italian one and the Cannes regulations insisted that only the original English version was eligible. (A double irony I have already mentioned was that the *Palme d'or* that year was snatched away from Visconti by Bogarde's other mentor, Joseph Losey, with *The Go-Between*.)

I am afraid that my admiration for Bogarde suffered an abrupt disenchantment – and our relationship a hiatus – when he appeared in *The Night Porter* with Charlotte Rampling, one of those sharp coolly beautiful women he gets on well with, and a Euroactress who prefers, like he does, to live abroad. In the film, they played a couple who practised in peacetime the sado-masochistic games that their characters had begun playing in

Auschwitz where she had been a captive Jewess and he a sadistic guard. Bogarde by now should have learnt to avoid prolonged orgies on screen: they usually look very silly. Sarah Miles once told me *vis à vis* Losey's *Servant*, "Joe had absolutely no idea what people *did* in an orgy." Liliana Cavani, who directed *The Night Porter*, unfortunately had, and very silly it looked, with strawberry jam insinuating itself into the couple's lustful encounter, perhaps in the hope that it would enhance its perverseness the way that a half-pound of butter had shared the love-making of Marlon Brando and Maria Schneider in that other story of chamber-sadism, Bertolucci's *Last Tango in Paris*.

Bogarde was distinctly sulky at my refusal to be impressed and was, forgivably, irritated by the adverse review of the film that appeared prematurely in the *Evening Standard*. It had apparently been anticipated that one would write about the film – it was experiencing distribution difficulties – only if one had *liked* it. Critics shouldn't get caught in these gentlemanly *ententes*. (The sad story can be found, told from Bogarde's side, in his memoirs.)

It seemed to me – and unrepentantly it still seems to me – that the film missed the point that degradation without illumination doesn't invite interest, after a basic curiosity about people's peculiar perverse tastes has been satisfied. Bertolucci's film in contrast, brought dawning understanding of why people play desperate games of pain and humiliation; *The Night Porter* only brings disgust.

Bogarde went on to get his "heart's desire" by working with Alain Resnais in *Providence*, as a cuckolded husband whose mien is so chilly you expect icicles to form on his lips, not words. (Considering the verbose script, icicles would have been preferable.)

John Gielgud stole the film; but then to put Gielgud in a film, *any* film, is rather like asking a kleptomaniac to tea – don't be surprised when you come to count the silver.

I think it worth recalling this extraordinary Gielgud performance. For although the film earned respectful reviews, they were the kind laid like wreaths on the coffin of a not much loved notability: a prudent gesture rather than a demonstrative joy. Gielgud's memorial notices may well neglect his appearance in it, even though it achieves some kind of cinema "first" by giving us sight of our senior knight ensconced on the loo – at least I took those patrician ankles to be Sir John's – or stuffing a suppository up himself all the while lamenting the "great spheres of fire" he is passing in tones of self-punishment that would do justice to a penitent Richard II. Sir John on the rack, being worked over by the Spanish Inquisition, could not have put up a better orchestrated symphony of phonetic anguish. By turns malicious, piteous, mocking, infantile, stoic, he evoked more mood music through voice and visage than any other actor alive could conduct – he was the Von Karajan of this world of aches and pains. Bogarde, by contrast, sounded very one-note. But then only the very great – or very innocent – actors can admit to themselves that the text adds up to a load of balls and decide to let their own feelings loose on it.

Bogarde was persuaded by Richard Attenborough – who, after all, would not be? – into making a brief return to British heroics by playing Lt General Sir Frederick "Boy" Browning in the story of the Arnhem paratroop disaster, *A Bridge Too Far*. The film showed Browning accepting blame for the balls-up. Bogarde's role had even more blame heaped on it in the letters column of *The Times* by Browning's widow, the novelist Daphne du Maurier, and other members of the Military Establishment (Rtd.). I wonder if he felt the shudders as deeply as when his young punk played the cop-killer in *The Blue Lamp*. Possibly not. By this time, he was part of a foreign field as well as an acre or two of French olive orchards.

A role in Fassbinder's *Despair*, with an accent zat would cut *sauerkraut*; and then he came back to act in England on the small screen, in his own adaptation of Graham Greene's *May We Borrow Your Husband?* and most recently in a banal piece of "future shock" called *The Vision*. Now he has come back to live in England (*pro tem*, anyhow). He felt himself, in his French fastness, becoming like the tortoise marooned in the rabbit hole. When he had first moved to the Alpes Maritimes region, the nightingales were singing and the peasant farmers cultivating the *roses de mai* for the perfume factories. But the area had long lost its birdsong and its scents as the holiday villas of Sloane Rangers and rich *déraciné* Arabs marched up the hillside towards him and the peasants took off to the litoral to work the cash registers

261

in Cannes and Nice. A pattern of melancholy stoicism, fostered and deepened by the "gathering in" of his friends, was communicated to us when he made a public burning of his letters, diaries and notebooks during a television interview – a pyre for the past tantalisingly lit in public to frustrate posterity. There are apparently to be no more memoirs now that life has reined in its expectancy, has been reduced to a state of "one thing at a time" endurance and has lost even the verities that looked as if they would remain reasonably eternal: *English* rites like the mucking out of the pool, the dividing up of the water lilies (imported from Angmering, Buckinghamshire) and the culling of the celandines (French) down by the cesspit.

Bogarde's late-blooming career as a writer has supplied formidable compensations. It's provided him with a smaller but certainly more satisfying fanship than his heyday as a Rank *matinée* idol. When he sticks his head out of his shell nowadays – the metaphor has now been consciously adopted by the memoirist – he usually chooses to make himself visible in the persona of a writer or a stoic (often the same thing). In 1987, in a room devoted to literary figures, I saw a painting of him hanging in the National Portrait Gallery – surely a rarer kind of credit than any film titles could bestow. The artist had posed him in a bare room of the French farmstead that's now been sold – no doubt to some rich vulgarian – wearing a pullover (the knitting-pattern feeling still hovers round his shoulders) and an expression that, although resigned and reclusive, looks reasonably self-sufficient.

Though Bogarde has made *The Vision* for television since coming back to settle in London, so far, he has made no cinema movies. He has happily recovered from a slight stroke and lives a sheltered life, determinedly untheatrical, unshowy, the social equivalent of his best acting style. Yet there is a certain measure of defiance as well as forebearance in all of this. No one is going to "crack" him open. That kind of resolution lends distinction, in English eyes, anyhow, to the lustre he has gained abroad: he doesn't really need other tributes, like the Hon.D.Litts. they insist on thrusting on him – and, anyhow, degree ceremonies dangerously expose him to public view. He is more preoccupied with what goes on behind the closed doors of his life than with the painful self-inspection that the big screen invites. Like the good, the *very* good actor he has made himself into, Dirk Bogarde knows the value of holding back, of leaving something to be guessed at.

When Kenneth Tynan was *dramaturg* at the National Theatre, he used to try and set people at their ease before an interview with Laurence Olivier by telling them, "Larry's a blank page. You've got to tell him what part you expect him to play, and then he's all right."

Somehow, I hadn't quite believed this. I'd always assumed "our greatest living actor" would be articulate enough about his art, or, if he was feeling off-colour that day, artful enough to dissemble satisfactorily. A remark of Olivier's I'd heard him make at a British Film Academy awards night had reinforced this impression of pert if sly certitude. Unbelievably, some idiots had nominated Olivier for his performance as Air Chief Marshal Sir Hugh Dowding in *The Battle of Britain*. Stiff, gruff, tenacious (or pigheaded) in the rightness of Dowding's wartime battle strategy, Olivier's playing stood out like an article of faith in a film that was otherwise a gestural tribute to "The Few". But to urge Olivier's claim to be the "Best Supporting Actor" should have sounded an alarm siren in the heads of everyone who voted for him: it was simply the BFA's way of flattering its self-esteem. Worse still, he won; worst of all, he seemed grateful for the honour until, holding the trophy, he turned to go back to his table, hesitated, and then said in a dry clear voice: "Thank you again . . . It will be a great encouragement to me in my career." Brilliant! I thought. He'd rebuked his court circle for the vainglory it had thrust on him, unasked, without at the same time signifying that it was unacceptable. The sarcasm fitted the sycophancy of the occasion perfectly, as if Solomon arrayed in all his glory had prepared the court for one of his famous judgments, and then ordered himself a shoeshine.

Memories of that occasion warmed me to an even quicker acceptance, a year or so later, when I was invited to act as moderator between Olivier and a cinema audience. It was rare, *very* rare for him to "do" a show like that, I was told. But he'd directed *The Three Sisters* as a record of his own National production in which his wife, Joan Plowright, played Masha and he had taken the role of Dr Chebutikin. It had a special place in his heart, I was informed: a work of admiration and affection undertaken in the Oliviers' tenth year of marriage. It must have touched Olivier's sensibility deeply, and not just his craftsmanship to have persuaded him to appear in public after the showing at the Screen on the Green cinema, Islington, and answer questions without the protection of rehearsals or re-takes.

We were to meet for dinner at Robert Carrier's restaurant in Camden Passage, eat while the film was showing and then, crammed with good food and enough wine, give the audience *its* fill of words – self-assessing and, if possible, not too self-serving. It sounded great.

I got to Carrier's at about 6.45 p.m., when it was of course emptier than it would be when the tidal flow of diners began. I looked in the restaurant to see six places set for our group, who included Romaine Hart, director of the Screen on the Green and (eventually) several more "Screen" cinemas; and when I stepped back into the small entrance hall, Olivier had just taken off his top-coat. His wife hadn't been able to make the engagement for reasons I suspected had to do with her diffidence about discussing her work. Olivier immediately looked concerned to see me. "So sorry, so sorry to have kept you waiting for me." – "Not waiting," I said, "anticipating." *Wrong! . . . Wrong! . . .* I heard a little censor in my head cry out: *Don't top his line. Actors don't like that.* Olivier closed the distance between us with a firm handshake. *Start again*, was the feeling he gave me. *Let's find out what kind of play we're in.* Then he put his foot in it. "Congratulations on your award," he said. *Award? . . . What award?* Had he mistakenly got hold of *my* dialogue? *His* award, surely: the one I'd seen him accept so laconically for *The Battle of Britain. I* should be doing the congratulating . . . But then I recalled a journalism prize that had gone my way a few months before. And it was suddenly clear that some National Theatre aide of his, some secretary appealed to when day and date and time had been irrevocably set for *The Three Sisters* talk-back, had forearmed him with this sort of pacifying bone for this Hound of the Baskervilles, this critic, whose enormous footprints were going to overlay his trail that night – *on the scent of his secret.* For the very first time in my life, I realised how nervous great actors could be.

Romaine Hart led us and the others in the party in to dinner. We were a camp-fire huddle in the corner of the still empty restaurant.

I'd imagined that Olivier making small talk would be like Richard III feeling solicitous for someone with a cold in the head. Not at all. He was shy and awkward. Olivier *is* the Ordinary Man far better than he *acts* the Ordinary Man; just as Chaplin miming a drunk in his two-reel comedies was far better than Chaplin playing one for real in *Limelight*. A paradox maybe: but in Olivier's case, revealing an interesting territorial limitation to his commonwealth of talents. Eight years earlier, reviewing *Term of Trial*, I'd noted the discomfort he felt in trying to fit the skin of a nondescript character – in that case, an ineffectual schoolteacher in a Northern town, grasping at the cane like a straw of salvation in the sea of misery and frustration he's drowning in. His attempt at a realistic portrait of a washed-out pedagogue failed by as much as his parody of a worked-out music-hall artist succeeded in *The Entertainer*. What we admired in the Osborne play was a brilliant *"déclassé"* double act: Olivier the great classical actor "slumming" it on the vaudeville stage. In those days, at the end of the 1950s, the class-conscious, status-ridden West End theatre which had been the kingdom of "Larry and Vivien" was under siege by the New Playwrights in their bailiwick at the Royal Court. For Olivier to appear as Archie Rice at the "Court" seemed to many equivalent to the social *faux pas* of going to live "north of the Park". All right for a Green Room Rag or a one-night charity "do", but for one partner in the demi-royal double act of "The Oliviers", it was going just a bit far, don't you think?

Olivier's success silenced that kind of talk for ever. His "crossing over" into Osborne's theatre gave his career its second wind – and, incidentally, brought him his third wife, Joan Plowright. He didn't cease to be the King; it just meant that he didn't have to play him all the time. And yet the "Little Man" continued to defeat him on stage and screen. Those who saw him in the play, *Semi-Detached*, noted with dismay how awkward he looked playing a very common "commoner" – and *Term of Trial* simply magnified his reliance on techniques that didn't quite work, now that a pitiful character had to be acted rather than a stylised caricature assembled. It was only when Olivier's

265

schoolteacher stepped into the dock in *Term of Trial*, to face a charge of indecent assault, that he showed a flash of his old and still unrivalled power to harrow one's heart. Facing the magistrates, he made a plea for mercy in strangulated tones that quavered with apprehension and indignation. Nondescriptness is the kind of sackcloth that doesn't suit him; self-torture, on the other hand, is a state of exposure he can make indescribably painful.

When he came to publish his autobiography in 1982, he called it aptly *Confessions of an Actor*. For what, after all, is acting but a kind of confession that takes place inside the "box" of a character's *persona*? Whenever a part has penance written into it, Olivier's response hits a public nerve magnificently.

His discomfort increased after we'd ordered at Carrier's and were waiting for the first course. By now I was ready to jump aboard any boat that our desultory conversation brought sailing by; but it looked as if only an icebreaker would get through. Then he turned towards me. 'Mr Walker, may I ask you a perhaps impertinent question?" – "Of course." – "Where do you *come* from?" – "What do you mean?" – "Where were you born?" – "Oh, in Ireland . . . in Northern Ireland." – "*Ahhhhh*." More syllable than word, more death-bed sigh than detective-story exclamation, the sound escaped from Olivier with unmistakable relief. He had got me placed! He had me ticketed! And as he proceeded to show, he was now at ease with the character sitting opposite him; he could construct his own performance around me. My vocal identity established, I became "flesh". I ceased to be a "critic", and turned into a "character".

Plenty of recorded occasions testify to Olivier's "suddenly" getting a character that he's trying to construct – "getting the green umbrella", as his biographer, Felix Barker, colourfully tagged the moment when the essential key to a role is discovered: like the mink with its tongue frozen to the ice that gave him the tonal clue to his chilling scream in *Oedipus*; or the moustache he wore for Othello that added the necessary illusion of Negroid thickness to his thin Caucasian upper lip; or the stammering over the letter "w" that impelled him to take the un-starry role of Hotspur in *Henry IV* so that he could die with the additional pathos of attempting (and failing) to utter his own epitaph of becoming "dust and food for w-w-w . . ." and leave it, as Tynan noted, to Prince Hal to supply the words ". . . worms, brave Percy".

Physical make-up takes hours of Olivier's time in front of the mirror, after he's made preliminary sketches, in profile and full face, on a photograph of himself. But the soul of so many of his performances is vocal. In this respect, the voice acquires an enhanced importance since it is the one item in an actor's repertoire that the speaker cannot "hear" – at least not as others hear it, despite the advent of tape recorders. Some actors seem to spend their life straining to hear their own voices. Richard Burton was a notable casualty and, as I mentioned earlier, always seemed to be vocally narcissistic.

Olivier's screen roles register him as indelibly on the sound track as his image does on the celluloid emulsion. Sometimes, the vocal register is the stronger. He appeared in *David Copperfield* in 1970 – oh yes, he did; though even he couldn't make that flat film memorable – teamed with another actor with a fine ear, Richard Attenborough. Olivier was Mr Creakle, the sadistic headmaster; Attenborough, Mr Tungay, the peg-legged usher. I am sure the two of them worked it out between them, like schoolboys in collusion. Olivier's classroom threats were pitched in a voice that was barely audible – while Attenborough, as his creature, repeated them in a parade-ground amplification of his master's whisper: a perfect Dickensian double-act. I have only a hazy memory of how they looked; but how they sounded still echoes through my head.

So when Olivier's distant early warning system detected a classifiable "something" in my own voice, he had homed in on it and not given it clearance until it had identified itself. (Later, he told me he had taken it to be Scots-Canadian – half-right, though the border that runs through my accent is not the 49th parallel.) Orson Welles once told Olivier he ought to mount a production of *Othello*. "You'd make a marvellous Iago, Larry." I believe several silent beats ensued. Then, tilting his eyes at his dinner-table companion – those orbs of Olivier's seem to swivel on their own secret axis like a Rubik's cube – Olivier said quietly, "Why not Othello, Orson?" – "You haven't a deep enough voice, Larry." No reply, until nearly 20 years later, when he *did* play Othello. By purposeful work, he had acquired the black velvet

267

voice to go with the impressive, if ethnically questionable, coloured skin of the Moor – well, at any rate, Afro-Moor. I admired the Negroid impersonation he gave, though I didn't really enjoy it. I had to laugh, but in sympathy, when I later heard the story of Olivier arriving, at dawn, at the studio where they were committing his *Othello* to film, spending hours coating himself in body make-up, giving a final polish to the visible highlights, and then going on-set where one of the co-stars – was it the wicked Maggie Smith? – used to greet him daily with the languorous drawl, "How now, brown cow?"

But I liked and enjoyed, both hugely, his performance as the Mahdi in *Khartoum* in 1966. He had altered Othello's *basso profundo* into a counter-tenor's sing-song (we forget Olivier had once been a zealous choir-boy, and a good one, too, by his own proud accounting) and he sported the lucky "V" shape space that the warrior had in his front teeth. How well the researchers had done their work! Or was it maybe Olivier's own historical delving that had turned up that bit of Identikit (or Inden*talk*it)? Even the way he pronounced the place-name of the title served the character – "Khar-toum!" uttered midway between a cough and a retch, as if the Mahdi were clearing the sand out of his throat.

Charlton Heston, who had broken lances in so many epics, played General Gordon. He now actually experienced a lance being broken in *himself* when he met the Mahdi's men on the palace steps. Heston is one of the few really scholarly Hollywood stars, though I think he worries too much about whether such-and-such a role is worthy of him. He had no doubt about Olivier's worth, however. "He's quite marvellous in the part," he generously entered in his diary, ". . . complete African characterisation, borrowed from Othello perhaps, but utterly valid for this. On top of it he has superimposed a careful Sudanese enunciation. The whole thing, down to painting the inside of his mouth, is an example of the total devotion to the role that is probably part of his success. Part of it. He also happens to be an incredibly good actor." Yes, let's not forget *that* when analysing the "parts" of him.

How Olivier got to be such a good screen actor is a story told many times. Olivier in particular relishes re-telling it. I've watched him in several interviews, squirming with satisfied recall as he relates how William Wyler, who had cajoled him into playing Heathcliff in *Wuthering Heights* in 1938, publicly humiliated him on the set, berating him for the snobbish condescension that he, a *stage actor*, was bringing to the chore of film acting. He was disdaining the greater naturalism demanded by the camera, giving a stiff-necked, coarse-grained performance in the repeated "takes" that Wyler demanded – even earning himself a rebuke from Merle Oberon for unintentionally spitting at her as he said his lines. Wyler laid his tongue across Olivier's theatrical hoity-toityness; his insistence on take after take after take physically wore the actor down to the point where he was almost indifferent to his fate, virtually welcoming it the way Christian martyrs did, as earthly purgation preceding admission to Paradise or, in Olivier's case, a boat-ticket home to Britain. The religious analogy isn't inappropriate. I've commented in my biography of Vivien Leigh on the purgation Olivier found in such trials and tribulations and compared it to Vivien Leigh's childhood upbringing in a Roman Catholic school where the conventual rule insisted that stubborn wills had first to be broken and then re-set in God's way. Olivier's will was broken and re-set in Wyler's.

Like an epiphany, he perceived there and then that there was a truth to film acting he had never suspected – a different truth from stage acting, which still held his primary allegiance – but one that he now embraced with fervour the way a convert does who accepts a faith that belong to the hitherto despised infidels. He did penance – and learned to be a star.

When Vivien Leigh reached Hollywood, whither she had rushed to comfort him in the hour of his humiliation (and, additionally, to push her own claim to the role of Scarlett O'Hara), she found an Olivier who was cured, converted and intent on "Christianising" the heathen with a zealousness that Olivier's own father, a High Churchman who lost and then recovered his vocation, had demonstrated when he set himself to make good his years of lost grace.

"[The cinema] was for me a new medium, a new vernacular," Olivier said of the creative breakthrough that had literally occurred inside a day or two. The development of his skills in realistic film acting dates from those few days.

Anyone looking at the film roles Olivier played before and

269

after *Wuthering Heights* must be struck by this transfiguration. Previously, sporting the looks of a Cypriot waiter laying claim to Ronald Colman's moustache and the zeal of a conventional juvenile lead, he had languished in an indifferent succession of pictures "done for the money". Love at least animated him in *Fire Over England* when Vivien Leigh was his co-star on screen and his mistress off it. In subsequent films for Korda, like *The Divorce of Lady X* and *Q Planes*, he had to cope with Ralph Richardson stealing whatever scenes were worth the heist (precious few). Richardson's presence in a film with Olivier was an ambivalent comfort. Off-screen, he was Olivier's boon companion and respected guru; on-screen, he had a natural "presence" that Olivier then lacked. I think that whatever madness lurked in Richardson, behind eyeballs like "crazed" glass, within a voice of Alpenhorn other-worldliness, rendered him proof against any dull, *sane* role they handed him. Richardson had only to look at it and it was enchanted. If Olivier eventually emerged as the tribal leader of the Great British Actors, Richardson remained their witch doctor. And there was always a caginess between the two of them.

Heathcliff gave Olivier his first really popular romantic role. Overnight, he became the bobbysoxers' favourite, the way that the young Sinatra did in his line of entertainment. With Vivien Leigh's success as Scarlett O'Hara to reinforce the dual image of screen romanticism they presented when written up in the papers and magazines of the 1940s, their performances in *Lady Hamilton* were able to borrow fire from the adulterous flame that they had had to keep under decent cover while *Gone With the Wind* was in the making, in case scandal impaired its box-office potential. Lord Nelson in *Lady Hamilton* is a canny piece of acting, necessarily underplayed, since Olivier had to incarnate national virtues appropriate to Britain's wartime valour, whereas he would have liked to give Nelson his quota of human weaknesses – especially the fleshly ones. But Vivien Leigh's own passion for Olivier lets him bathe in the reflection of it that her Emma Hamilton provides. And the Olivier voice is the quantity that gives the illusion of weight to a cardboard mariner. It is an "official voice", but resonant with passion for England, Emma and, of course, duty.

The two Hollywood films he did soon afterwards, both with-

out Vivien Leigh, actually gained from the irritation he felt at
David O. Selznick denying his beloved Vivien's wish to be his
co-star. In both *Rebecca* and *Pride and Prejudice*, he had to be
unbending towards the heroine; and seeing only Joan Fontaine
and Greer Garson in the roles Vivien had coveted helped to
preserve the gap between him and the ladies that the respective
plots insisted on for a large part of the story. One wonders what
went through his thoughts as he played these roles. Maxim de
Winter, in *Rebecca*, is a man pursued by guilt over a first wife
with whom he could reach no marital accommodation; and
Olivier was still in some torment over *his* first wife, Jill Esmond,
whom he had abandoned for Vivien just over two years earlier.
His acting has a ponderousness that suits the character's secret
self-reproach; but it is, for him, oddly un-nuanced. Selznick
crisply summed up the deficiency when he wrote in a producer's
memo: "[Olivier looks] as if he were deciding whether or not to
run for President instead of whether or not to give a ball."

Olivier's Darcy in *Pride and Prejudice* is a perfectly
miniaturised stage reading of the role, impeccably right in its
upper-class aloofness, its self-conscious posture, its suppression
of passion until the petrifying code of convention Darcy
observes has been thwarted by love. Olivier spent the time
between takes literally sketching out the stage production of
Romeo and Juliet he was planning to take across America with
Vivien. Sometimes his acting suggests a man impatient to get
back to the drawing board – not inappropriate for Darcy's
brush with provincial society.

As we ate our way through dinner at Carrier's talk turned to
Olivier's three great Shakespeare films. He bore with it gallantly:
a tour guide concealing his sinking heart as he leads his inquisitive party up to the landmark for the Nth time.

People forget, he said, that *Henry V* owes its origins to a
radio adaptation by the BBC producer Dallas Bower, which
was intended to boost Allied morale by recalling the parallel
invasion of Europe by King Henry. That explained much about
the movie, he said. Radio equalled narrator; narrator in
Shakespeare suggested Chorus; but Chorus had to have a habi-
tation and that meant the boards of the old Globe Theatre. Thus
he had hit on the concept for the film's first third, rooted in a
realistic tour of an Elizabethan playhouse; then came the dis-

solve into stylised cinema; finally, the epic naturalism of Agincourt. He made it sound simple, logical; but I imagine a lot of it was intuitive.

Olivier has a "radio ear". And why not? He grew up in the radio age, like two other directors, Welles and Kubrick, whose powerful visual sense has been supplemented (and sometimes, I think, prompted) by the way their "radio days" had formed their imaginations. Kubrick was a fascinated radio listener; Welles was of course a celebrated practitioner and radio was his calling-card to Hollywood after he had panicked America with his scary simulation of the invasion by Martians in *The War of the Worlds*. *Citizen Kane* is a film, yes; but listen to it, with your eyes shut, and it is a brilliant radio play. If we don't count *Spartacus*, which he always regards as the work of a hireling in Kirk Douglas's employ, then all but two of Kubrick's films since *Killer's Kiss* have featured a narrator's voice. Olivier likewise knows and enjoys exploring the sheer power of story-telling through the voice. This is a great part of the pleasure in *Henry V* and *Richard III*, with their soliloquies and their "asides": one film addressing us formally, regally; the other colloquially, slyly, gloatingly. *Hamlet*, for me, does not convey that kind of enjoyment because the film has a hero who "ignores" us. It uses the internal monologue to convey the Prince's thoughts on the soundtrack while his lips stay shut – or open only to snap out a particularly painful line or two. Olivier admits he had fallen in love with cinema techniques when he came to make *Hamlet*; they distance his intimacy – and place us too, at a remove from him.

Melvyn Bragg has noted how Olivier's "Englishness", or his "birthright", as he himself called it, has been diffused throughout his theatre work and especially in his whole appreciation of Shakespeare. He was filming *Henry V* in 1943 when he bought his country house, Notley Abbey, formerly a 13th-century foundation once endowed by the same Henry – surely a good omen. To the son of a cleric who had marked his return to the faith by divesting himself of his lovely serene old Queen Anne rectory – a punishment visited on his family, too, in Olivier's view – and moving to a jerry-built minister's house in a prosaic garden suburb, the acquisition of Notley Abbey meant that Olivier could return to both "the Church" and "the English earth". And he did so at a time when his own patriotism had been vindicated by the approaching victory in Europe and his artistry confirmed by his immensely successful film of *Henry V*.

Richard III channels another kind of "Englishness" directly to us, for at his malicious best, Richard has the ego-tripping autocracy of an English actor-manager. We know Olivier based his peduncular villainy on the looks of Jed Harris, the Broadway impresario, who had been his tormentor on a pre-war appearance on the New York stage; but it is the licence of an English theatrical autocrat that Richard enjoys and exercises with such relish.

Macbeth is Olivier's great might-have-been movie: cancelled in the mid-1950s because Rank wouldn't finance it and Korda, the moneyman he went to in such straits, had recently died. "Why couldn't you have gone back to it later?" I asked Olivier over dinner. (We both of us, tactfully, ignored the "Hallmark *Macbeth*", the film that had come out after the collapse of Olivier's project, underwritten by – of all patrons for such a play! – the manufacturers of greetings cards.) Olivier looked bleak. "I couldn't – couldn't really. I'd invested so much in it, so much hope. I even found a Scottish island where the bracken used to turn blood red in season – what a battlefield that would have made!"

Vivien Leigh, who would have played Lady Macbeth, was suffering one of her most severe manic-depressive attacks; and this alone, as well as the ominous reputation of "the Scottish play", would have been tempting fate (and finance) too much. Anyhow, Olivier never returned to the project. And the loss of *Macbeth* is a bitter one to him, and to us.

"Why do you play so few comedy roles in films?" I asked Olivier. He looked at me quizzically. I wondered if I'd inadvertently reminded him of the judgment that he was a tragedian by talent and a comedian by instinct. "With my mug?" he finally said. One of those enquiry-stoppers; I didn't pursue it.

But Olivier must often have given himself fun in the parts he accepted – otherwise there was no reason, apart from the money (which may be reason enough, of course) for accepting them. Otto Preminger cast him in *Bunny Lake Is Missing*, hoping perhaps he'd give a stand-out performance by making the most of a Scotland Yard man. Instead, Olivier decided to make the least of the part – but in a magical way. "A mere detective," Isabel

Quigly said in her *Spectator* review, "paring his personality down to its merest." I'd never seen him do this trick before and haven't seen him repeat it. Just as some actors "make a character" out of a sketch, Olivier solemnly reversed the process. "He sits like a paperweight on his own personality," I wrote in 1966, "so that a flat character lies even flatter. Only a great actor dare make himself this small." A case of taking the money and vanishing.

Then there was *The Betsy* . . . By this time, 1978, the money had become huge. A million dollars was Olivier's asking price in the late 1970s, following the "money notices" he'd got for *Marathon Man*, and for quite a few years, I'm told, he got not a cent less and sometimes quite a few cents more. When you think of the premier actor of the British stage hiring himself out to play Harold Robbins's randy octogenarian motor tycoon in *The Betsy*, it does seem shameful evidence of what money can buy. Yet Olivier works up a Falstaffian appetite for such junk food and makes an enjoyable meal of it, suggesting that the sex drive rather than overdrive is what powers the tycoon's automobile empire. He even turns his own confinement in a wheelchair – a medical requirement for Olivier at this time, following a series of debilitating illnesses – into a plus factor by making it appear as if the motor mogul has to be anchored thus in order to stop him gate-crashing every female's bedroom. His performance is Basic Big Daddy, but he knits it together without dropping a stitch.

By the 1970s, however, Olivier had embarked on his return journey to the bravura performances of his stage heyday, only now he gave them on the screen – incorporating dozens of ingenious little artifices but staying a degree larger than naturalism. His appearance in *Sleuth*, with Michael Caine as the only other member of the cast, was a *tour de force* of stamina and *trompe l'oeil* in every sense of the phrase. "His face is a study of split-second metamorphoses," Jay Cocks wrote in *Time*, about the malevolence of his chameleon-natured crime writer. "He does so much with it so fast that sometimes, in a close-up, he gives the impression of a multiple exposure."

He does more than take a part and put his patent on it. He can enlarge or contract it to fit the film he's in. Even a "small Olivier" is a collector's piece. He is especially good at the

reductio ad absurdum approach to Great Men which such
cameo roles invite, skewering the blimpish World War One
commander Sir John French in *Oh, What a Lovely War!* on a
single line of dialogue ("We're not under any obligation to the
French – we've our own war to fight") and putting eloquence
into a groan in *Lady Caroline Lamb* when his Duke of Welling-
ton is importuned by a socialite touting for a commission for
her son. Olivier contradicts Boswell's opinion of Milton; he can
carve heads on cherry stones *and* cut a Colossus from the rock.

Marathon Man is proof of the latter. The film made him not
only a fortune but fashionable, as it were, among the Hollywood
superstars and producers for whom the notion of employing a
British knight or a Peer, or acting opposite one, became almost a
conditional clause of any contract they signed. Except for Ralph
Richardson, Olivier and his peers (lower-case here, please) each
had one huge box-office hit to which they had lent their prestige:
Guinness's Magus-figure dispensing "the Force" in *Star Wars*;
Gielgud as Dudley Moore's butler in *Arthur* giving silver tongue
to four-letter words as if they were letters being proffered on a
salver; and Olivier personifying sheer evil in *Marathon Man*. He
played a hard-up Nazi war criminal lured back to New York
from his hide-out up the Amazon to retrieve a nest-egg of diamonds he'd stashed away against just such a day in the rain
forests. If Olivier had stood well back in *Bunny Lake Is Missing*,
looking like a man anxious not to catch a cold from anyone, in
Marathon Man he was the source of all infection.

Personally, I'm not overfond of John Schlesinger's film; I
think it a commonplace thriller. But it does bear out Hannah
Arendt's too often repeated, too seldom corroborated observation about the "banality" of evil. Olivier's Nazi *is* banal, but
utterly, irredeemably evil. His very appearance explains what
one sometimes feels on looking at, say, Klaus Barbie or some
other sometime-Nazi exposed to the light of judgment after decades of concealment among quotidian ordinariness: how could
such debilitude have once been demoniac? The drawstring line
of tiny wrinkles around Olivier's lips are like seismic cracks out
of which hate and fear eventually seep; the face itself looks like
painted lead, a toxic thing that poisons all decencies. And up the
sleeve of his featureless raincoat, the man keeps a horrendous
trick in reserve – a flick blade. The snake's bite. When cornered

at the end, Olivier summons up and expectorates a massive gob of spittle to assault Hoffman. The snake's venom.

The great scene in the film is *not* the one we're constantly seeing and hearing on television or radio, the one where Olivier keeps on repeating, "Is it safe?" prying the answer out of Hoffman with his dental tools. (I still don't know what William Goldman's script means by that line.) No, it is the scene where Olivier is recognised in New York's diamond district by a Jew with a long memory for the concentration camps. And suddenly the monster is like a vampire defanged. A hunted old man wishing to hurry but fearing to run, he becomes kith and kin to Peter Lorre's child-murderer in *M*, but without the claim on our compassion that Lorre exercised. I think this is Olivier's last great "transformation scene" on the screen.

It had one unforeseen consequence: it popularised Olivier's German accent to such a degree that it made him first choice for any similar role and, for a time, it looked as if the greatest English-speaking actor would end his box-office days speaking in Teutonic strain. He was a sad-moustached, frail-bodied but stubborn-willed Viennese Nazi-hunter in *The Boys from Brazil* (an amusing role-reversal after *Marathon Man*); he was *The Jazz Singer*'s Yiddish father in the Neil Diamond remake; he was Van Helsing, the Dutch vampire hunter, in the 1979 version of *Dracula* in which he pursued the thirsty fiend with sharpened stakes like a man who has just drawn stumps at the end of a cricket match. It was no good telling Olivier he was prostituting his talent. He even played Rudolf Hess! Demand can breed indifference: just as familiarity, contempt. He was "hot". So why not strike for the fees that were his due, even if they came with parts that were not his equal?

Such pardonable opportunism led to an encounter with Olivier that I still recall with a wince. It took place in Beverly Hills in the late spring of 1979. I'd just attended the *première* of George Roy Hill's *A Little Romance*, in which Olivier played an elderly Frenchman on a bike, a sort of fairy godfather, who incited two runaway kids to fulfil their romantic daydream by running off to Venice for a kiss beneath the Bridge of Sighs.

Unexpectedly, Olivier's French accent was like his cycling – all over the place. It wandered into the "German" territory of his earlier Teutonic roles, so that one charitably thought that it must have originated in Alsace-Lorraine before that disputed pocket of land was given to the French by the Treaty of Versailles. The film was limply received, but Olivier made a speech in front of the screen that would have been more appropriate to a triumph. Ken Tynan was sitting beside me and buried his face in his hands, uttering an Oedipal groan of mock agony as "the Lord", without irony this time, thanked everyone for their encouragement. Later on at the supper, though, Olivier sat there looking duly crestfallen and his long and loyal agent, Laurie Evans, easily persuaded me to come over and at least say hello. (Tynan had slipped away – and, as it turned out, slipped out of my life, for I wasn't to see him again before his death, just over a year later, after the terrible battle with emphysema that his widow Kathleen has chronicled so heartrendingly.)

Olivier reacted to my presence gratefully – too gratefully. He reached over his banquette table and grasped my arm, pulling me towards him with unexpected strength, so that I became bent over the table like a schoolboy about to be spanked. "Dear friend . . . dear friend, have you come all this way?" I had; but assuredly it hadn't been simply to see *A Little Romance*. Then, contriteness or confidentiality intervening, Olivier gave me that sudden, sharp, *Richard III* look – the upward one from under heavy lids – and added, if I heard his words correctly, "I do it for the children." Embarrassed, and additionally panicked in case I'd be polled for my opinion of the film, I heard myself blurting out, as if I were giving dictation, "How – many – chil-dren – do – you – have?" The grip was instantly surrendered and, sweating, I made my excuses and left.

Some English actors, if they are eminent and old enough, revert to being Great Victorians. There is a lot about Olivier that is Tennysonian, not just the agonies of his private life to which he has attested in *Confessions of an Actor*. Both men were rectors' sons; public figures with inward-turning, melancholy natures; laureates in their respective arts; sociable with friends, suspicious of unknown admirers; prodigiously creative right into their eighties; peers of the realm; Tennyson buried in Westminster Abbey, Olivier, it would be agreed, destined for the same national shrine, though likely to opt for a more private place.

277

I think it delights Olivier to play himself smaller than he is, frailer than he looks; then to throw off the guise and take a bow. *Fooled you!*

In 1982, I was preparing an Olivier retrospective for the Manila International Film Festival and had put in a "form's sake" request through Laurie Evans for 20 minutes of Olivier's time to film him recalling his career. It was a long shot, and a cheeky one. He had just been paid a reported £250,000 to do much the same thing with Melvyn Bragg on *The South Bank Show*, a two-parter lasting two hours. We had 22 minutes of film and barely £2,000. But on the dot of 11.00 a.m. he showed up at the St James's Club. We'd all been wondering if he would come and were consulting our watches, as if we were expecting Phileas Fogg to bound in at the last second and announce he had just circled the globe in 80 days . . . and at first we didn't really connect with the man wearing a soft hat and a frail attitude who materialised on the threshold backed up by an Italian chauffeur like an enormous black bear. He looked shrunken, a "Little Man" out of a Straub cartoon, so that once we'd pulled ourselves together, we rushed forward to make sure he didn't fall apart. "Do sit down, Sir Laurence . . ." "Would you like a cup of tea . . .?" "Can we put a bit of make-up on . . .?" (A very expensive girl had been hired for the morning from Vidal Sassoon.)

"I don't want *make-up*," he said querulously, spitting the word out like wine gone sour. Then, pointing at me: "Put some on him – *he* needs it."

That he was playing the role of a cranky old man in order to deter nuisances like us became plain only by stages. Melvyn Bragg had already discovered that and he was to recall it in a piece he wrote in *Vogue* for Olivier's 80th birthday in May, 1987. I feel I owe Bragg some thanks; after all, he'd acted as a "warm-up man" in his own *South Bank Show* for the Olivier who was gracing our frugal 20 minutes that morning, and for free. By way of gratitude, let me quote the vivid transformation Bragg witnessed at a dinner he'd arranged in honour of Sir William Walton at the Garrick Club quite a few years earlier:

"When the man in the over-large pin-stripe suit trudged into the room, I had no idea who he was. The spectacles were City clerk-ish heavy; the clothes correct but a little crumpled; the air deeply diffident; in all, a brilliant disguise for one of the most famous faces and forces in the theatre this century. Laurence Olivier, the retired old gentleman, well dug into his shell, only wispily, only accidentally, it seemed, taking the odd peck at the outside world . . . But as a lizard on a rock, he was only waiting for the moment to start . . . As in a fairy tale, the little old gentleman in the over-large pin-stripe came on, released a cluster of fireworks – anecdotes, brilliantly exact mimicry, coy-seeming self-satires, cannonades of belly-laughter stories – and then said it was time for him to go home."

"Our" Olivier looked so wilted that I feared to have the arc lights turned on until a minute or two before we were – before *he* was – ready to roll. Dejectedly he'd asked which country he was doing this for. *Utter alarm.* "Manila . . . the Philippines," I said. – "What language do they talk there?" – "English" – "Oh" – He looked even more dejected. "I thought it was a foreign country." – "Well, it is in a way." *Desperation.* "They've got 52 dialects." He brightened a bit; again the linguistic lubricant oiled the conversation. – "What do they sound like?" – "I only know *tagalog* . . . a few words, anyhow." – "Speak a bit. What's *tagalog* for 'Hello'?" – "*Mabuhay.*" – "What?" – "*Mabuhay*" – "Oh." He lost interest again and seemed momentarily to doze. But it was "the lizard on the rock". As I said, "Lights . . . camera . . ." to our mini-crew, the transformation happened.

Olivier suddenly became as self-possessed, as *formidable* as he'd been in *Marathon Man*. And up his sleeve, on this occasion, too, he'd secreted another little surprise. As I finished my own nervous introduction (sound only: we had no film to spare) and said, ". . . Laurence Olivier", he gave the camera a wide, generous smile. "*Mabuhay,*" he enunciated.

They could not believe it when they heard it in Manila. *Laurence Olivier speaking tagalog!* He was on television . . . every hour . . . every quarter-hour . . . all four channels . . . *Laurence Olivier saying "Mabuhay"* . . . *"Mabuhay"* . . . *"Mabuhay"* . . . *"Mabuhay"*. The word had given him his "role".

But at Carrier's restaurant that night in 1970, he wasn't yet sure what his role was going to be . . . what part the audience would expect him to play when I introduced him from the stage.

"Laurence Olivier", obviously; *but that was no role! How could he play himself?*

By the time we arrived at the cinema, *The Three Sisters* was coming to an end. We stood at the back, watching over the heads of the usual mute, undemonstrative audience. Even I began to feel uneasy. At the same time, I heard the theatre cat's low nasal mewling. Only, when I looked its way, it was no cat: Olivier was nervous. He said, "Oh, I wish Joanie were here." – Joan Plowright, Lady Olivier.

I had a "cotton-wool throat" as I led him up the aisle a half-minute later. *It was going to be a disaster.* We sat down on the sort of chairs that are always too low and feel like a sick-bed. The first question came. "Why did you direct this film?" (Oh, God, no! Not *that* one!) I repeated it in Olivier's direction, putting as cheerful a shine as I could on the ball.

And then Olivier began to hum. I don't mean "hum" with his lips, like humming a tune. He began to hum like a piece of equipment switched on. Everything about him became energy – mental, moral, physical, psychic perhaps. The massive chest that all Shakespearean actors develop more powerfully than their non-classical confrères began vibrating as he took in air. He was pumping his vocal muscles, feeding their galvanising current into his circuitry. I was three feet away from him and I was *hearing* it!

What Olivier actually said, I have only an imprecise recollection. I imagine you will find something of his opinion on *The Three Sisters* in his 1986 book, *On Acting*, maybe even *all* of it, though he made his written opinion of Chekhov, which is scarcely 14 lines long, stretch to 60 minutes by the most artful-artless piece of acting that night. He played up to the audience shamelessly, acting out the questions that had any dramatic content to them, acting baffled when he didn't understand the question, acting humble when he came to praise his cast . . . acting . . . acting . . . acting.

They very properly gave him a standing ovation as he passed through them again and straight out of the cinema. A round of hand-shakes, and the limousine that had been waiting to take him to Victoria Station in time for the last train to Brighton pulled away. It travelled a few yards, stopped, then reversed back to where I was still standing making small-talk with my hosts about the evening's success.

The window whirred down. His hand reached for my arm and dug into the flesh again. "Dear friend . . . dear friend," pulling me down to his lips . . . "I couldn't have done it without you," he whispered. He sounded as false as hell.

INEXACTLY
EXPRESSED
SENTIMENTS
ABOUT THE
MOST PRIVATE
PERSON
I KNOW

There are times, I think, when Stanley Kubrick must wish he could be written out of his own life – left to lead it incognito, unobserved and (especially) unreported.

A lot of what follows he will not like: simply because, well, *mainly* because it has been written down. Writing, with all its palpably vulnerable chances for inexactness, seems to perpetrate an assault on his persona he would rather not suffer. I continually try to understand this. I tell myself it is rather like the fear among primitive people that the tourist's camera snapshot will filch away part of their soul. But that analogy, too, is inexact. Kubrick himself handles a camera without fear and can nearly always ensure that others pointing it at him handle it with deference. Cameras hold no terrors for him. Words do.

He is the most private man I know. "Know" is how that last word ought to be written; quotation marks at least denote an honest doubt, a questionable assumption. Few *know* Kubrick these days. Yet before the world became so bothersome to him, it was possible to meet him quite easily. I did in New York, at the end of the 1950s, by no more byzantine way of introduction than writing a letter and telling him he was the most exciting film-maker I'd encountered in my work as a critic. I write no such letters these days – not out of professional etiquette, rather because I know too much about new directors to ever find them exciting.

That wasn't true of Kubrick in the 1950s. Who on earth was he? I asked myself that after I'd caught *Killer's Kiss*, which I still think is the most perfect shortish film (64 minutes) ever made. I'd expected an action-thriller – hadn't we all: Gavin Lambert, Lindsay Anderson, Richard Winnington, all those who, like me, were astonished at its unAmerican tone? The mood of urban loneliness when nothing visible happened yet everything crystallised around a character-mood; the sexual obsession that beat like a pulse just below the skin of a tenement melodrama; above all the feeling of fable in its tale of a beautiful girl abducted by an ogreish dancehall owner infatuated with her and rescued by a valorous young boxer with antecedents in knight-errantry. Later, oh much later, I recognised the theme had eerily anticipated *Lolita*, which wasn't published until 1955, a year afterwards. I've no idea how this strange concurrence could have happened. But there must have been some self-fulfilling prophecy about it, for of course Kubrick and Nabokov collaborated on the darker enchantment of the film of *Lolita*.

Soon after seeing *Killer's Kiss*, I saw *The Killing*. Again a revelation – again an anticipation. This time a foreshadowing of one of Kubrick's favourite themes: how the "flawless" plan is pushed forward step by predetermined step while, simultaneously, chance, accident and the irrational are undoing it and ensuring its failure.

Along with a few other London critics I wrote to the distributors of *The Killing*, which was then playing in a tawdry little cinema on the Tottenham Court Road. We begged United Artists to bring it into the West End. They didn't, of course; but their publicity director, a man who shared the pleasure that films gave even though he had to promote their profit, wrote back and said that the *next* Kubrick, a war film, – *Paths of Glory*, it turned out – would definitely open in a city-centre cinema. I used that letter as my "calling card" for Kubrick.

He was then living (I think; for he won't of course verify my recollection) on the East Side in an apartment that was being cannibalised into the one next door. The debris forced us out. We ate at a restaurant with an Austrian bias to its menu, drank many *steins* of beer and talked until midnight. I went up to the apartment to collect my overcoat and as I left – it was now about 12.30 a.m. – bright tin cans of film were off-loaded out of a delivery van into the elevator. I squinted at their titles. They were in Japanese. But one or two had English words – just enough to give me a clue to their content.

"Are you going to make a film about Outer Space?" I asked. Even now I can see the dark suspicious glance I got.

"*Please*," said Stanley, "*be careful what you write.*"

I *was* careful . . . I was careful for ten years, until there was no hiding the fact that *2001: A Space Odyssey* was under way. (The

Japanese films, I surmised, had been ordered up to show him the state of the art in special effects.)

Today, Kubrick engenders not only curiosity among those who don't know him, but apprehension among those who do. I was recently telephoned from New York by one of his past associates, a man who has now achieved his own distinguished career as a naturalist and communicator, with books and television series about the vanishing American wilderness. He was thinking of writing his autobiography. "But what do I do when I get to the chapters on Stanley?" he asked. The book hasn't yet appeared; perhaps he hasn't decided how to solve the problem. Perhaps, for him, the problem is forever unsolvable.

Just how Kubrick exerts his will-power, it's hard to say. There have been times when I've imagined myself exposed to a steady concentration of will playing on my suggestibility. Nothing malign. But a kind of cerebral concentratedness expressed by the voice – low and hard – and the eyes – large and dark – so that one is locked into it like a radar beam. I've tried occasionally to "break" the spell by telling him something that distracts him, some peripheral anecdote or other, only to find the story has acquired a baleful relevance to one or other of Kubrick's own basic interests. Thus I once told him how Werner von Braun made a practice of never hiring anyone for a job who sprinkled salt on their food before tasting it. I suspect this "test" is now appreciatively filed away in Kubrick's memory bank. Lucky are those of us who break bread with him: but watch the salt.

For him, each day seems to be a battle to curb the chaos that filmmaking unleashes. Kubrick is an evolutionary pessimist: the worst that can go wrong, will. "Only maybe not just yet," I interject, hoping to defer Armageddon. But no, there is never any time to spare. "Don't save the day: anticipate it," is the order of battle. Many an apocryphal anecdote about Kubrick fashions its basic material out of his intense and – I must admit – usually well-founded desire for total control. One true story is about the time he wanted a New York cinema's interior painted matt black because light-coloured walls would distract audiences from the finely graded colour photography in *Barry Lyndon*.

"Too late," howled his American distributors, "the film opens the day after tomorrow."

287

Without leaving the home near London – he has been resident in Britain since coming here to make *Lolita* in the 1960s – Kubrick opened a New York "Yellow Pages" under "Painters and Decorators". The black surcoat that was put on the screen surrounds overnight was barely dry before the film premiered later in the day.

But even this was not as close a call as *The Shining* suffered. The film had been playing to packed cinemas in America for three days, in 1981, when Kubrick's personal emissary turned up at the projection booth in the first-run houses in New York. His instructions: to delete one single scene. It was barely two minutes in length, but the director believed it was delaying the film's enigmatic conclusion. Paul Eluard observed that poems were never finished, only abandoned. With Kubrick, it is films.

But to conduct one's affairs in this way, at a distance yet omnipresent, one has to have the self-confidence that total power confers. In Kubrick's case, that means *legal* power – not just the right to the final cut, but the right to the first say.

That recurring theme in Kubrick's films, the flaw in the machine that converts it into an instrument of retribution or annihilation, is what their maker tries to foresee in the fine print of film contracts. His patience and persistence are his strongest weapons. When lawyers hold meetings over some point he raises, time may as well take unpaid leave. One has to have a creative will of tungsten not to get worn out with "mere" process when all one's impatient urges are to "go" with the product. Kubrick has adapted to this pre-production wheeling and dealing with more uncompromising tenacity than any other filmmaker I know. Like the movie mogul who boasted he didn't have ulcers – he *gave* them, Kubrick doesn't let himself be worn out, he wears out others.

Not surprisingly, perhaps, chess is his favourite game. He plays it – or at one time did so – to tournament standard. In chess, the aching preliminaries to a move can make the players appear paralysed, but they are the imperatives to controlling the game. As many as six years can elapse between Kubrick's films. But then they are not being made under tournament rules; he doesn't have to make an obligatory move inside a fixed span of time. The only reliable lesson is: if you start before you're ready, you'll lose.

I imagine it was the bad experience he had directing *Spartacus*, in 1959, that hardened his resolve never again to serve under anyone else's generalship. Kirk Douglas, the film's eponymous star, was its producer, too, and he brought Kubrick in after one director already had been fired. The temperamental differences between himself and Douglas would probably have prompted Kubrick to quit had he not been obliged by legal restraints to remain with the production. Hence the bitter in-joke of "I am Spartacus, set me free" that later found its way into one of the "goonish" quips uttered by Peter Sellers, as Quilty, in Kubrick's *Lolita* – a sardonic echo of the director's own experience of contractual slavery.

Spartacus had collected its international cast of stars by giving each member of it the impression that his role stood out to better advantage than that of any of his co-stars. But the script they received on arrival on location showed greatly reduced possibilities. The ones who arrived earliest did better than the late-comers in clawing back their vanished scenes and lines. Olivier, with his own devious skills in the unexpected emphases on performance and sly up-staging of his co-stars served himself very well; others, like Charles Laughton, who went in physical fear of the muscular Douglas, were not so lucky. But of course Peter Ustinov played with the cunning of an old lag in the dock and had the courtroom in a roar. While the haggling and bargaining went on among his actors, Kubrick withdrew to plan his gladiatorial moves. The training sequences are generally acknowledged to be the best in the film. They also give a curious foretaste of the film he was to make nearly 30 years later, *Full Metal Jacket*; in both films about war and popular revolution, individuals are welded into an efficient killing machine.

Yet the acting in *Spartacus* is far more individually nuanced than in most historical epics of similar pretensions. Kubrick probably learned much from such masters of character invention as Olivier, Laughton and Ustinov. A director couldn't wish for better godfathers. I once asked him what Olivier had thought while making *Spartacus*, and got the laconic reply that Olivier knew what shit it was. I later asked Olivier the same question and he answered, "Stanley knew it was shit." Well, yes, but when we are watching, *we* don't. Kubrick possesses the uncomfortable virtue – uncomfortable, anyhow, for those working with him –

of gauging just how far the creative flame needs to be turned up under a player in order to convert a raw performance into one so subtly cooked that the recipe is a source of wonder to others. Kubrick would say, of course, that getting good ingredients helps. But it's in the quality of the preparation that the heaviest investment is made.

Consider Jack Nicholson's casting in *The Shining*. Prior to signing him, Kubrick viewed most of Nicholson's previous films. One set of characters, he noted, were played on an "up" current of energy; another set were dominated by Jack in a more mordant mood. Either way might have been appropriate for *The Shining*, though each would have produced a different film. Kubrick chose to go with the flow of manic energy, the "Jack in the Box" springiness that gives devilish glee to the gruesome events. "Jack brings such power to a part," Kubrick told me at the time, "that he fills all the moments."

"What do you mean exactly?"

"Well, most actors, when they're not actually required to do something, are, at best, just paying attention. But Jack stays switched on. There's the scene where he's applying for the care-taker's job over the winter season when the hotel's closed and he's asked if his wife and child will be able to put up with the extreme isolation of the place and he replies coolly, 'Oh, they'll love it.' But you're watching his eyes and what *they* are saying is, 'What the hell has it got to do with them?' Jack can articulate a part and deliver it on camera so that it *shows*."

The opposite is true, of course: an actor who is under par has to be helped top up a performance. If this means hurt feelings, so be it. For Kubrick, the proof of a performance lies in its improvement.

Unfortunately for him, not everyone can be present throughout the long and sometimes painful process to see how the performance is improving. The gossip mills are only inter-ested in keeping an inventory of how many takes the director put his actor through. "Sadism" or "wastefulness" are words too often spoken at the inquest. Few things irritate Kubrick more than this canard of being in the sadistic line of descent from Von Sternberg. He always vigorously rebuts the slander that he gives actors an unnecessarily hard time of it. He insists it's not "per-fection" he's after – it's "creativity". And what might that be?

Something he recognises growing to the film's advantage in the gruelling give-and-take between director and actor as they are shooting the scene. To Kubrick, a priceless asset but one he can't put in an advance order for.

The late Peter Sellers and Kubrick were of one mind and art in this respect. Both began working on a part in the dark, so to speak, using the instincts of blind men who, feeling their way, receive powerful suggestions of shape and size that the sighted would not notice because their literalness makes them take things for granted. To watch (as I did) Sellers improvising his monologues in *Lolita* and *Dr Strangelove*, with Kubrick feeding him the oxygen of his own inspiration when the actor grew short of creative breath, was to be witness to a rare double act. "Writing" had scarcely no meaning for these two filmmakers when they were in creative collusion. Kubrick, in any case, views a written script the way he'd contemplate a balanced diet. It might be good sense to stick to it, but how dull! And Sellers viewed acting like a gourmand – his appetite grew by feeding. It is a tragedy that Sellers died so early, when he and Kubrick had such an affinity with each other. If only the latter had directed Sellers's penultimate film, *Being There*. Its mockery of human self-delusion needed the mix of Kubrick's misanthropy to provide a blacker shade of comedy for Sellers's apparition of shining innocence to materialise against.

Not all actors, however, recognise they're doing their best work when they collaborate with Kubrick. Some only discover it later.

The story is told that George C. Scott asked to see *Dr Strangelove* before it opened publicly. He sat through it in silence – then was seen to stalk out of Columbia's screening room, broodily uncommunicative. Reports had him in a state of extreme irritation at having witnessed his hulking Pentagon warmonger, General Buck G. Turgidson, being continually cut every time he reached the peak of his "pre-emptive strike" evangelism – so that he looked like a jackal repeatedly illuminated in a flash of lightning. Savage cutting frequently feels like a slap in the face to actors as "driven" as Scott. But by constantly imprinting the general's caricatural posture on one's retina, Kubrick ensured one should never see him other than in manic overdrive. Later, Scott called *Dr Strangelove* one of the best films he'd made.

* * *

What one could call "the works" – the machinery that puts emotions in gear, shapes screenplays, manipulates audiences – fascinate a man like Kubrick who is so concerned to conceal his own "works". It is part and parcel of his fascination with methods and systems, of course; but there can be pure aestheticism in it, too.

On one of the last occasions I visited him at his home near London, I noted a beautiful white Porsche standing in the forecourt of the mansion. It was a thoroughbred among the work-horse Range Rovers and trucks in the adjoining film-company's stable. ("Stable" is an exact word here, since it is in an out-building once used for quartering horses, a structure itself as large as many a country house, with its own gates and a bell-tower, too, where Kubrick has established his offices, editing rooms, etc.). Now Kubrick's concern for physical safety is well known. He doesn't ever use commercial aircraft, considering the skies too crowded and air-traffic controllers too readily identifiable with the fateful vulnerability that governs events in his own films. He views speed with the same scepticism. He has been known to ring off on his car phone if he is approaching an intersection, then call back once he has safely negotiated the crossing. So I was surprised to discover the Porsche belonged to him. Yet considered simply as a piece of superb engineering, the car makes a statement about its owner that has absolutely nothing to do with status. It is "the works" in it that he admires.

He seeks, *needs*, reliability around him. Over the years, he has assembled a domestic *apparat*, every part of which has been tested and found true. His choice of transport was influenced by the West German army's adopting the same make of truck. If it was good enough for them, Stanley felt, it would serve his own purposes, which fell somewhat short of war.

His immediate family extends into his filmmaking one. He has been married three times: first to a girl he was at high school with; then to Ruth Sobotka, a ballet-dancer with the Balanchine company whose strange, forlorn *pas seul* performed in a memory-sequence of *Killer's Kiss* adds to that film's fairy-tale tone; and to his present wife, Christiane, an exhibiting artist as well as an actress, once cast before her marriage as the nervous German girl soothing the war-weary infantry with a ballad like a mother's lullaby at the end of *Paths of Glory*. Kubrick's brother-in-law,

292

Jan Harlan, a member of a German family distinguished on stage and screen, functions as his executive producer. His son-in-law Roy Hobbs was associate producer on *Full Metal Jacket*. His third daughter Vivienne composes music for her father's films and keeps the "family album" of him at work on them with her own Super-8 and now with video. Her television documentary on the making of *The Shining* recorded a rare view of Kubrick as both demon and daddy – saturnine when not actually satanic, then at times surprisingly sweet and funny.

The reality of the family man contrasts with the largely fictional account of his megalomaniac ways as a filmmaker. When "privacy" becomes reclusiveness, the media scene is set for the appearance of "Citizen Kubrick", a secretive eminence whom legends have gathered around like Gothic shrouds. They have succeeded in making a monster out of a man who has simply a mole's preference for keeping out of sight. Indeed I fancy an empathy exists with that unseen but obstinate and subversive little underground creature every time I cross the lawn of Kubrick's home with him by my side; for I have never heard him even refer to, much less deplore the mole hills that have reared up to turn parts of it into a miniature Western Front in World War One.

Some of the most frequently repeated anecdotes about him have either no basis in fact, or else possess an entirely rational explanation. Just for the record, it never happened that he evacuated his entire household – he was then living in a different part of England – and took his wife, children, servants, cats and golden retrievers off to a hotel in order to have a crop-dusting airplane fly over his grounds and spray them with insecticide to keep down the particularly high incidence of garden pests that summer. No truth at all in that.

Nor was it some Howard Hughes phobia to do with germs which made him decree that everyone must wear surgical masks while shooting certain sequences of *2001: A Space Odyssey*. The truth had to do with economy, not hygiene. The enormous and expensive light bulbs essential for the front-projection images of a prehistoric landscape in "The Dawn of Man" prologue were so fragile that they would crack, even explode, if anyone as much as breathed on them. At hundreds of dollars a time, that was some heavy breathing. Surgical masks filtered air expelled by technicians' lungs before the drops of moisture in it could shatter the hot glass.

It is true, though, that during the great English summer drought of 1976 he laid down a cellar of mineral water. Most of the bottles lay there – for all I know, still do – undrunk by the end of the dry season, but in store for another possible sign of the apocalypse. The "survivalist" attitude is ingrained in Kubrick. Had a distant ancestor of his been featured as a primate in the "Dawn of Man", be sure he would have been The One who found a new use for the bone he'd just picked clean. (Not by turning it into the first weapon, however – that would not be characteristic of a law-abiding man who personally abhors violence.) He used to have a passion for knowing the time. But it's quite some time now since I heard his wrist-watch alarm buzzing fractiously, to indicate that someone, somewhere, should be getting a call from him. Perhaps this is because his working life-style has deranged chronology so completely that it no longer applies to what he does day and night. The man who once bought wall clocks by the half-dozen, so as never to be too far away from one, now seems to keep no regular hours about work, food or rest. In that respect, he does remind me of Howard Hughes – and David O. Selznick. Those men were devotees of "natural sleep", in other words collapsing into unconsciousness when exhaustion finally overtook them. This comes hard on eight-hours-a-night subordinates.

What does Kubrick do to relax? I heard of him taking a vacation – once. He went over to Normandy and made a fascinated reconnoitring of the German fortifications that – the flaw in the perfect plan again! – proved ineffectual when the Allies invaded on D-day.

It's not that Kubrick finds travel abroad boring – not exactly. More that he simply finds it unnecessary. "Going to a place doesn't necessarily increase the reality of it," he said, when I questioned his decision to build a facsimile of South-East Asia for *Full Metal Jacket* in South-East England. He was right. There is a "location" reality and there is a "film" reality that the mind sometimes accepts more easily, more satisfyingly, even though one is masquerading for the other. Thus Kubrick found a square mile of gas-works – "Put that way, it sounds terrible," he concedes – on the Thameside marshlands with container ships clearly visible (though not in the finished film) going up and down the river. He noted the architectural resemblance it bore to industrial complexes in Vietnam – especially after a breaker's ball-and-chain had been employed to "improve" the abandoned look of British Gas into the blitzed look of high-rubble Hué. For Kubrick, "reality" is what the mind accepts. Movies for him are a state of wakeful dreaming.

The power of his films derives, in part, from the way his chosen route can skirt the surreal or penetrate directly its heightened suggestiveness. The battlefield behaviourism of a film like Oliver Stone's *Platoon* is one kind of reality. But it does not transcend reality. Stone's film was shot in a foreign field (not Vietnam, admittedly, but the Philippines – a duplicate location, all the same). Kubrick's film set is another world. One man is recalling his own experiences of battle; the other is constructing his own universe of the unreal.

A Kubrick film always feeds the aesthetic senses; it *looks* visionary even when it is as literal, as functional, as the scene, say, in a barrack-room loo in *Full Metal Jacket*. The latrines have the sort of transcendent whiteness that Hollywood traditionally used to represent Heaven. It's not just because the shattered cranium of a suicidal Marine creates splotches on the pure-white tiles like a Sam Francis painting; the whiteness of the ceramic walls and lavatory units has an unearthliness that takes it out of this world. And the awesomeness that extreme order generates – even before it is desecrated by violent death – is assisted by the *double row* of toilet pedestals, facing each other, as if waiting to be inspected by an honour guard rather than actually used by anyone. The two rows were installed on Kubrick's orders – one row is deemed sufficient to meet all Marine needs at boot camps like the Parris Island one in the film. But a second row preserves the symmetry that Michel Ciment's illustrated study of Kubrick's themes and motifs shows to be his most characteristic signature.

Such concern for design in a man who has no concern for his own appearance always strikes me as vaguely amusing; though it's a cliché that a great artist hardly knows and never bothers what colour, shape or fit his own clothes are, so long as they meet minimum standards of decency and convention – or indeed rebel against them. (Sometimes, I'm delighted to report, Stanley has been unsettled by a close encounter of the sartorial kind when he's strayed into an alien environment – like the West End hotel where we had dropped in to have tea on a Sunday afternoon. It was dominated by a *maître d'hôtel* who was, with difficulty, reconciled to a tieless Kubrick only because Stanley's beard could be persuaded to hide the deficiency.)

I think it's the sheer elegance of his aesthetic images that disturbs audiences and leaves some critics feeling that even the human beings are *objets d'art*. This has exposed Kubrick to the old canard of being a "cold" director. Admittedly, he doesn't often touch our hearts. But then does Coppola? Does Cimino? Does Scorsese? Yes, of course, there's Spielberg. But *his* films are pure feelings laid out on the storyboard with accompanying instructions for transplanting into audiences. Kubrick designs his films in his mind's eye and feeds their ideas back into viewers' psyches. Spielberg's sentimentality often hits the right place in the heart for the wrong reasons. Kubrick's detachment operates on the twilight zones of the unconscious mind. Spielberg has the ingratiating come-on of the warm-up man with a studio audience. Kubrick operates with the stealth of an infiltrator on the individual sensibility.

He himself is well aware of his so-called "heartlessness". If taxed about it, he'll laconically recall the words of Herman Kahn, the A-bomb apologist, who was reproached with a similar lack of caring. Yes, Kahn admitted, his apocalyptic overview of annihilation might have gained more adherents if he had introduced some warm human stresses into it.

Kubrick in film after film has taken an overview of mankind that allows the race little evolutionary credit. Thornton Wilder thought we'd scrape through the worst by the skin of our teeth. Kubrick's blackest comedy doesn't hold out even that hope. As the Bomb goes off in *Dr Strangelove*, triggering a Doomsday Machine that spreads serial annihilation across the globe, the satirical counterpoint of Vera Lynn's song "We'll Meet Again" may seem to hold out some faint terminal promise of continuity – but it is noticeably vague on exactly "how" or "when", never mind as "what", we'll do so.

2001: A Space Odyssey begins by depicting man as a risen ape; it ends by suggesting that man-of-the-future will be a fallen angel. That last shot of the recycled cosmonaut, transformed into a Star Child with shining eyes turning curiously towards

Earth, is one of the greatest images in cinema. And, for a man
like Kubrick, curiously hopeful and touching. Up to a point,
anyhow. That "point" expires with the beginning of his next
picture, *A Clockwork Orange*, which follows the angel's earthly
progress. Its first shot of Malcolm McDowell as the satanic Alex,
all angelic sweetness modulated into demonic gloating, introduces a society that will draw its repressive energies from just
such a delinquent anti-hero. The individual can't win in a
Kubrick universe. *Barry Lyndon* ends with its eponymous
parvenu drummed out of the social class he'd attempted to gate-
crash – short of one leg, too, as a permanent reminder of his
presumptuousness in social climbing. *The Shining* suggested that
a man's fate is irreversible, however hard he tries to leap-frog in
time over his destiny. *Full Metal Jacket* suggests a man should be
grateful for the small mercies he can now write large, having
gone through hell on earth and survived. "We have nailed our
names in the pages of history enough for today," Private Joker
reflects at the end of the film. "I am in a world of shit . . .
yes. But I am alive. And I am not afraid." And with the Mickey
Mouse Theme from the American children's TV programme on
their lips, a juvenile jingle superseding the Marine Corps drill
chorus, Joker and his fellow "grunts" march down against the
sunset sky to bivouac for the night on the banks of the Perfumed
River. "Enough for today" all right. One is grateful for the
unexpected grace note.

But the impression remains of an Olympian gazing down on
these *misérables*.

My favourite photograph of Kubrick on the set of a film shows
him peering out of a Black Forest of camera equipment, pensive,
detached, and for some reason black-gloved. I think it was taken
during the making of *The Shining* and he may have slipped on
the kind of gauntlet that, on Peter Sellers' hand in *Dr
Strangelove*, developed a mutinous life of its own, although on
Kubrick's hand a glove is a glove is a glove.

The photo has the feel of a thinking hermit about it – quite
unlike the one that Kubrick took of himself when *Newsweek* put
him on its *"Clockwork Orange"* front cover in January 1972.
There he was, a close-bearded, full-face Stanley, like a benevolent
illusionist, very white-of-eye, caught perhaps in mid-command,
wielding a hand-held camera that suggests a mask that he's just

297

slipped off his face to reveal its humanity – "The Phantom of the Movies". I believe he was the first subject permitted by *Newsweek* to take his own picture for its cover – it was that or nothing, he insisted. By the time of *Barry Lyndon*, however, Marisa Berenson was on the cover of *Time*.

It is as if the first *Newsweek* picture is trying to say (as Kubrick once said to me): "I ought not to be regarded as a once-happy man who has been bitten in the jugular and compelled to assume the misanthropy of the vampire." Then I look at the other photo of him in more sombre mien that hangs in my workroom and it says to me, "My films have changed because life has changed. The opportunities for feeling deeply but pessimistically are far more frequent today than they used to be."

The immensely long labour-period a Kubrick movie goes through can take years – and now, as a rule, does – and commits him and his associates to stretches of patience beyond the ordinary or, some have thought, the tolerable. He had to cope with one rare crisis like this on *2001* when a highly placed technical adviser reportedly made his grievances known to MGM executives back in Hollywood. It was "no contest"; the "mutineer" self-destructed and that extraordinarily placid looking film, in which even mortality is reduced to a straight line silently signalling the terminal failure of a man's vital functions, betrays no hint of the disturbance.

Every detail of pre-production on a film has to be "justified" before Kubrick accepts it. This makes life hard for associates. They know that the questions he puts to them at the start of the day's work have to have been answered by the time work ends.

Ken Adam, one of the cinema's great production designers, imagined Stanley was easy to work with the first time they met on *Dr Strangelove*. Adam did a doodle on his pad for the War Room set. It was enthusiastically received. But a week later, when it had been elaborated into a multi-level model, it was abruptly rejected; it couldn't be lit for the effect Kubrick was after. Adam admits he felt like a man in a plane that's hit an air-pocket. But urged to fly higher, his imagination soared to the ceiling that was set by Kubrick's demands. The result was the spectacular triangular bunker in the film. The shape was scientifically justified, too – it was the best one to withstand an A-bomb blast.

298

The Shining must be one of the few filmed ghost stories in which the lights stay on all the time. Again, reality is the reason. "It's the way a hotel would be lighted," Kubrick said when I remarked on it. "You'd need illumination if you were a caretaker in the off-season – lights would be left on in the main rooms and corridors." The usual horror-film lighting was never even considered. "You've got to make people believe in what they're seeing. That's the second most pressing problem."

"What's the first?"

"Making sure what they're seeing is interesting."

Of course!

"A simple naturalistic style is best. I'm sure it is. Kafka approached the same problem in the same way. Kafka deals in the unreal and fantastic, but he describes things in a deceptively simple, journalistically factual manner. Conversely, the films based on Kafka's novels have never done themselves any good by using baroque lighting and sets that are half-consciously 'Kafka-esque'. Kafka should be filmed like *Marty*, and acted that way, too. There isn't any dark at the top of the stairs in *The Shining* for the same reason – and it's well-lit at the bottom, too!"

The same thinking is behind Kubrick's penchant for long, unbroken camera movements. They may have started out as a young filmmaker's sympathetic homage to Max Ophuls, but he soon saw how effective they were for accumulating tension. A sudden cut may make people jump, but an uninterrupted movement keeps them uneasy. The same applies to music. Many well-laid plans to surprise an audience are spoiled when the music on the sound track gives advance warning of it. The electronic music composed by Abigail Mead for *Full Metal Jacket* was designed to sound like no earthly orchestra – thus depriving an audience of all the conventional music cues. It was an eerie score on its own; it was as if the very land of Vietnam were exhaling its last painful sigh as the Marines advanced nervously over it. The sound of alien pain.

"Music," says Kubrick, "helps narrow the decisions."

"What do you hope to find when you start going over a scene with an actor you've cast?" I asked him once. I think we were driving home from the huge outdoor set of the maze that had been built on the back lot of the old MGM studios at

Borehamwood. It was a full-sized, three-dimensional maze, with hedgerows seven foot high, and liberally dotted with off-camera signposts; maps were issued to those entering it as a supplementary precaution.

I'd been watching Kubrick directing Shelley Duvall in the crucial scenes of *The Shining* when, as Nicholson's wife, she was starting to have misgivings about her husband's sanity; soon these would turn into dread, then into naked fear. Kubrick was concentrating on the *exact* tone of voice he wanted her to have as she discussed Dad's strangeness with their young son.

She had to keep on walking, as well as talking, endlessly turning one corner of the maze after another.

Kubrick had hooked himself onto the belt of the Steadicam photographer. This was the only place where he could give directions and at the same time monitor what the camera was seeing in a tiny TV screen attached to the Steadicam. As Shelley Duvall and the kid advanced, he and the operator were obliged to walk backwards through the maze for quite some distance. Anyone outside the skin of a pantomime horse who has ever tried retreating in synchronised step with his partner-in-harness will know the tricky elements that had to be juggled smoothly together to simulate, on the screen, the impression of a woman losing her bearings in the real world of the maze that was seen to suggest a huge vermiculated brain cortex.

"Generally, the better an actor is, the more he or she enjoys work," said Kubrick. "First, we go for the specifics of the scene. Are there ways of playing it which are more interesting than others? Stanislavsky used to say that either an actor doesn't understand what the words he's saying really mean or what his emotional attitude to them should be, or else he's not believable – simply not *interesting*. The best actors already have a perception of the part and can articulate it – deliver it – even while they are discussing it with you.

"But the source of many a good thing is still the imagination, not the intelligence."

Later, I asked him about the moment Jack Nicholson sank the axe through the door panel and heralded his attack on a cowering Shelley Duvall with a mocking aberrant parody of the vainglorious announcement that always introduces Johnny Carson to his television audience: "He-e-e-e-re's Johnny!"

300

"That came to me 'born whole', so to speak; it was never in the script. It's the bonus you suddenly receive amidst the unbelievable pressures of the production. And of course to have an actor like Jack, who can articulate it at peak performance . . . It's the quality of what you give a player to work on that often determines the sort of performance he or she gives you."

The dialogue in the film took on a tonal value over and above its meaning; the tone was Nicholson, but Nicholson modulated by Kubrick.

Likewise, while making *A Clockwork Orange*, Kubrick found Malcolm McDowell's high, sharp, autocratic tones – he tends, in my opinion, to speak a decibel higher than is strictly necessary – suggested the vocal level at which to pitch the aggressive Nadsat slang of Anthony Burgess's teenage "droogs".

Matthew Modine's contribution to *Full Metal Jacket* was visual rather than vocal. His shaven head increased his vulnerable "baby" look and concentrated all the attention on whatever sensitivity he could make visible on the permanent features that the Army barber had spared.

"If Gary Cooper and Henry Fonda had had a baby, he would be Mathew Modine," Kubrick remarked about Modine's image of macho sensibility – someone on the receiving end, but no weakling.

For this director, however, the greatest problem any film sets is preserving the generative shock of his first encounter with the story of the idea.

"The effect is at its most exciting the very first time you read something that ignites a desire in you to want to film it. It gets weaker and weaker the more often you refer back to it. The deeper you get into it as the filming gets under way, the more you're tempted to operate on instruments – not instincts – and that can be fatal."

A man like Kubrick has a quality of obsession that seems to me considerably further east, geographically speaking, than his Middle European origins in Austria suggest. It is nearer Dostoevsky and the obsessions of the Russian mind. That impression appeared to me, in all its self-concentrated force, late one night at Elstree Studios.

It was shortly after *The Shining* had opened in New York.

Nine o'clock at night is not a usual hour to be visiting most film

301

studios. And the guards in the gate-house checked me out carefully and dubiously. "Is anyone working this late?" they asked. "One is," I said.

I found him in a rented storage block, identified only by the sign "HAWK FILMS – KEEP OUT" which had been turned into a general-command post. Its open-plan space was already cluttered up into something like the ominous maze in the film with all the paraphernalia of a film company, the trestle tables, electric typewriters, the cold remains of meals on paper platters: the high tech side-by-side with the unhygienic.

Sitting in a pool of light and hemmed in, bunker-like, by rack upon gleaming rack of bright tin cans of film containing every single shot, used in the film or not, wearing his usual uniform of casually mismatched items that might have been left over from the last war, Kubrick was holding a telephone to his ear and had an outsize magnifying glass clamped to his eye. He nodded to me to sit down. Spread in front of him was a copy of that day's edition of the *New York Times* which must have been flown in to him only a few hours before. It was open at a full-page display advertisement for his new film.

He was talking in low, contained but intense tones – angry, yes, but reprimanding whoever it was at the other end of the line with the force of irony, not ire.

"Doesn't it strike you as strange that you're 3000 miles away in New York and here I am in London telling you that the 1.00 a.m. extra screening scheduled for *The Shining* has been left out of the ad in today's *Times*?"

I had to admire the tenacity. What filmmaker, having spent at least 15 million dollars, and an exhausting three years of his life, in fleshing out the fantasies in his mind's eyes, could muster the energy to monitor the small print in a current advertisement for a cinema thousands of miles distant? Only Stanley Kubrick.

"WHY THIS ONE AND NOT THAT ONE, WHY ONE EVENT AND NOT THE OTHER?"

Film critics spend more time in the dark than their colleagues who go to the theatre, opera or ballet. I was born lucky: I could employ the dark at both ends of the day. Insomnia is an affliction to some: to me, since early childhood, it has been a welcomed accomplice. Most of this book was written between the hours of ten at night and three (or three-thirty) in the morning. It is the schedule by which I work best, can concentrate hardest for the longest continuous time.

But I have also kept my fellow critics company in the artificial darkness at noon that gives our trade the feeling of a tribal ritual. It's privileged – it's a bit perverse, too – to be sitting in the dark, having a mass entertainment screened for so few of us at an hour when "the masses" are living or working by the light of day. Sometimes we're reproached by the filmmakers on these very grounds. We've "lost touch" with "our audience", we're told. If only we could see and hear the response of "ordinary folk for whom the films are made", we would lose our fanged or furred inheritance that the people in the industry who feel the bite of the vampire or the snarl of the werewolf believe we creatures of the night carry in our genes. Human company would make us human, too: they hope.

But every film column is an act of communication with those who weren't there when we watched the film: every book a critic writes is a search for company to share his experience.

A film critic enjoys a lot of privileges. Privileges, please note, not power. One should use them to bear witness, on as many occasions as possible, to the huge human and industrial diversity of the film business. Any time some particularly depressing week's filmgoing makes my spirits sink, I remind myself that seeing films is only part of what it's all about. Encounters off screen as well as on are obligations to be pursued. Frequently, they enrich one's perception: almost certainly, they extend it.

It's my hope that this book has suggested something of the range of experience that being a film critic encompasses. My choice in the matter has been personal – idiosyncratic rather than representative. Why this one and not that one, why one event and not the other, why these names and not those: the only explanation I can offer recalls the Borges story about the man who started to paint a fresco of the world and ended up with a picture of himself. Everything in the foregoing pages bears witness to some of the multitude of human talents and events which have struck me as particularly worth preserving and sharing. If there is any other common element beyond the sensibility they were filtered through, it is the uncommon gifts possessed by almost everyone I have written about. How far I've succeeded in analysing the unique and reconstructing the significant isn't for me to judge. But of one thing I am very sure: the pleasure it's been to bear witness.

INDEX

308

309

310

311